Learning AirWatch

Learn to implement, manage, and deploy the latest Enterprise Mobility Management (EMM) platform offered by AirWatch

Mark Dunkerley

BIRMINGHAM - MUMBAI

Learning AirWatch

First published: March 2015

Production reference: 1260315

Published by Packt Publishing Ltd.
Livery Place
35 Livery Street
Birmingham B3 2PB, UK.

ISBN 978-1-78439-167-6

www.packtpub.com

Credits

Author

Mark Dunkerley

Reviewers

Jason Bayton

Nathaniel Adam Briggs

Justin R. Kellen

Emil Novakov

Sunil Sarat

Commissioning Editor

Dipika Gaonkar

Acquisition Editor

Vinay Argekar

Content Development Editor

Arwa Manasawala

Technical Editor

Madhunikita Sunil Chindarkar

Copy Editor

Deepa Nambiar

Project Coordinator

Purav Motiwalla

Proofreaders

Mario Cecere

Maria Gould

Bernadette Watkins

Indexer

Hemangini Bari

Production Coordinator

Shantanu N. Zagade

Cover Work

Shantanu N. Zagade

About the Author

Mark Dunkerley is currently the manager of messaging, mobile, and video services at the Adventist Health System. He was born in Newcastle upon Tyne, England and currently resides in Orlando, Florida. He holds a bachelor's degree of science in business administration and a master's in business administration.

He has worked in the technology field for over 12 years and has experience in several technical areas. He has earned certifications from AirWatch, Microsoft, CompTIA, VMware, AXELOS, Cisco, and EMC.

Mark is currently involved with unified communication and mobility strategies and deployments in his current role. He recently spoke at several conferences for AirWatch and Microsoft and published several case studies. To view more information on the work Mark has done, you can visit his LinkedIn profile at www.linkedin.com/in/markdunkerley.

About the Reviewers

Nathaniel Adam Briggs is the founder of eGenerations Network and Synthetic Magic Advanced Business Services. He has over 21 years of experience in professional design, technology, and business solutions.

He has worked with American Express (AXP), LifeLock, Paxson Communications/ION Media Networks (ION), AON Corporation (AOC), International Speedway Corporation, McNichols Corporation, DuPont Registry, Colliers International, Florida Holocaust Museum, Laubeck, ReMax Realty, Outhouse, Qualisys, Biovision Sports, and Netwolves, to name a few.

Nathaniel has developed over 40 successful products as a team member, and sometimes as the sole engineer. His vision and innovation have been recognized in the fields of advanced computer graphics, the Internet, visual effects, grid computing, broadcast television, marketing, and CRM segments of the technology arena. He has served as a guest speaker at several industry events, and is a member of the Association for Computing Machinery (ACM), National Physique Committee (NPC), and SIGGRAPH.

Nathaniel began his career by learning to develop software in the fourth grade. 2 years later, he was among the top 10 winners of the National Science Olympiad in earth science. Later, he served in the United States Marine Corps (Amphibious Assault), and earned a bachelor's in computer science (summa cum laude with 3.95 GPA) from the University of Advancing Technology, Tempe, Arizona.

I would like to thank Karma.

Justin R. Kellen is a 24-year-old man from Lakefield, Minnesota. He obtained his associate degree in system administration from Southeast Technical Institute in Sioux Falls, South Dakota. He also attended four semesters at St. Cloud State University before entering the workforce.

He has worked in IT for 2 years. At first, he was an intern at a company called LORAM Maintenance of Way. Currently, he is a technology specialist at Independent School District 177 in Windom, Minnesota. He is part of a team that oversees their 1:1 student iPad program. The program is in its second year. They have used AirWatch to manage these devices for about a year.

Learning Airwatch is the first book that he's reviewed for Packt Publishing.

I would like to thank Denis Zilmer and Stephen Farver at LORAM and Ryan Christoffer at ISD 177 for giving me the opportunity to learn new technologies and helping me progress in my IT career. I would also like to thank Pooja Mhapsekar and Purav Motiwalla at Packt Publishing for reaching out to me and guiding me through the review process. It's been a great learning experience!

Emil Novakov is the lead sales engineer for Central and Southern Europe at AirWatch by VMware, a leading enterprise mobility management (EMM) provider. As one of the first AirWatch employees in EMEA, he has helped numerous global organizations across different business verticals in designing and deploying secure and productive mobile strategies. He serves as a trusted advisor of many AirWatch customers in EMEA and acts as an evangelist for innovative mobility by speaking at numerous public events.

Prior to joining AirWatch, Emil worked in the telematics branch at the BMW Group and as a self-employed web developer. He holds a master's degree in mobile networks and services from the French Institut Telecom as well as a master's degree in electrical and computer engineering from the Georgia Institute of Technology.

Sunil Sarat is the vice president of cloud and end user transformation services at an India-based global hybrid IT infrastructure services provider.

He played a key role in setting up and running this practice dealing with emerging technologies such as public/private cloud, hybrid IT, enterprise mobility, VDI, app virtualization, associated transformation services, and so on. His role is to strategize, create, roll out, and manage services in these technology areas.

Sunil is a technology and business leader with varied experience. He has handled diverse functions such as innovation/technology, service delivery, transition, presales solutions, and automation.

He has authored white papers, blogs, and articles on various areas related to technology and service. He reviews technical books and is a speaker at cloud-related events. He holds various industry certifications in the areas of computing, storage, and security, and also holds an MBA in marketing.

www.PacktPub.com

Support files, eBooks, discount offers, and more

For support files and downloads related to your book, please visit www.PacktPub.com.

Did you know that Packt offers eBook versions of every book published, with PDF and ePub files available? You can upgrade to the eBook version at www.PacktPub.com and as a print book customer, you are entitled to a discount on the eBook copy. Get in touch with us at service@packtpub.com for more details.

At www.PacktPub.com, you can also read a collection of free technical articles, sign up for a range of free newsletters and receive exclusive discounts and offers on Packt books and eBooks.

https://www2.packtpub.com/books/subscription/packtlib

Do you need instant solutions to your IT questions? PacktLib is Packt's online digital book library. Here, you can search, access, and read Packt's entire library of books.

Why subscribe?

- Fully searchable across every book published by Packt
- Copy and paste, print, and bookmark content
- On demand and accessible via a web browser

Free access for Packt account holders

If you have an account with Packt at www.PacktPub.com, you can use this to access PacktLib today and view 9 entirely free books. Simply use your login credentials for immediate access.

Instant updates on new Packt books

Get notified! Find out when new books are published by following @PacktEnterprise on Twitter or the *Packt Enterprise* Facebook page.

Table of Contents

Preface

The ability to become fully dependent on our mobile devices is a reality we are faced with today. With the rapid growth of mobile usage in the consumer space, enterprises are challenged with providing the workforce with the ability to access corporate resources easily and, most importantly, securely. This is where we need to fully understand the bigger picture of mobility and the security implications that come with it. As technical experts, we are not only responsible for installing and providing the solutions to the end users, but we are also fully responsible for understanding the risks associated with providing access to corporate information and the possible leakage of that information. As we are all aware, there is a constant growth of societies worldwide that are constantly looking for ways to penetrate confidential information, and as technical experts, we are tasked with minimizing the risk.

In order to provide the level of security and usability to our users, we need to understand the tools available on the market today. The latest toolset available that encompasses all manageability of mobile devices is currently known as Enterprise Mobility Management (EMM), which was recently known as Mobile Device Management (MDM). MDM is now part of the overall suite of EMM. EMM tools include the ability to manage mobile devices, applications for the device including a catalog, content on the device, secured containers, integration with enterprise tools, full security over all information, and much more.

Throughout this book, you will learn how AirWatch by VMware has provided the toolset needed to manage all the components of EMM, allowing you to deploy a secure and robust mobile environment. As you travel through the chapters, you will gain a thorough understanding of what is involved in EMM and the benefits it can provide to your workforce. Mobility has exploded in the recent years and is growing at an incredible pace, forcing us to implement solutions to meet the needs of the workforce. This book will allow you to view the bigger picture of mobility and provide you with the information that will allow your organization to become ahead of the curve and provide solutions to the users before they start demanding them from you.

The days of providing only e-mail to mobile devices are behind us, and we need to be innovative as technical experts. If your organization hasn't already done so, it needs to start looking at it as mobile services and invest in a mobility team or provide dedicated resources to allow growth in the area. Today, a mobile strategy is critical for your organization, especially with the growth of the younger generation moving into the workforce and their dependency on mobile devices to do everything.

What this book covers

Chapter 1, Getting Started, gives an introduction to AirWatch along with providing you with an overview of the different management suite options available. It continues onto the hosting and support options available to the customer as well as the learning and deployment services available. The chapter then shows the devices supported by AirWatch, the different types of ownership supported and a walk-through setting up your environment.

Chapter 2, Administration, covers how you access the Admin Console once you complete the installation of AirWatch. You will then be shown the Getting Started wizard and how it will help with the deployment. Following the Getting Started wizard is an overview of the console before covering all aspects of the console in detail.

Chapter 3, Enterprise Integration, provides an overview of the enterprise integrations available, then covers core enterprise integrations. The chapter continues onto covering AirWatch Cloud Connector and how to install it as part of your deployment. Once AirWatch Cloud Connector is installed, you will learn how to integrate with the core enterprise systems. The chapter will then finish off with an overview of Mobile Application Gateway, Secure Email Gateway, and other available enterprise integrations.

Chapter 4, Mobile Security, gives an overview of mobile security today and covers the more popular compliances you can expect the need to adhere to. You will then be shown the security controls available within AirWatch before being shown how to implement the controls to secure your mobile fleet.

Chapter 5, Mobile Device Management, provides an overview of Mobile Device Management and then describes the different device ownership types for the admin to understand. You will then be shown what the organization and smart groups are along with how to set them up and configure them. After organization and smart groups, you will learn how to create and publish a profile and what is needed before you enroll your device. You will then learn how to enroll a device, manage your device through the Self Service Portal while finishing off, and un-enroll a device.

Chapter 6, Workspace Management, shows an overview of workspace management and goes into detail about bring your own device and why workspace management is a good fit for it. You will then go over organization groups and smart groups again for workspace management before configuring the workspace options. Next, you will go through the pre-enrollment steps before enrolling a device into workspace management. The chapter then finishes off with managing workspace on the device, how to use the Self Service Portal to manage your device and un-enrolling the device from AirWatch.

Chapter 7, Mobile Email Management, gives an overview of Mobile Email Management and the importance of protecting e-mail. You will then learn the supported deployments within AirWatch before covering how to integrate with the Secure Email Gateway, PowerShell, and Direct Google. The chapter then covers the security configurations available with AirWatch and then demonstrates how to set up and configure an e-mail profile. The chapter then finishes off with managing and removing e-mail.

Chapter 8, Mobile Content Management, provides an overview of Mobile Content Management and the importance of protecting content. The next section will cover Mobile Application Gateway for proxy and content before covering the security configurations available. Next, you will learn how to configure content management and then be shown how to access the configured content before learning how to manage and remove the content from a mobile device.

Chapter 9, Mobile Application and Mobile Browser Management, covers Mobile Application Management by providing an overview before showing how to set up and configure Mobile Application Gateway per-app VPN. You will then learn the different application types and how to deploy applications and manage them. The second part of the chapter covers Mobile Browser Management with an overview of what it is before finishing off with the configuration and deployment of browser management.

Chapter 10, Multiuser and Laptop Management, demonstrates what Multiuser Device Management is by providing an overview to the admin before showing how to configure and deploy multiuser devices into the environment. The second part of the chapter covers laptop management, giving an overview of what it is. You will then learn how to configure and deploy laptop management into the environment.

Appendix, The Future of Mobility, gives an overview of where mobility has come from, what we are seeing it being used for today and an overview of what we could potentially see in the future with mobile devices.

What you need for this book

In order to use this book, you will need the following for each of the chapters that require software/hardware:

- For *Chapter 1, Getting Started*, you can deploy the environment on-premise but it is not recommended unless there is a good reason to keep it on-premise. If you aren't a customer of AirWatch and don't have a SaaS environment, you can sign up for a 30-day trial to work through the book at `https://forms.air-watch.com/en/free-trial/?_ga=1.222733083.10488847.1417965363`.

- For *Chapter 3, Enterprise Integration*, you will need Windows 2008 R2, 2012, or 2012 R2 Server with basic requirements to deploy AirWatch Cloud Connector. To perform the integrations, you will need active directory, certificate authorities, and other enterprise systems available to provide integration with AirWatch.

- For *Chapter 5, Mobile Device Management*, you will need an iOS device and an Android device to install the MDM agent and enroll into the environment.

- For *Chapter 6, Workspace Management*, you will need an iOS device and an Android device to install the Workspace application and enroll into the environment.

- For *Chapter 7, Mobile Email Management*, you will need Windows 2008 R2, 2012, or 2012 R2 Server with basic requirements to deploy Secure Email Gateway. You will also need an iOS device to deploy e-mail with the native mail application and an Android device to install AirWatch Inbox to deploy e-mail to it. In order to provide enterprise e-mail to the device, you will need the Exchange and Google Apps for Business environment.

- For *Chapter 8, Mobile Content Management*, you will need a Windows 2008 R2, 2012, or 2012 R2 Server with basic requirements to deploy Mobile Access Gateway for Windows. In addition to server, you will need an iOS device and an Android device to install Secure Content Locker to access corporate content. In order to access your corporate content, you will need to have access to a supported content repository, such as File Share and SharePoint.

- For *Chapter 9, Mobile Application and Mobile Browser Management*, you will need Linux CentOS 6.5 64-bit server with the basic requirements to deploy Mobile Access Gateway for Linux. You will also need an iOS device and an Android device to install AirWatch App Catalog and AirWatch Browser.

- For Chapter 10, *Multiuser and Laptop Management*, you will need an iOS device and an Android device to set up and configure multiuser access. For laptop management, you will need a Mac OS X and Windows 8.1/RT laptop. To enroll, you will need the AirWatch MDM agent for the Mac OS and to configure Windows Workspace and the AirWatch Protection Agent for Windows.

Who this book is for

Learning AirWatch is intended for technical professionals who are looking to implement Enterprise Mobility Management (EMM) or those who are currently managing EMM. This book will give those with no knowledge of AirWatch the information they need to set up, manage, and deploy EMM and mobile solutions. For those who are already experts, this book will provide opportunities in other areas of EMM that they may not have deployed yet. This book will also help organizations who are looking at EMM solutions to better understand the functions, features, and capabilities of AirWatch to provide a better informed decision. By the end of this book, you will have a full understanding of EMM and all the functions involved in deploying the enterprise solution. This book will give the reader the knowledge and confidence to represent EMM and develop mobile opportunities to help drive innovation within their organization.

Conventions

In this book, you will find a number of text styles that distinguish between different kinds of information. Here are some examples of these styles and an explanation of their meaning.

Code words in text, database table names, folder names, filenames, file extensions, pathnames, dummy URLs, user input, and Twitter handles are shown as follows: "The AWCM server external URL should be `server.domain.com` with no HTTPS in front of it."

Any command-line input or output is written as follows:

```
keytool -list -v -keystore $JAVA_HOME\jre\lib\security\cacerts
```

New terms and **important words** are shown in bold. Words that you see on the screen, for example, in menus or dialog boxes, appear in the text like this: "Check **Enable API Access** if not already checked and validate whether an API Key is shown and click on **Save**."

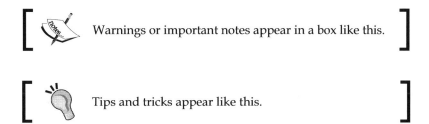

> Warnings or important notes appear in a box like this.

> Tips and tricks appear like this.

Reader feedback

Feedback from our readers is always welcome. Let us know what you think about this book—what you liked or disliked. Reader feedback is important for us as it helps us develop titles that you will really get the most out of.

To send us general feedback, simply e-mail feedback@packtpub.com, and mention the book's title in the subject of your message.

If there is a topic that you have expertise in and you are interested in either writing or contributing to a book, see our author guide at www.packtpub.com/authors.

Customer support

Now that you are the proud owner of a Packt book, we have a number of things to help you to get the most from your purchase.

Downloading the color images of this book

We also provide you with a PDF file that has color images of the screenshots/diagrams used in this book. The color images will help you better understand the changes in the output. You can download this file from http://www.packtpub.com/sites/default/files/downloads/1676EN_ColoredImages.pdf.

Errata

Although we have taken every care to ensure the accuracy of our content, mistakes do happen. If you find a mistake in one of our books—maybe a mistake in the text or the code—we would be grateful if you could report this to us. By doing so, you can save other readers from frustration and help us improve subsequent versions of this book. If you find any errata, please report them by visiting http://www.packtpub.com/submit-errata, selecting your book, clicking on the **Errata Submission Form** link, and entering the details of your errata. Once your errata are verified, your submission will be accepted and the errata will be uploaded to our website or added to any list of existing errata under the Errata section of that title.

To view the previously submitted errata, go to `https://www.packtpub.com/books/content/support` and enter the name of the book in the search field. The required information will appear under the **Errata** section.

Piracy

Piracy of copyrighted material on the Internet is an ongoing problem across all media. At Packt, we take the protection of our copyright and licenses very seriously. If you come across any illegal copies of our works in any form on the Internet, please provide us with the location address or website name immediately so that we can pursue a remedy.

Please contact us at `copyright@packtpub.com` with a link to the suspected pirated material.

We appreciate your help in protecting our authors and our ability to bring you valuable content.

Questions

If you have a problem with any aspect of this book, you can contact us at `questions@packtpub.com`, and we will do our best to address the problem.

1
Getting Started

As you read through the chapters, you will get a full understanding of all the tools included in **Enterprise Mobility Management** (**EMM**) with AirWatch by VMware's mobile management suite. We will go through each of the toolsets available to ensure that you understand what is available and how to set up and configure each of them. The intention of this book is not to dive into extreme detail of AirWatch's EMM but to give you the knowledge needed to understand, represent, and set up the configurations. Understand that the mobile space is an extremely fast-growing market and some of the information might have already been updated. The information presented in this book is current as of AirWatch 7.3.

In this chapter, we will take a look at what is needed to get started with AirWatch; we will explore the different licensing options and what hosting methods are available with support. We will also look at the different types of devices that are supported along with the different profile options to manage the devices. Toward the end of the chapter, we will look at setting up the environment in preparation for the following chapters.

The following will be covered in this chapter:

- An overview of AirWatch
- Management suite options
- Hosting options
- Support options
- Learning and deployment services
- Supported devices
- Device ownership
- Setting up your environment

An overview of AirWatch

AirWatch is based in Atlanta, USA, with offices worldwide. AirWatch has a presence in more than 150 countries, providing usability in 17 different languages. They were founded in 2003 and began their journey with the management of wireless and rugged devices. Today, AirWatch has been recognized by Gartner as the current leader in EMM. In 2014, AirWatch was acquired by VMware, the industry leader in virtualization software for $1.54 billion.

As an EMM platform, AirWatch has built its solutions to support organizations with its mobility deployments and strategies with ease of use and security in mind. With AirWatch's EMM platform, you will be able to implement (depending on the license) the following components:

- Mobile Device Management
- Workspace Management through containerization
- Mobile Application Management
- Mobile Content Management
- Mobile Email Management
- Secure Browser Management
- Enterprise File Synchronization and Sharing
- Multiuser Management
- Laptop Management
- Profiles for personal (BYOD)/corporate-owned/shared devices
- Mobile Security
- Enterprise Integration
- Application store
- Full inventory of all mobile assets
- Management portal

Understanding and implementing these components will allow you to provide corporate information to your work environment. This will allow employees to become more efficient in what they do best, whether it's an executive who is able to retrieve and modify documents securely on their personal device, a pilot who now has their flight plan always up to date contained within a mobile device, or a physician who is able to access patient information securely from their mobile device. These are just a few examples of the power of EMM and the opportunities available with AirWatch and its fully integrated, single pane of glass solution.

Visit `http://www.air-watch.com/` for additional information.

Management suite options

Before you get started with your AirWatch deployment, you will need to decide and select which suite you will implement. AirWatch currently has its management structure broken down into four different color suites: **Green**, **Orange**, **Blue**, and **Yellow**. Each of these suites offer different features depending on what your organization is looking to deploy with EMM.

The following is a breakdown of each **Management Suite**:

Management Suite \ Feature	Green	Orange	Blue	Yellow
Mobile Device Management*	●	●	●	●
Workspace (Container)	●	●	●	●
App Catalog	●	●	●	●
Inbox**		●	●	●
App Wrapping+			●	●
Browser			●	●
Secure Content Locker View			●	●
Secure Content Locker Collaboration++				●
Telecom				●
Chat	Available as an add-on to any of the above Management Suites			
Video	Available as an add-on to any of the above Management Suites			

In the previous figure:

*AirWatch MDM includes native e-mail management with PowerShell integration.

**AirWatch Inbox includes AirWatch SEG.

+AirWatch App Wrapping includes AirWatch Tunnel (iOS only).

++AirWatch Secure Content Locker Collaborate includes AirWatch Secure Content Locker View.

The preceding information was extracted from AirWatch's website at the time of this writing. Review and validate any changes to their suites by visiting http://www.air-watch.com/pricing.

Depending on your mobile strategy and current initiatives, your organization is working on with mobility will depend on which suite to start with. Here is a quick summary of the possible usages of each management suite:

- Green Management Suite:
    - This will be sufficient for those organizations that own all corporate assets
    - For **Bring Your Own Device (BYOD)** initiatives, this suite could create security and legal concerns

Chapter 4, Mobile Security, Chapter 5, Mobile Device Management, and *Chapter 6, Workspace Management* discuss further the security and legal concerns with BYOD.

- Orange Management Suite:
    - This will be sufficient for those organizations with BYOD-only e-mail deployments to provide e-mail security with SEG
    - This suite will not provide protection to attachments without the **Secure Content Locker (SCL)** unless you prevent attachments being delivered to the mobile device

- Blue Management Suite:
  - ° This will most likely be the suite needed for most organizations in order to deliver corporate content with BYOD and meet security requirements
  - ° This will allow for full functionality over all features with the exception of the edit feature within SCL
  - ° SCL will allow for full attachment control within e-mail and access to other repositories
  - ° This has enhanced app features to build on application initiatives

- Yellow Management Suite
  - ° This includes the ability to modify documents within SCL
  - ° This adds the ability to provide EFSS as a service to the users

- The chat and video add-on
  - ° These are the latest features that provide the chat and video functionality with your EMM deployment

You might also have a need to implement multiple suites within your environment to save costs. For example, you might only want to deploy the Green suite for all your corporate-owned assets and the Blue suite for your BYOD deployment. By identifying the business needs and aligning with the mobile strategy, you will be able to select the Management suite that best meets your needs as an organization.

Hosting options

AirWatch currently has both on-premise and cloud offerings for your organization. Making the decision of hosting AirWatch in the cloud or on-premise will be purely determined by your organization's stance on cloud services. There is no difference between the services offered in the cloud or on-premise with AirWatch.

 On premise, the infrastructure will be needed for enterprise integrations whether you are in the cloud or not.

As we have all witnessed over the past few years, there has been a tremendous growth in cloud offerings. This isn't any different with AirWatch and as with many other organizations, AirWatch provides the option of using the cloud to host your EMM suite, also known as their **Software as a Service (SaaS)** offering.

There are a lot of questions regarding migration to cloud environments with security and data privacy and the concerns with the possibility of technical positions being eliminated. For the security concerns, hosting companies are providing the encryption and controls to meet organizations security requirements. For the most part, I'd imagine enterprise-grade cloud services are providing more than what you are able to provide on-premise, including the latest hardware and software with both physical and software security in place along with high availability and disaster recovery. With an AirWatch SaaS deployment, you are only storing the device information in the cloud environment and there is no corporate data being stored in the cloud, thus providing less risk with using that environment.

For the technical personnel concerns, there will be a change, but it doesn't necessarily mean positions being eliminated. Traditionally as technicians, we tend to spend most of our time dealing with installations, upgrades, patches, and failures of the services (both hardware and software). Because of this, our positions have become more of an operational role, taking the focus away from the service being provided and being able to improve on these services for the customers. Now that we are able to offload the heavy burden of our everyday jobs, we can focus more on the solutions/integrations with the product, allowing us the ability to provide a more service-oriented workforce and better user experience. Also, the mobile space is currently an extremely fast-growing area and won't slow down anytime soon. Because of this, eliminating as much management as possible by moving to a cloud environment will also allow us to focus on the end user service and experience, which is what really matters.

By moving to a cloud environment, we are seeing a shift in the structure of teams. Cloud, service, innovative, architecture are some of the names that are starting to appear in team names as we are seeing a shift in the way, as we have traditionally seen **Information Technology (IT)** move to more of an **Information Service (IS)** era.

The following is a breakdown of the hosting options provided by AirWatch:

Hosting options	Description	
On Premise	You have full control over your deployment, installation, and upgrades.	
Cloud SaaS	**Shared SaaS** • The custom URL for an environment setup as redirect • Migration between SaaS and on-premise with re-enrollment • The environment is automatically upgraded based on the quarterly release schedule • Hotfix updates are applied regularly and automatically	**Dedicated SaaS** • The custom URL for environment as setup as CNAME • AirWatch Console access by an IP range • Migration between SaaS and on-premise with no re-enrollment • The environment is upgraded, which requires the customer's approval • Hotfix updates applied require the customer's approval

 AirWatch is also being provided and packaged by other IT hosting companies as a service.

Now that you have all the information on the Management suite and Hosting options, you can make a decision on what best fits your organization. The licensing cost is dependent on which suite you select and the hosting plan you move forward with. The Cloud offering is subscription based per device annually or subscription based per user (up to three devices) annually. The cost includes the standard hosting. The on-premise solution has an initial per device cost with a perpetual annual maintenance fee at a smaller cost of the initial fee.

 For the latest pricing, visit `http://www.air-watch.com/pricing`.

Support options

AirWatch has significantly improved its support model over the recent years. The following table demonstrates the different support options available for your organization:

	Feature	Basic	Enhanced	Enterprise
myAirWatch (Web Support)	Knowledgebase	Full access	Full access	Full access
	Forums	Full access	Full access	Full access
	Documentation	Full access	Full access	Full access
Reactive support	Support channels	Web and phone	Web and phone	Web and phone
	Support requests via web	Unlimited	Unlimited	Unlimited
	Support requests via phone	10 calls/year	Unlimited	Unlimited
	24 x 7 response times for severity 1	Yes (1 hr)	Yes (30 min)	Yes (30 min)
	Weekend response times for severity 2	No (5 x 12)	Yes (2 hr)	Yes (2 hr)
	Priority queue	-	Yes	Yes
	Dedicated support line	-	-	Yes
	Number of supported administrators	3	5	7
	Root cause analysis for severity 1	-	-	Yes
Proactive support	Technical account manager	-	-	Yes
	Annual business reviews	-	-	Yes
	Health checks	-	1/year	2/year
	Road map reviews	-	-	1/year

In the preceding table, severity 1 incidents requiring 24 x 7 coverage must be submitted via phone, and severity 1 incidents are not counted toward calls. This table was extracted from AirWatch's website at the time of writing this book. Review and validate any changes to their support by visiting http://www.air-watch.com/services/support.

Deciding on your support option entirely depends on the extent of your EMM deployment. If you have a small organization with a minimal deployment in the cloud, you might only need Basic Support model. If you have a large enterprise with an on-premise deployment, you will most likely need to go for the Enterprise Support model to ensure that you are receiving the most responsive support with all the proactive features included.

As stated in the preceding table, myAirWatch is available to all customers with a lot of valuable resources. From this portal, you are able to manage support requests, access training, view product documentation, collaborate via forums, view analytics, search, FAQs, view announcements, download software, access best practices within EMM and more. This portal will help empower you as an administrator with instant access to a lot of valuable information. As a customer, you can access the myAirWatch portal at https://my.air-watch.com.

Learning and deployment services

AirWatch also includes the option of purchasing their services to deploy your implementation. These services are standardized based on Management suite you select or can even be customized to meet your deployment and needs.

 To learn more on AirWatch's Professional Services, visit http://www.air-watch.com/services/professional-services.

In 2013, AirWatch created AirWatch Academy. AirWatch Academy is a certification program that provides administrators an avenue to learn and become accredited as an expert in EMM with AirWatch.

AirWatch's Certification program consists of three different levels:

- Associate Certification
- Professional Certification
- Expert Certification

In addition to AirWatch Academy, AirWatch also has its Partner University program to allow AirWatch partners to be fully prepared when it comes to selling, deploying, managing, and supporting the product and solutions.

AirWatch provides opportunities to learn in the following formats:

- Product documentation including architecture designs, how-to guides, checklists, white papers, and installation guides
- ASK knowledgebase with a community of experts
- Live webinars of training, new features, enhancements, and more
- OnDemand Training that provides recorded sessions of instructor-led classes
- Instructor-Led Training on-site, at a training center, or online

 Visit `http://www.air-watch.com/services/training` for additional information on training and certification

In order to become accredited by AirWatch, you will be required to take an exam:

- Questions are focused on real-world examples
- These are multiple-choice questions

It is extremely important to invest and promote time and money with learning. Learning opportunities provide benefit to both the technician and the organization. Having technicians on staff who fully understand the product they are managing and show the incentive to learn will only help drive a successful deployment and service for the organization.

Supported devices

AirWatch supports a wide array of platforms within its EMM suite. Not only is the platform portfolio limited to phones and tablets, but manageability is also available for rugged devices (Android and Windows mobile), Mac OS, Windows PC, and Apple TV. Let's take a look at all the different supported platforms and the functionality available within each of them:

Platform	Manageable Features
Android Version 2.3 or higher	Passcode, Restrictions, Wi-Fi, VPN, Email Settings, Exchange ActiveSync, Application Control, Bookmarks, Credentials, Secure Launcher, Global Proxy, Date/Time, Sound, Display, Advanced (Additional Options), Custom Settings
Apple iOS (Version 4.0 or higher)	Passcode, Restrictions, Wi-Fi, VPN, Email, Exchange ActiveSync, LDAP, CalDAV, Subscribed Calendars, CardDAV, Web Clips, Credentials, SCEP, Global HTTP Proxy, Single App Mode, Content Filter, Managed Domains, Single Sign-On, AirPlay Mirroring, AirPrint, Advanced (Additional Options), Custom Settings
Apple Mac OS X (Version 10.7.0 or higher)	Passcode, Network, VPN, Email, Exchange Web Services, LDAP, CalDAV, CardDAV, Web Clips, Credentials, SCEP, Dock, Restrictions, Parental Controls, Security and Privacy, Login Items, Finder, Accessibility, Printing, Messages, Global HTTP Proxy, Mobility, Managed Domains, Content Filter, AirPlay Mirroring, Custom Settings, Software Update, Directory, Disk Encryption, Login Window, Energy Saver, Time Machine, VMware Fusion
Apple TV (Version 7.0.2)	Restrictions, Wi-Fi, Credentials, Custom Settings
Blackberry (Version 5.0 or higher)	Device, Telecom, Advanced (Additional Options), Custom Settings
Blackberry 10 (Version 10.0.9 or higher)	Passcode
QNX	Custom Attribute
Symbian (Version 3.1+ and S60)	Passcode, Restrictions, Wi-Fi, Exchange ActiveSync, Credentials, Launcher, VPN, Time Sync, Shortcut, Time Zone
Windows Mobile (Version 5.0 or higher including CE 4+)	Passcode, Wi-Fi, Credentials, VPN, Shortcut, Restrictions, Exchange ActiveSync, Launcher, Time Synch, Time Zone
Windows Phone (Version 7.0.0 or higher)	Passcode
Windows Phone 8 (Version 8.0.9900 or higher)	Passcode, Restrictions, Wi-Fi, VPN, Email, Exchange ActiveSync, Application Control, Assigned Access, Credentials, SCEP, Custom Settings

Platform	Manageable Features
Windows 8 / 8.1 / RT (Version 8.0 or higher)	Passcode, Wi-Fi, VPN, Credentials, Restrictions, Firewall, Anti-Virus, Encryption, Automatic Updates, Web Clips, Exchange ActiveSync, SCEP, Custom Settings
Windows PC (Version Windows XP 5.1.0 / Windows Vista 6.0.0 / Windows 7 6.1.0)	Wi-Fi, VPN, Credentials, Shortcuts, Exchange Web Services, Encryption, Passcode

 Some functionalities might not be available on all platforms as they are provided through traditional MDM APIs provided by the operating system.

Device ownership

AirWatch has built its enrolment around three types of ownership: corporate dedicated, corporate shared, and employee owned. As you build your mobility initiatives, it's important to align your deployments with the different ownership types from AirWatch. These different types of ownership grant a different level of access to the device. The configurable options available for each of the device ownership are:

- GPS
  - GPS data

- Telecom
  - Carrier/Country code
  - Roaming status
  - Cellular data usage
  - Call usage
  - SMS usage

- Applications
  - Personal applications

- Commands
  - ° Full wipe
  - ° File manager access
  - ° Remote control
  - ° Registry manager

As stated here, these options are customizable for each of the device ownership types within the administrator console and will most likely be different for each of the ownerships:

- Corporate – Dedicated:
  - ° Should be used for devices owned by the organization
  - ° Will most likely have all options enabled for full access to device

- Corporate – Shared
  - ° A device supplied by the organization to also be used personally, which is also known as **Corporate Owned Privately Enabled (COPE)**. An example of this is a corporate phone that is also allowed for personal use.
  - ° A device supplied by the organization but used by multiple users, which is also known as a **Multiuser Device.**
  - ° This will most likely have most options selected with the exception of some to allow some personal privacy but will depend on the policies enforced by the organization.

- Employee Owned
  - ° This ownership type will be used for personal devices
  - ° There shouldn't be any options enabled as the device is personal and can potentially create a conflict with privacy
  - ° These options will come preconfigured by default but you will want to make sure you set up and document each of the ownership types. For Employee Owned, I recommend that you make this available to users to view as a document or by creating customized Terms of Use for users to read and accept. There will be questions with regard to the ownership type with personal devices. Users are very sensitive with their personal devices and you will at some point be explaining to them exactly what you can see on their devices.

Setting up your environment

Depending on which hosting option you selected, your setup can be as easy as simply logging in with a newly provided user account to the cloud or consist of a lengthy configuration and set up with the on-premise deployment. The following are the requirements needed to get your environment set up based on your choice of deployment:

Shared SaaS

With the SaaS environment, you will have two options for deployment:

- Pure Cloud
- Integrated Cloud

The Pure Cloud option will have no integration with any of your enterprise systems. All accounts will be managed locally and there will be limitations on your deployment. This option might serve a purpose for a smaller organization that doesn't have enterprise systems or is just looking for a simple deployment of AirWatch.

If you move forward with this option, there could potentially be a lot of management needed with local accounts that need to be created and deleted.

The Integrated Cloud option or better known across the industry as Hybrid Deployment provides the same SaaS environment for management with the addition of integrations with your enterprise systems using **AirWatch Cloud Connector (ACC)**, **Mobile Access Gateway (MAG)**, and **Secure Email Gateway (SEG)**. These integrations do require on-premise deployment of servers, which will be covered in *Chapter 3*, *Enterprise Integration*, and *Chapter 7*, *Mobile Email Management*.

With both of these options, getting started is easy. You will be provided with the URL to your environment and login details to gain access. Your URL will look something like `https://cnxxx.awmdm.com`, where xxx will be replaced with a number. Once you have this information and your login details, you are ready to start.

You can set up your own custom URL that is redirected to your SaaS environment.

Dedicated SaaS

The dedicated SaaS environment follows the same options as mentioned previously with the exception of the differences listed in the table present in the *Hosting options* section of this chapter. There are a few reasons to select this option but the primary reason is to gain more control over when updates and Feature Packs can be deployed.

To get started with your dedicated SaaS, you will be provided with the URL to your environment and login details to gain access. Your URL will look something like https://cnxxx.awmdm.com, where xxx will be replaced with a number. Once you have this information and your login details, you are ready to start.

> You can set up your own custom URL using a CNAME DNS record. The recommended configuration is to set up your CNAME record to point to the AirWatch CNAME record, which will direct to the AirWatch Host A record. The reason for this is to allow AirWatch to gain control over where the records point in the event of a failover. If you point your CNAME record directly to the AirWatch Host A record, you will delay the time of a failover, as you will be required to update your DNS records.

On-premise appliance

As an alternative to setting up and configuring your on-premise deployment, AirWatch provides us with the opportunity to use an appliance. The appliance is preconfigured by AirWatch, shipped to the customer ready to simply deploy in the network and turn on.

The following is the sizing chart provided by AirWatch:

Max number of devices	100	500	1,000	2,500	5,000
Number of appliances	1	1	1	1	1
CPU cores	3	3	4	4	4
RAM (GB)	4	4	4	8	8
Hard disk (GB)	21	35	50	95	185

The following are important to know as part of the appliance deployment:

- It is not recommended to enroll more devices than stated per configuration
- Windows server and SQL licenses are included with the appliance
- You will need multiple appliances and your own load balanced solution to provided HA/Failover

On-premise deployment

The last option is the on-premise deployment, that is, giving the customer full control and flexibility over the deployment. This option will require a lot of planning and involvement from multiple teams in order to make it successful.

Since this book is focused more around learning AirWatch, I will not go into deep detail on all the different architecture and options with setting up AirWatch, as this information can easily present itself in its own book. Instead, I will give a high-level overview of the options and requirements to get AirWatch set up.

Before you get started with your on-premise deployment, you will need to fully review the architecture and pre-installation documents provided by AirWatch. You will need to size your environment correctly based on the number of devices you plan to enroll plus future growth.

For the setup and configuration, you will need to involve multiple technical teams with the deployment:

- The Application/Mobility team (Application owner of AirWatch)
- The Database team (SQL database installation and management)
- The Systems management team (provide servers and monitoring)
- The Storage team (provide all storage requirements)
- The Network team (provide Firewall changes, HLB, and other network changes)
- The Security team (validated configurations meet security needs)

Components

For your on-premise deployment, there are three required components:

- **AirWatch Admin Console**: This is the web console used by administrators to set up, configure, and manage devices

- **Device services:** This component allows AirWatch to communicate with the devices

- **SQL database**: All AirWatch information is contained within the SQL database

In addition to the required components, there are several optional components:

- **AirWatch SEG**: Allows greater integration, control, and security with enterprise e-mail systems. This will be covered in detail in *Chapter 7, Mobile Email Management*.

- **AirWatch Cloud Messaging (AWCM)**: AWCM allows AirWatch to directly send commands to Android, Symbian, and Windows mobile devices and push products to PCs and Mac OS X. This allows the elimination of **Google Cloud Messaging (GCM)** for Android devices and reduces security concerns by eliminating communication over public networks.

- **AirWatch Cloud Connector (ACC)**: ACC provides enterprise integrations with multiple different components within the network. This will be covered in more detail in *Chapter 3, Enterprise Integration*.

- **AirWatch Mobile Access Gateway (MAG)**: MAG allows secure integration with enterprise applications and sites and content repositories. This will be covered in more detail in *Chapter 3, Enterprise Integration*; *Chapter 8, Mobile Content Management*; and *Chapter 9, Mobile Application and Mobile Browser Management*.

- **AirWatch App Wrapping**: This allows an organization to add additional security and data loss prevention by wrapping the applications before deployment. This will be covered in more detail in *Chapter 9, Mobile Application and Mobile Browser Management*.

Configurations

There are multiple configurations available with all the different components provided by AirWatch. In summary, the following configurations are provided as examples from AirWatch:

- Basic/Single Application Server Deployment
    - This is recommended for managing less than 1,000 devices
    - This includes all the components on a single server
    - This allows simplified installation, configuration, and integration

- Hybrid Server Deployment
  - ° This is recommended for managing between 1,000 and 5,000 devices but can be used for less if desired
  - ° This solution combines only the Admin console, AWCM and Device Services components onto one server
  - ° Dedicated server for SQL database
  - ° Dedicated server for SEG and other optional components

 Plan to deploy the application server within a **DMZ** if possible for additional security.

- Multiple Server Deployment
  - ° This is recommended for managing more than 5,000 devices but can be used for less if desired
  - ° This solution allows the deployment of components on their own dedicated servers
  - ° Provides greater security by deploying specific components within the DMZ and others on internal network

 Because of the complexity and requirements for this deployment, it is recommended to work with AirWatch on the architecture and configuration.

Requirements

The following tables will give you an idea of the hardware requirements needed for your on-premise deployment:

Application server

Max number of devices	100	500	1,000	2,500	5,000	10,000	25,000
Admin Console	1 standard app server for all roles Virtual Machine / 2 CPUs / 4 GB RAM					1 app server per 50 concurrent admins	
Device Services						1 app server	2 app servers
Device Services with AWCM						1 app server	2 app servers

Database server

Max number of devices	100	500	1,000	2,500	5,000	10,000	25,000
CPU cores	1	1	2	2	2	4	8
RAM (GB)	4	4	4	8	8	16	32
DB size(GB)	10	20	25	50	100	175	250
Trans log size(GB) (Log backups every 15 minutes)	3	5	10	20	40	50	100
Temp DB (GB)	3	5	10	20	40	50	100
Avg IOPS (DB and temp DB)	30	30	30	75	150	300	750
Peak IOPS (DB and temp DB)	40	50	60	150	300	600	1500

There are also minimum requirements and deployment architecture for 50,000 or more devices that can be provided by AirWatch.

Console and device services connectivity prerequisites

Before you can get started with the installation of the console and the device services connectivity server(s), you need to meet all the prerequisites. The following is a breakdown of what is needed before you can start the installation:

The hardware requirements are as follows:

- A VM or physical server

The general requirements are as follows:

- Remote access to Windows servers
- Notepad++ (recommended)
- Firefox or Chrome (recommended)
- Service accounts for authentication to enterprise systems
- Test devices (iOS, Android, Windows Phone 8)

- Corporate Apple ID—if your deployment includes iOS devices, you will need to generate Apple APNs certificate, which is available at `https://appleid.apple.com`

- Corporate Google ID—this is required to search Play Store and push applications to the devices

The software requirements are as follows:

- Externally and internally registered DNS (public IP addresses)

- SSL Certificate from trusted third party with Subject or **Subject Alternative Name (SAN)** of **Domain Name System (DNS)**

- Windows Server 2008 R2 or 2012 or 2012 R2

- Installation of IIS Role with the following services from Server Manager:

  ○ **Common HTTP features**: Static Content, Default Document, Directory Browsing, HTTP Errors, HTTP Redirection

  ○ **Application development**: ASP.NET, .NET Extensibility, ASP, ISAPI Extensions, ISAPI Filters, **Server Side Includes (SSI)**

  ○ **Health and diagnostics**: HTTP Logging, Logging Tools, Request Monitor, Tracing Security: Request Filtering, IP, and Domain Restrictions

  ○ **Performance**: Static content compression, dynamic content compression

  ○ **Management tools**: IIS Management Console, IIS 6 Metabase Compatibility

 Note that Ensure WebDAV is not installed.

- Installation of the following features from Server Manager:

  ○ **.NET Framework 3.5.1 features**: Entire module(.NET Framework 3.5.1, WCF activation)

  ○ **Message queuing**: Message Queuing server

  ○ Telnet client

- Installation of 64-bit Java Runtime Version 7 or higher

- IIS 443 binding with the same SSL certificate (device services only)

- Installation of .NET Framework 4.0

- Microsoft URL Rewrite Module 2.0

Additional proxy software might be required for communication to Apple devices, App Store, and Google Play Store.

The database and reporting services requirements:

- SQL Server 2008 R2 or 2012 running in the 2008 compatibility mode
- Creation of AirWatch database
- SQL collation is `SQL_Latin1_General_CP1_Cl_AS`
- SQL account permissions:
    - ◦ `db_owner` on the AirWatch database
    - ◦ `db_datareader`, public, and SQLAgentUserRole on MSDB
- Ensure Full-Text Search is installed on SQL database
- Reporting services installed and configured in SQL Management Studio
- Reporting services configured with user, password, and database
- Validate SQL account permissions:
    - ◦ `db_owner` on the `ReportServer<Instance>` database
    - ◦ `db_owner` on the `ReportServerTempDB<Instance>` database
- Validate that the Web services URL is reachable
- Validate that the Report Manager URL is reachable
- Validate that the Web services URL is reachable from Console server

The network requirements are as follows:

There are multiple ports that need to be opened on your corporate firewall in order to allow AirWatch to work correctly. The following will need access to internal and/or external Internet resources:

- Admin console server
- Device services server
- SQL server reporting
- Devices (Internet/Wi-Fi)
- Apache Tomcat server

You will need to work closely with your network team to ensure that all the ports on the firewall are opened correctly. There is over four pages of protocol/port configurations to multiple external URLs needed. The required protocol/port configurations can be found in AirWatch On-premise technical architecture guide.

It is highly recommended to implement redundancy with a load balancer. These configurations should be implemented: Round Robin, Session Persistence for Device Services, and Admin Console and redirect all HTTP requests to HTTPS.

The preinstallation check

After implementing all the requirements, you can use AirWatch's preinstallation tool to validate that your on-premise environment is ready to install AirWatch Application server. Once the tool is open, select **Application Server** and then follow the instructions to validate. You will be presented with the results and what needs to be resolved if there is anything.

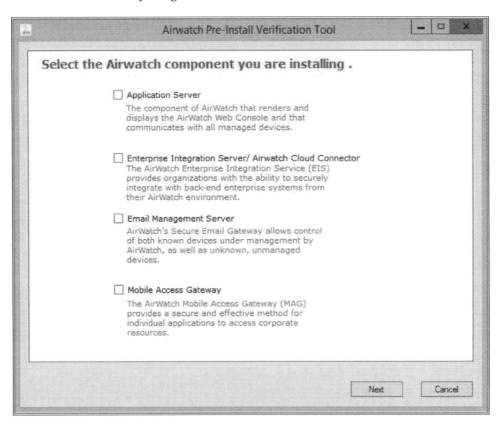

Once you have everything set up correctly, you will be ready to install your environment. AirWatch will provide you with the necessary installation files and services to get your environment up and running on premise.

Deploying AirWatch On-premise will require a lot of preparation and planning, which will require a dedicated senior-level architect/engineer to fully understand the complexities and requirements needed to set up the environment. Unless your organization has a no-cloud policy, it is highly recommended to move forward with a SaaS deployment to allow your teams to focus more on the services being delivered and more importantly, a successful mobile strategy.

Summary

In this chapter, you learned about AirWatch and their product portfolio with mobility. The mobile industry has moved towards an EMM solution. Moving forward with one EMM will allow organizations to simplify their mobile strategy and create more efficient solutions for the end users.

We looked at the different management suite options provided by AirWatch; whether you would need all features or just some depends on the scope of your deployment and the needs of your initiatives. There are different options to host your AirWatch environment, of which SaaS is a popular option. We also looked at the support, learning, and deployment services available from AirWatch and the different options available with each of them.

We also looked at the supported devices within AirWatch along with the different ownership types that devices can be enrolled as (corporate dedicated, corporate shared, and employee owned). To finish the chapter, we reviewed the requirements for setting up the AirWatch environment depending on your deployment type. This leads us to the next chapter, which demonstrates how to access and manage the AirWatch environment once set up.

2
Administration

Now that the infrastructure is set up, we can take a look at the administration of AirWatch by VMware. AirWatch has provided a centralized web-based console to manage its EMM suite, or as its being referred to more often these days, a single pane of glass for management.

As Admin Console is web based, there is no requirement for additional software, plugins, and so on. The latest browser on your desktop will allow you to simply log on and manage your environment. This is a significant benefit over other products that I have had to manage that require additional installations, plugins, configurations, and so on to manage them.

AirWatch Admin Console has improved quite a lot as it's grown from version to version. Currently, at the time of writing this, Admin Console is at Version 7.3. The console is very simple to learn and administrate. As we take our journey through this chapter, I will guide you through all sections of the console, so you'll have a full understanding of where everything is and where to navigate to manage each piece of the EMM suite.

The following will be covered in this chapter:

- Accessing Admin Console
- The Getting Started wizard
- Admin Console overview
- Admin Console in detail

Accessing Admin Console

AirWatch Admin Console is browser based, and it's recommended to use the latest version of Firefox or Chrome for management. By this time, you should have your URL set up whether you received it from AirWatch for your SaaS environment or you created your own custom URL with a dedicated SaaS or on-premise deployment. To access the console, open up a browser and enter your URL as `https://myenvironment.domain.com`. Once you are at the login screen, enter the username and password that were provided or set up during the installation:

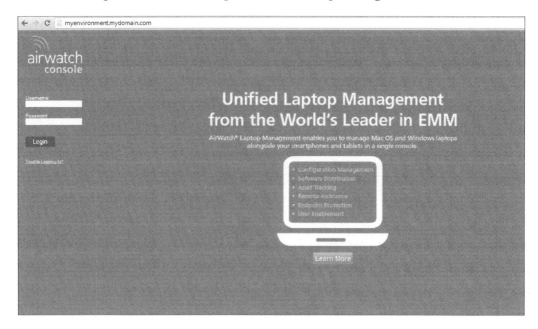

The first time you log in, you will be presented with a screen to set up a four-digit security PIN for your account. The Security PIN will serve as the second factor of authentication for specific tasks within Admin Console to prevent accidental deletion of specific components, device wipes, and so on.

The Getting Started wizard

The next screen you will see once you set up your Security PIN will be the Getting Started wizard. The Getting Started wizard serves as a guide to ensure that you are successful in setting up and configuring your AirWatch environment.

Within the Getting Started wizard, you will be presented with the following tasks:

- The **Setup** menu will consist of the following submenus:
    - **Setup**: This submenu will consist of the **Apple MDM, Apple Certificate**, and **Email Domain** options
    - **Enroll**: This submenu will consist of the **Add User, Enroll Device, Dashboard**, and **Hub** options
    - **Secure**: This submenu will consist of the **Passcode And Encryption, Restrictions**, and **Compliance Policies** options
    - **Configure**: This submenu will consist of the **Profiles, Applications, App Catalog, Privacy**, and **Terms of Use** options
    - **Grouping**: This submenu will consist of the **Organization Groups, User Groups**, and **Smart Groups** options

- The **Configuration** menu will consist of the following submenus:
    - **Enterprise Integration**: This submenu will consist of the **Cloud Connector, Directory Services, Directory Enrollment, Mobile Access Gateway, Certificate Authorities**, and **Certificate Templates** options
    - **Content**: This submenu will consist of the **Upload Content, Install AirWatch Content Locker and Download Content**, and **Content Repository** options
    - **Advanced Enrollment**: This submenu will consist of the **Add Device Restriction** and **Additional Enrollment Customization** options
    - **Workspace**: This submenu will consist of the **Enroll Workspace device** and **View App Profile Settings** options
    - **Email Management**: This submenu will consist of the **Email Integration** option
    - **Administrator Accounts**: This submenu will consist of the **Administrator Roles** and **Admin Accounts** options

- The **Advanced** menu will consist of the following submenus:
    - **Shared Device, Telecom, Mac Management, AW Browser, Customization** and **Advanced Content**

You can disable/re-enable the Getting Started wizard at any time by navigating to **Groups & Settings | All Settings | System | Getting Started | Select or deselect the check box | Click Save**.

You can only configure the Getting Started wizard when **Organization Group Type** is set to **Customer** within **Organization Group Settings**.

Admin Console overview

AirWatch Admin Console consists of a header menu in the top-right and a main menu that flows vertically on the left of the console. The main screen will display the information from the menu item selected. In addition to the two menu items, there is a dropdown to change your organization group in the header menu. In the following screenshot, where it states **Company X Parent Organization Group**, this is where you can change your organization group to manage.

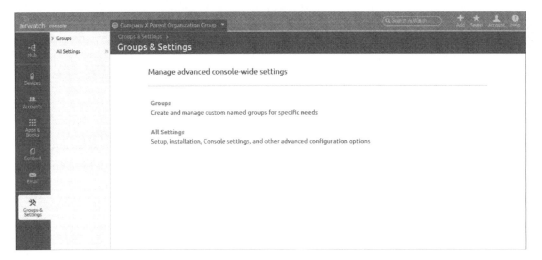

The header menu contains the following options from left to right on the top and bottom rows:

- **Search**: The search feature allows you to search for anything within AirWatch Admin Console.

- **Getting Started**: This option allows you to launch and continue the Getting Started wizard at any time if the wizard is enabled.

- **Add**: This allows you to add an admin, device, user, compliance policy, content, profile, internal application or public application without needing to browse the menu.

- **Saved**: This allows you to access any features you have saved (similar to Bookmarks) within Admin Console.

- **Account**: This allows you to view and change the roles assigned to your account. You can also configure your **Account Settings**, which includes **User Information** and **Security Settings** (security PIN, password, and password questions).

- **Help**: This will launch the online help portal for documentation on Admin Console.

- **Refresh**: This option refreshes the current screen.

- **Available Selections**: This allows you to display/hide items within the main screen.

- **Export**: This allows you to export information presented in the main section.

- **Home**: This navigates back to your homepage within Admin Console.

- **Save**: This allows you to save pages for quick access from the **Saved Pages** option.

The main menu navigation contains all the primary features for you to configure and set up your environment. The options available from top to bottom on the left-hand side of the console are as follows:

- **Hub**: This is the area that gives you a high-level overview of your entire environment including items such as devices enrolled, compliance, profiles, and so on.

- **Devices**: This section includes all management for your devices including profiles, enrollment status, dashboard, and so forth.

- **Accounts**: Here you can manage all your users and administrators, including roles and groups within your environment.

- **Apps & Books**: This section contains management of the app and books catalog along with Apple **Volume Purchase Program** (**VPP**). Other settings include smart groups, app groups, and Geofencing to name just a few.

- **Content**: This is where you manage and upload all content made available to the users. Here you can also manage the content repositories and user storage, along with some other settings related to content.

- **Email**: Here you can view all devices enrolled for e-mail, view reports on devices enrolled with email, and manage all email compliance policies.

- **Telecom**: This section allows you to view and manage telecom usage for those devices configured to collect this information.

- **Groups & Settings**: This is where you manage your organization groups, smart groups, app groups, user/admin groups, and structures related to these groups.

Admin Console's main menu

Now that we have logged in and are familiar with Admin Console, we will go into detail on each of the main menu sections and what can be viewed, set up, and configured within each of them.

Hub

The first of the main menu items is **Hub**. When you click on **Hub**, you will be directed to the **Overview** section by default and presented with a submenu that appears to the right of the main menu, as shown in the following screenshot:

An overview

In the main screen of the **Overview** section, you will be presented with multiple different graphs and reports of the environment. You will find the following **Overview** submenus within the AirWatch **Hub**:

- **Devices**: This submenu consists of the **Status Breakdown, Platform Breakdown**, and **Enrollment History** options

- **Compliance**: This submenu consists of the **Compliance Violations, Top Violated Policies, Devices with Blacklisted Apps** and **Devices without Required Apps** options

- **Profiles**: This submenu consists of the devices without **Latest Profile Version**

- **Apps**: This submenu consists of the devices without **Latest Application Version** and **Most Installed Apps**

- **Content**: This submenu consists of the devices without **Latest Content Version**

- **Email**: This submenu consists of **Policy Violations**

- **Certificates**: This submenu consists of the **Expiring Certificates**

 You can toggle between **Chart View** and **List View** by clicking on the icons in the top-right corner of each view.

Reports & Analytics

Below the **Overview** submenu, the second of the submenu items you will see is **Reports & Analytics**. Within the **Reports & Analytics** submenu, you are presented with two additional menu items, **Reports** and **Events**.

The **Reports** submenu contains two options: **List View** and **Subscriptions**. Within the **List View** section, you are provided with an extensive list of predefined reports from AirWatch. You can also create custom reports on specific criteria and schedule them to be automatically sent to recipients. Within each of the reports, you have four options. The magnifying glass option allows you to view/create the report; you will select the options required and export the report to one of the desired formats (such as PDF, Excel, and CSV). The second option allows you to add the report as a subscription, automating the delivery to selected recipients. The third option allows you to add the report to **My Reports** for easy retrieval and the last drop-down option provides a sample of what the report will provide. These options are shown in the following screenshot:

The **Subscriptions** menu item will take you to the **Report Subscriptions** section, which is within the **Settings** menu. **Report Subscriptions** are those reports you have subscribed to for automatic delivery to a specific user or set of users.

If you see this icon next to a menu item, it will take you to the **Settings** section of Admin Console.

Within the **Events** submenu, there are three additional menu items. The first is **Device Events**, which consists of all events from the devices enrolled within your environment. Within **Device Events**, you can filter within **Date Range**, **Severity**, **Category**, **Module**, or even **Search** to help drill down to what you are looking for. This section can be very useful when it comes to troubleshooting. The **Console Events** section provides all events related to Admin Console. Here you will see any changes, configurations, additions, and so on to Admin Console and by whom. Again, you can filter within **Date Range**, **Severity**, **Category**, **Module**, or even **Search** to help drill down to what you are looking for. This will help identify any misconfigurations and troubleshoot unexpected changes. The last section within **Hub** is the **Syslog** section. This item will direct you to the **Enterprise Integration** section within **Settings**. Here you will be able to configure your **Syslog** settings to output the logs into an enterprise logging server. We will go into more detail about this in *Chapter 3, Enterprise Integration*.

 AirWatch DataMart is a tool that can schedule automatic data exports from AirWatch for statistical analysis and reporting. AirWatch also provides integration with SCCM to allow the export of data automatically to SCCM.

Devices

The next section in the main menu is **Devices**. In this section, you will see all **Devices Enrolled**, **Profiles**, **Compliance Policies**, **Certificates**, **Printers** and other device-specific configurations. In the upcoming screenshot, you can see an overview of the all the submenu options available.

Dashboard

The first submenu within **Devices** is **Dashboard**. Similar to the **Overview** section within the **Hub**, **Dashboard** provides a high-level overview of all enrolled devices within your AirWatch environment. The following is presented on **Dashboard**:

- **SECURITY**: This shows the percentage of devices that are compromised, have no passcode, or that are not encrypted

- **OWNERSHIP**: This shows how many devices are Dedicated corp, Shared corp, Employee Owned, or Undefined

- **LAST SEEN OVERVIEW**: This shows the number and percentage of devices that have been seen recently
- **LAST SEEN BREAKDOWN**: This shows the last time devices were seen with respect to number and days
- **PLATFORMS**: This shows how many devices are enrolled for each platform
- **ENROLLMENT**: This shows how many devices are enrolled, unenrolled, and registered

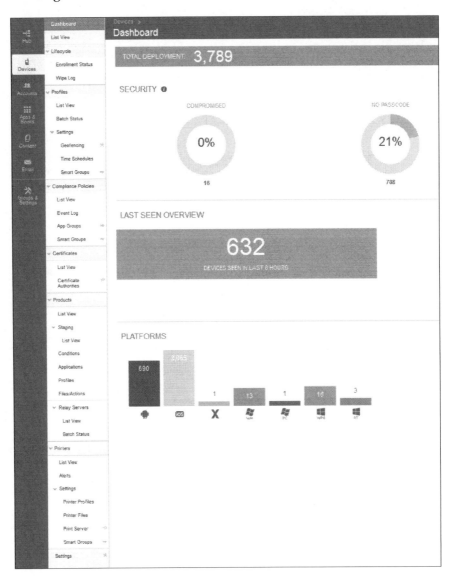

List View

The **List View** section displays all enrolled devices within your organization and allows you to filter your search based on **Management, Ownership, Smart Groups, Platform, Security, Status,** and **Advanced**. Here you can view the status of a device and view additional detailed information of the devices to assist with troubleshooting. You can customize the information being displayed in the main section by customizing the layout within the **Layout** option in the top-right corner. Here is a screenshot for your reference:

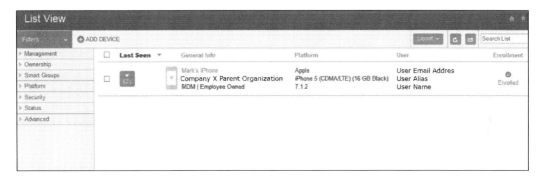

Lifecycle

The next submenu item is the **Lifecycle** section, which contains the following two items:

- **Enrollment Status**: This is where you can view the status of **Enrolled, Registered,** or **Blacklisted Devices**.

- **Wipe Log**: Here you can view the status of any device or enterprise wipes that were sent to a device. You can filter the results by **Date Range, Wipe Type, Status, Source,** and **Ownership**.

Profiles

Next on the list is the **Profiles** submenu with multiple options within it. Profiles are what are configured to manage the devices. This is where you configure all the settings, configuration, policies, and so on for the devices that are enrolled. We will go into more detail about profiles later in the book. Within **Profiles**, you have the following submenus:

- **List View**: This is where you manage all of your profiles within your organization. Here you can add, delete, view, and edit the profiles for your organization. You can also view which platform the profile is for, enable or disable the profile, and even view how many devices the **Profile** is installed or assigned on.

- **Batch Status**: Here you can view the status of any batches that have been set up to import profiles or other specified actions.

- Within **Settings**, you have the following submenus:

  - **Geofencing**: Geofences allow you to define a geographical area that a profile is bound to. If the device falls out of the scope of the geographical area, you can deny access to content or features. This submenu will link you to the **Settings** section to view the configurations.

> Geofencing is available for iOS and Android devices. The device must be connected to the Internet and have GPS capabilities in order for this to work. iOS devices must have **Location Services** enabled also.

  - **Time Schedules**: This allows you to configure when profiles can and can't be used based on the time of day. Once you set up your time schedule, it can be applied to your policies.

  - **Smart Groups**: This is a shortcut to the **Smart Groups** section within the **Groups & Settings** item in the main menu and this will be covered later in this chapter.

> If you see this icon next to a menu item, it is a shortcut/link to another item within Admin Console.

Compliance Policies

Next in the submenu is **Compliance Policies**. This is a critical part of your deployment and allows you to ensure that your users are adhering to the policies put in place. If they aren't, AirWatch allows you to take actions against those devices. For example, you could have a policy that looks for a rooted device. If it detects your device is rooted, you can have AirWatch send an email with a warning email to restore the device back to normal within 24 hours. If they fail to do so, you can then send a command to enterprise or device wipe the data on the device until it is no longer rooted. There are multiple rules that can be put in place with several different actions for each of the rules.

Within **Compliance Policies**, there are three submenus:

- **List View**: Here you can see all compliance policies and whether they are active or inactive. You can also view the number of devices the policy applies to and how many devices are compliant or compromised.

- **Event Log**: This will list all events that have occurred from the compliance policies.

- **App Groups**: This is a link to the **Apps Groups** section within **Apps & Books**, which will be covered later in this chapter.

- **Smart Groups**: This is a shortcut to the **Smart Groups** section within the **Groups & Settings** item in the main menu, which will be covered later in this chapter.

Certificates

Next within **Devices** we have the **Certificates** submenu. This is where we can view any certificates that have been installed on devices enrolled into AirWatch. Within **Certificates**, there are two submenus:

- **List View**: This lists all certificates that have been installed onto enrolled devices.

- **Certificate Authorities**: This is a link to the enterprise integration settings showing certificate authorities that have been configured to be used with AirWatch. We will go into more detail in *Chapter 3, Enterprise Integration*.

Products

Products is the next submenu within **Devices** and allows for enhanced remote device configuration. Product provisioning allows you to deploy an installation of different features based on conditions you set and always ensures that your devices are up to date. This section has grown exponentially with Version 7.3 and this is the section that will be primarily be utilized by rugged devices.

> The bulk of this section has just been introduced in Version 7.3 and won't be covered in detail in this book. Rugged device management is becoming a bigger piece of **Mobile Device Management** (**MDM**) and is moving into a new era as we are seeing the opportunity to leverage these devices with the latest Android OS, allowing for more usability and flexibility over the traditional Windows mobile OS.

Within **Products**, you have the following submenus:

- **List View**: This is where you can create and edit your product provisioning configurations and view the status
- Within **Staging** you have the following submenu:
    - ○ **List View**: This is where you can set up your devices to be automatically configured and enrolled into AirWatch using rapid deployment
- **Conditions**: This is where you can set up conditions that can be applied to your provisioning products
- **Applications**: Here you can add applications that will be used for your provisioning products
- **Profiles**: View, modify, or create profiles that have been created for your provisioning products
- **Files/Actions**: This is where you can create actions and upload files that can be used in your provisioning products

- Within **Relay Servers** you have the following submenus:

  ○ **List View**: Here you can view, manage, and add relay servers to your deployment

  ○ **Batch Status**: Here you can view the status of any batches that have been set up to import relay servers

 Relay server is an FTP(S) server that is used to push products to your devices and for staging your devices. This is a new feature that has just been added as part of the **Product Provisioning** section.

Printers

The second last option is the **Printers** submenu. Here you can view and manage all printers within your AirWatch environment:

- **List View**: This is a view-only dashboard of all printers within AirWatch
- **Alerts**: Here you will be able to view any **Printer** alerts generated
- Within **Settings** you have the following submenus:

  ○ **Printer Profiles**: Here you can add and manage all your printer profiles. At the time of writing this, **Zebra Printers** are the only available profile.

  ○ **Printer Files**: This is where you can upload files to **Printers**. Again, this is currently scoped to **Zebra Printers** at the time of writing this book.

  ○ **Printer Server**: This is a shortcut to the **Settings** section where you can add a print server to the AirWatch environment.

  ○ **Smart Groups**: This is a shortcut to the **Smart Groups** section within the **Groups & Settings** item in the main menu, which will be covered later in this chapter.

Settings

The last submenu in **Devices** is the **Settings** option. This is a shortcut to the **Devices** and **Users** sections within **Settings** that will be covered in more detail later in this chapter.

Accounts

Following **Devices** in the main menu is **Accounts**. This is where you will manage all users, groups, roles, administrators, batches, and so on. The following screenshot displays all menu items within the **Account** section:

The submenu within **Accounts** is divided into two main sections, **Users** and **Administrators**.

Users

The first section we will cover is the **Users** submenu:

- **List View**: This is where you can view and manage all user accounts within the AirWatch environment. These users can either be basic (local) or from an enterprise directory source. Within **List View**, you can add a new user, batch import users, manage a current user, send a message, or remove a user.

> It is recommended that you integrate with an enterprise directory for centralized management of user accounts. Directory Integration will be covered in *Chapter 3, Enterprise Integration*.

- **User Groups**: These are groups that are either created locally or imported from an enterprise directory source and contain users for enrollment. Groups allow you to be more restrictive on enrollment for users by assigning groups to profiles and only allowing members of a specific group to enroll.

- **Roles**: This section is where you can view the different roles that can be applied to a basic user account. These permissions are what define the level of access a user receives with the self-service portal. By default, there are two roles: basic access and full access. You can also create custom roles and assign them to the users.

- **User Migration**: This is where we can migrate any basic user accounts to an LDAP user.

- **Enrollment Status**: This is a shortcut to the **Enrollment Status** section within the **Devices Menu** option.

- **Batch Status**: This section lists all batch imports that have been created. From here, you can also create a batch import to bulk upload users and devices into AirWatch.

AirWatch has a `Template CSV` file for reference for the upload.

- Within **Settings** you have the following submenus:
    - ○ **Directory Services**: This will direct you to the **Directory Services** section within **Enterprise Integration** in **Settings**.
    - ○ **Enrollment**: This will direct you to the **Enrollment** section within **General** in **Settings**.
    - ○ **Terms of Use**: Here you define your terms of use for users to accept and agree to before proceeding. The terms can be applied to different organization groups and can be applied to enrollment, applications installations, and access to Admin Console. You can create and customize as many terms of use that are needed.
    - ○ **All Settings**: This will direct you to the entire **Devices & Users** section in **Settings**.

Administrators

The second main section within **Accounts** is **Administrators**. This section is very similar to the **Users** section with the exception that the admin accounts are those that are used to manage the AirWatch environment and user accounts are those used for enrollment:

- **List View**: This is where you can view and manage all admin accounts within the AirWatch environment. Similar to the user accounts, the admin accounts can either be basic (local) or from an enterprise directory source. Within **List View**, you can add a new user, batch import users, manage/edit a current user or remove a user.

 Make sure that you have more than one global administrator account active in the event something happens with one of the accounts.

- **Admin Groups**: These are groups that are either created locally or imported from an enterprise directory source and contain admins for management. Admin groups allow you to define what specific management tasks an admin can do and where they can do these tasks.

- **Roles**: This is where you can define what exactly an admin can manage within the AirWatch console. There are several predefined roles that you can leverage and if none of them are sufficient, you can create a custom role and configure exactly what the admin is allowed to do. You can simply apply any of the default or custom roles to an admin account or admin group.

- Within **System Activity** you have the following submenus:

    ◦ **Batch Status**: This section lists all batch imports that have been created. From here, you can also create a batch import to bulk upload admins into AirWatch.

    ◦ **Login History**: This section will provide a list of all logins of admins for auditing purposes.

> Make sure that you create admin accounts that reference a user and don't create any generic admin accounts. This will allow you to more efficiently track changes, configuration, and so on within the AirWatch environment.

- Within **Settings** you have the following submenus:

    ◦ **Directory Services**: This will direct you to the **Directory Services** section within **Enterprise Integration** in **Settings**.

    ◦ **Terms of Use**: Here you define your terms of use for users to accept and agree to before proceeding. The terms can be applied to different organization groups and can be applied to applications' installations and access to Admin Console. You can create and customize as many terms of use that are needed.

    ◦ **All Settings**: This will direct you to the entire **Devices & Users** section in **Settings**.

Apps & Books

The next main menu item is the **Apps & Books** section. Here we will be able to view and manage all applications within the AirWatch environment, as well as being able to view analytics on apps, books, and orders. The following is a screenshot of all menu items within **Apps & Books**:

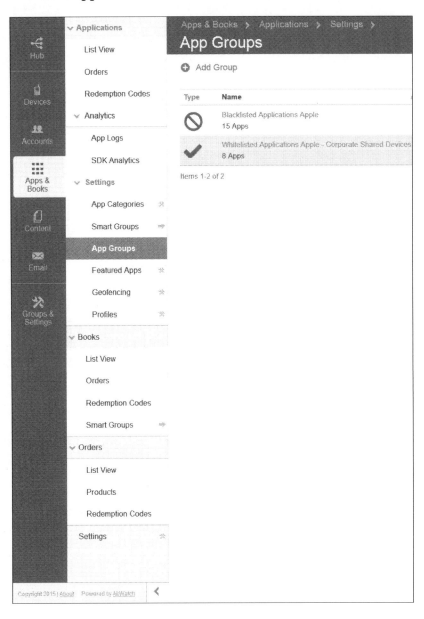

The submenu within **Apps & Books** is divided into four main sections, **Applications**, **Books**, **Orders**, and **Settings**.

Applications

Let's cover the **Applications** section:

- **List View**: This is where you can view and manage all internal, public, or purchased applications within the AirWatch environment. You have the ability to add an internal or public application and add any VPP orders that have been made.

- **Orders**: This is where you can view and add app purchases via Apple VPP. You can upload your public or custom order spreadsheet in CSV or XLS format.

- **Redemption Codes**: Here you can view all your VPP redemption codes.

- Within **Analytics**, you have the following submenus:
    ◦ **App Logs**: This is where you can view any information and warning or error logs related to the app. There are three different types of logs available: **App Log, Crash Log**, and **Device Log**.

    ◦ **SDK Analytics**: In this section, you can view all events related to any application that is using the AirWatch SDK. You can refine your search based on the application ID and event name.

- Within **Settings** you have the following submenus:
    ◦ **App Categories**: The first option within **Settings** is **App Categories.** This will direct you to the **Application Categories** section in **Settings**.

    ◦ **Smart Groups**: This is a shortcut to the **Smart Groups** section within the **Groups & Settings** item in the main menu, which will be covered later in this chapter.

    ◦ **App Groups**: This is where you can allow or deny access to applications within groups to specific organization groups. There are three types of groups that are available: **Blacklisted, Whitelisted**, and **Required** applications.

    ◦ **Featured Apps**: This will direct you to the **Featured Applications** section under **Settings | Apps | Catalog**.

    ◦ **Geofencing**: This will direct you to the **Geofencing** section under **Settings | Devices & Users | Advanced**.

    ◦ **Profiles**: This will direct you to the **Profiles** section under **Settings Apps | Settings and Policies**.

Books

The second submenu within **Apps & Books** is **Books**. This is where you can distribute and manage books. **Books** are better known as **iBooks** and are currently only available for iOS devices. The following menu items are contained within **Books**:

- **List Views**: This is where you can view and manage all internal, public, or purchased books within the AirWatch environment. You have the ability to add an internal or a public book and add any orders that have been made.

- **Orders**: This is where you can view and add book purchases via Apple VPP. You can upload your book order spreadsheet in the CSV or XLS format.

- **Redemption Codes**: Here you can view all your VPP redemption codes.

- **Smart Groups**: This is a shortcut to the **Smart Groups** section within the **Groups & Settings** item in the main menu that will be covered later in this chapter.

Orders

The third submenu within **Apps & Books** is **Orders**. This is where you can view and manage all Apple VPP orders within AirWatch. The following are the menu items within **Orders**:

- **List Views**: This is where you can view and manage all your app, books, and custom orders within the AirWatch environment

- **Products**: This is where you can view and manage all purchased products through VPP

- **Redemption Codes**: Here you can view all your VPP redemption codes

Settings

The last option within the **Apps & Books** menu is **Settings**. This will direct you to the **Apps** section in **Settings**.

Content

The next main menu item is the **Content** section. This is where you are able to configure and provide access to all your enterprise content to users on their mobile devices securely.

Dashboard

The first submenu in **Content** is **Dashboard**. Here you can get a high-level view of the content that has been deployed to the users. Within **Dashboard**, there are four data views:

- **STORAGE HISTORY**: Here you can view the storage history of storage available in your environment.

- **USER/CONTENT STATUS**: Here you can view users who are missing the required documents, latest version, or content that is near expiration. You can click on each of these items to view users and content listed.

- **CONTENT ENGAGEMENT**: This section will list the most and least viewed files by your end users. Clicking on the section will display up to 50 files, allowing you to better identify what is being viewed and what is not.

- **USER BREAKDOWN**: Here you will see the end user activity by **TODAY**, **THIS WEEK**, or **THIS MONTH**.

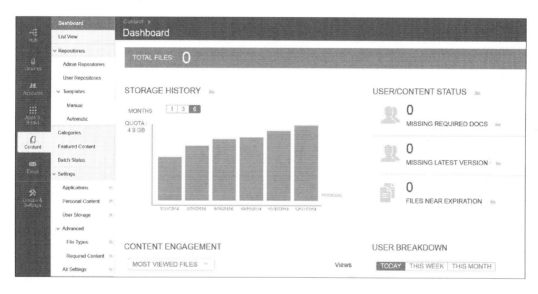

List View

The next submenu item is the **List View**. Here you can view and manage all content that has been published to the users. You can also add new content here and assign it to specific organization groups, so only specific users receive the content.

The maximum allowed file size is 200 MB.

Repositories

The next down the list is the **Repositories** section. This is where you will manage and create your repositories for the users to access their storage and documents. Let's have a look at its submenus:

- **Admin Repositories**: This is where you can set up and manage repositories that will be made available to your users in Secure Content Locker. Repositories include Network Shares, SharePoint, Office 365, Google Drive, and much more. These repositories will be published to everyone in the organization group it is published to.

- **User Repositories**: You can set up user repositories based on templates that allow users to access their content. Users can manage these repositories via **Self Service Portal (SSP)**. This section will display all User Repositories that have been made available to the user.

- Within **Templates** you have the following submenus:

  ○ **Manual**: This is where you can create and manage templates to allow users to manually add their own repositories from the SSP.

  ○ **Automatic**: This is where you can create and manage templates using lookup values to automatically create a user repository.

Categories

The next submenu item within **Content** is **Categories**. This is where you can organize your content and allow easier searches for your documents. It is recommended that you create your categories before you start uploading the content to allow an organized structure of content for your users.

 You do not need to manually create content categories if you integrate with an external content repository.

Featured Content

Featured Content is the next submenu within **Content**. Here you can manage content that has been added as **Featured Content** from the **List View** page of all the documents. **Featured Content** allows you to provide users with easier access to this content.

Batch Status

Next in the **Content** menu is **Batch Status**. This section allows you to batch import documents into the console via a CSV file to make available to the end users. If you aren't able to provide access to your repositories, this will provide an option to easily upload multiple files into AirWatch.

Settings

The last submenu item within **Content** is **Settings**. The following menu items are present within **Settings**:

- **Applications**: This will direct you to the **Applications** section within **Content** in **Settings**

- **Personal Content**: This will direct you to the **Personal Content** section within **Content** in **Settings**

- **User Storage**: This will direct you to the **User Storage** section within **Content** in **Settings**

- Within **Advanced** you have the following submenus:

   ◦ **File Types**: This will direct you to the **Advanced | File Types** section within **Content** in **Settings**

   ◦ **Required Content**: This will direct you to the **Advanced | Required Content** section within **Content** in **Settings**

- **All Settings**: This will direct you to **Content** in **Settings**

Email

Email is the next main menu item in the console. This is where you can view and manage all users and devices that have been enrolled for email within your environment.

Dashboard

The first submenu is **Dashboard**. Within **Dashboard**, you are provided with the following options:

- **MAIL CONFIGURATION STATUS**: Here you have a high-level overview of all **Blocked, Allowed, Blacklisted**, and **Whitelisted** devices.

- **MANAGED MAIL CONFIGURATIONS**: This lists the total number of devices with mail configurations.

- **POLICY VIOLATIONS**: This shows how many devices are not in compliance.

- **LAST SEEN**: Here you can see a breakdown of when the devices were last seen by hours.

- **MEM CONFIGURATIONS**: This lists all MEM configurations and how many devices are enrolled in each.

- **TOP 5 EAS DEVICE TYPES**: A view of the different types of devices accessing configured for email.

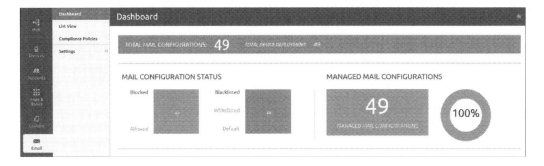

List View

The next submenu item within **Email** is **List View**. This section provides a view of all devices that are being managed by AirWatch for email access. You can list by **Device** or **User** and view the current status of the enrolled device, whether they are blocked, compliant, and so forth. There are also multiple filters to allow you to be more granular in your search, and you have the ability to whitelist or blacklist devices from here.

Compliance Policies

Compliance Policies is the next option within **Email**. Here you can provide additional security controls to your environment. The additional controls provided are grouped into three categories: **General Email Policies**, **Managed Device Policies**, and **Email Security Policies**.

 In order to leverage the compliance policies, you will need the SEG. This will be covered in *Chapter 7, Mobile Email Management*.

Settings

Settings is the last item within the **Email** menu; this option will direct you to the **Configuration** section within **Email** in **Settings**.

Groups & Settings

The last main menu item is **Groups & Settings**. This is where you will manage all of your groups within AirWatch. These groups include **Organization Groups**, **User Groups**, **Smart Groups**, **App Groups**, and **Admin Groups**. The last option in this menu is **All Settings**; here we are directed to a separate screen with all AirWatch settings. The following is a screenshot of all submenu items within **Groups & Settings**:

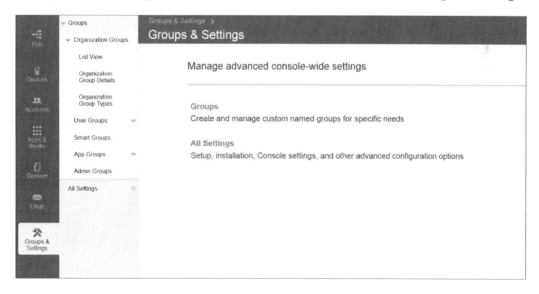

Groups

The first submenu of **Groups & Settings** is **Groups**. Within **Groups**, our first section is **Organization Groups**. **Organization Groups** are core to your deployment and it's extremely important that you set these up correctly from day one to best meet your organization's needs. There are many ways to set up **Organization Groups**, and there is not necessarily one correct way, as what works well for one company may not work very well for another. **Organization Groups** are what identifies users or devices receive when enrolled. During enrollment, your device is assigned to a specific organization group to which profiles are assigned. These profiles define what you have access to within your environment based on configurations from the admin.

It is important to understand your organization structure to set up your **Organization Groups** effectively. In my current role, we decided to create our **organization Groups** into **Bring Your Own Device (BYOD)** and corporate owned devices underneath the global organization group. Within BYOD and corporate owned devices, we created child **Organization Groups** pertaining to different BYOD and corporate owned initiatives. This has allowed us to keep our administration simpler by keeping our initiatives consistent for all our customers. If you work in a large enterprise that would prefer to delegate out to its different locations or facilities, you could create a hierarchy under the parent **Organization Group** based on location and/or facility. Within each location and/or facility, you could then create your child **Organization Groups** for each of your initiatives and delegate more granular admin access to only these child **Organization Groups**.

Before you start deploying into production, set up and test your organization groups to see whether they will work effectively. It may take a couple of times to create a hierarchy that better fits your organization, but it will help in the long-term management of the deployment.

The **Groups** menu consists of the following submenus:

- Within **Organization Groups** you have the following submenus:
    - **List View**: This is where you can view the hierarchy of all your organization groups.

List View

Organization Group	Active Devices	Inactive Devices
▼ Company X Parent Organization Group	1	0
▼ Location X	0	0
Initiative 1	0	0
Initiative 2	0	0
▼ Location Y	0	0
BYOD	0	0
Corporate Owned	0	0

- ○ **Organization Group Details**: This is where you can view and modify the details of all your organization groups and create a new child **Organization Group**.

- ○ **Organization Group Types**: Here you can create your own customized categories for your **Organization Groups**. This will help you organize and categorize your structure based on your organization.

- **User Groups**: This will direct you to the **User Groups** section under **Accounts | Users** covered earlier in this chapter.

- **Smart Groups**: This allows you to create customized groups to help define what applications and/or books an end user receives based on specific criteria.

- **App Groups**: This will direct you to the **App Groups** section under **Apps & Books** covered earlier in this chapter.

- **Admin Groups**: This will direct you to the **Admin Groups** section in **Accounts | Administrators** covered earlier in this chapter.

 To change organization groups, simply click on the drop-down arrow in the header of the console and select the desired group you would like to manage.

All Settings

The last item in **Groups & Settings** is the **All Settings** option. This will direct us to a separate screen to manage **All Settings** within the AirWatch environment.

As you can see in the preceding screenshot, there are a lot of options within the **Settings** screen. This is where the primary environment configurations will take place. The majority of these configurations can also be applied to specific **Organization Groups** for customized deployments. Simply click on the drop-down in the header as described earlier and select the **Organization Group** you would like to make changes to. Validate whether the **Override** option is selected to make the changes. The **System** settings will be covered at a very high level, and as we progress through the chapters, we will be revisiting a lot of these sections in detail as we cover each of the specific EMM components:

- The **System** setting consists of the following options:
    - ○ **Getting Started**: This was covered earlier in the chapter; here we can configure whether we want to view the **Getting Started** option.
    - ○ **Branding**: Here we can customize the branding for the environment. Customizations include logos, theme colors, and custom CSS.
    - ○ **Enterprise Integration**: This is where we will configure all of our enterprise integrations. We will cover this in detail within *Chapter 3, Enterprise Integration*.
    - ○ **Help**: This is where we can enable or disable the **Help** option.

- ° **Security**: This is where we can configure what actions require you to enter your security PIN for second factor authentication to prevent accidental deletion. We can also configure data encryption and secure private resources within the console.

- ° **Localization**: This is where you can specify which languages are available to be used within Admin Console.

- ° **Peripherals**: Here you can set up and configure any print servers to be used within the environment.

- ° **Reports & Alerts**: You can view and manage all reports you have subscribed to within AirWatch.

- ° **Terms of Use**: This is where you can create and manage all of your terms for users to accept for the console, enrollment, and application downloads.

- ° **S/MIME**: Here you can configure whether AirWatch should retain the S/MIME certificates or not.

- ° **Advanced**: Here you can view and configure your REST and SOAP APIs as well as view any API event notifications.

- The **Devices & Users** setting consists of the following options:

  - ° **General**: Within this section, you can configure all your **Enrollment** settings for when devices enroll into your environment.

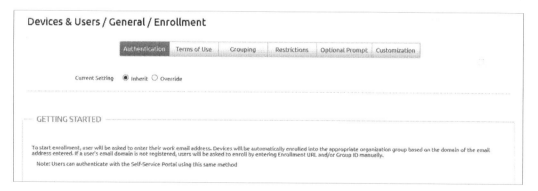

Other options within **General** allow you to customize the **Friendly Name** of the device, add custom **Lookup Fields,** and configure your **Shared Device** options along with some additional **Advanced** settings. You can also view/add/customize your **Message Templates** within the **General** section that allow you to e-mail, SMS, or push messages to the users for different scenarios. The **General** drop-down menu also contains the **Privacy** section. This is where you specify what can be viewed on each of the ownership types, as discussed in *Chapter 1, Getting Started.*

 It is important that you set up **Privacy** settings correctly from day 1 and that you understand any Privacy Laws that may apply within your State, or Country especially for BYOD deployments.

○ **Android**: This is where you can configure the **Agent Settings, Google Play Integration,** and **Service Applications** for Android devices.

- ° **Apple**: Here you have all your Apple-specific device configurations. Configurations in this section include the APNs for MDM, configurations for Apple iOS, configurations for Apple Mac OS X, and automated profiles can be created to be used in Apple Configurator, Apple's Device Enrollment Program, and SCEP enrollment.

- ° **Blackberry**: This is where you can configure your Blackberry device settings for your Blackberry 10 and Legacy Blackberry devices.

- ° **Symbian**: The only option available for Symbian devices is to configure **Agent Settings**.

- ° **QNX**: The only option available for QNX devices is to configure **Agent Settings**.

- ° **Windows**: Here you can configure all your device settings for Windows mobile, Windows Phone 7, Windows Phone 8, Windows PC, and Windows 8/RT.

- ° **Advanced**: **Advanced** options include **Bulk Management**, **Custom Fields**, **Device Groups**, **Geofencing**, **Tags**, **Wipe Protection**, and **Custom Attributes**.

- The **Apps** setting consists of the following options:

  - ° **Application Integration**: This section provides applications available that can integrate with AirWatch.

  - ° **Browser**: This is where you configure all your AirWatch browser settings, bookmarks, and notifications.

  - ° **Catalog**: Within the **Catalog** section, there are multiple options that can be configured. These options include **General catalog configurations**, **App Catalog without MDM options**, **App restrictions**, **Applications Categories**, **Application Workflow**, **External App Repository**, **Featured Applications**, **App Reputation**, and **VPP Managed Distribution**.

  - ° **Inbox**: Here you can configure your AirWatch **Email Client** settings and policies.

  - ° **Workspace**: Here you can configure your **Workspace** notification settings.

  - ° **Settings And Policies**: This section allows you to configure all **Security Policies**, **Settings**, and **Profiles** related to AirWatch apps.

- The **Content** setting consists of the following options:

  ○ **Applications**: This is where we can configure the settings for the **SCL Sync**, **Secure Content Locker**, and **Outlook Add-in**.

  ○ **Personal Content**: Here you can manage the personal content storage available to the users.

  ○ **User Storage**: This lists the storage usage for your enrolled users.

  ○ **Remote Storage**: Here you can configure **Remote File Storage** as an alternative from using AirWatch provided storage.

  ○ **Advanced**: This is where you can configure allowed **File Types** and require users to view the **Required Content** as part of the onboarding process.

- The **Email** setting consists of the following options:

  ○ **Configuration**: This is where you will configure your Mobile Email Management (MEM) Configurations within AirWatch.

- The **Admin** setting consists of the following options:

  ○ **Data Samples**: This is where you can view your data samples.

Summary

As you can see from this chapter, AirWatch has a lot of management options within Admin Console. Once you get familiar with all the components and understand where everything is to be managed, you'll find that the management of AirWatch is fairly simple. Having Admin Console available within a browser is also an added benefit as there is no requirement for additional software.

You first learned how to access Admin Console through the provided URL from AirWatch, or the one you customized or created for your on-premise deployment.

We then looked at Admin Console at a high level and in detail, giving an overview of all the available menu options. Now that you are familiar with Admin Console, we will move onto the next chapter, which will provide you with details on Enterprise Integrations available with AirWatch.

3
Enterprise Integration

Now that you are familiar with Admin Console and how to get around, the next component of EMM is the integration of AirWatch by VMware with your enterprise systems. It is critical and highly recommended that you integrate with your enterprise systems for greater security and control over your users and the environment. For example, if you already have an enterprise directory for your users, why duplicate the effort by creating the accounts again? I'd imagine you will also have a termination process in place with your enterprise directory. By integrating your enterprise directory with AirWatch, you create more efficient workflows by allowing your enterprise directory to manage the accounts and user information, which allows better scalability, especially if there are thousands of users within your deployment.

There are multiple enterprise integrations now available with AirWatch to provide that true EMM solution and allow you to leverage current implementations within your environment. This allows for a more integrated and secure solution. For your integrations, you will want to start with the core integrations into your enterprise systems. These core components include directory services, certificate services, e-mail integration, and logging. To integrate with these core components, AirWatch has its ACC tool. In this chapter, we will look at what is required to get the ACC tool configured and set up to provide the core integrations.

Once we've walked through the ACC setup and configuration, we will give you an overview of the other AirWatch integrations that include the SEG and the **Mobile Application Gateway** (**MAG**). To finish off the chapter, we will look at third-party enterprise integrations that are available with AirWatch.

The following will be covered in this chapter:

- An overview of enterprise integration
- Core enterprise integrations
- AirWatch Cloud Connector
- Configuration of Core enterprise integrations
- An overview of Mobile Access Gateway and Secure E-mail Gateway
- Other enterprise integrations

An overview of enterprise integration

As already mentioned, it is critical that you integrate your AirWatch environment with your enterprise systems. Enterprise integration is available for both on-premise and cloud environments to provide a more secure and robust deployment. Here is an overview of some of the enterprise integrations that are possible with your AirWatch deployment.

Directory services

AirWatch allows you to integrate with your enterprise directory services. This will most likely be your first integration to allow you to import your existing users and groups to allow easier management and efficient enrollment. Integrating with your directory services allows you to maintain consistency between your identities, as changes from your corporate directory will synchronize with AirWatch. This will also provide better security because when an account is disabled in your corporate directory, the changes will synchronize with AirWatch and disable the account, removing any profiles that have been installed on the user's device. One of the biggest benefits with the directory integration is the ability to leverage the current user account login information, providing a better user experience. When it comes to enrollment, it's as simple as instructing the user to enter their current username and password for enrollment; it does not require them to remember a separate username or password like it would with no-directory integration.

The following directory types can be used for integration with AirWatch:

- Active Directory
- Lotus Domino
- Novel e-directory
- Other LDAP

Certificate and Public Key Infrastructure

AirWatch also provides the ability to integrate with Certificate Authorities, **Public Key Infrastructure** (**PKI**), or third-party providers for advanced user authentication and security. Some of these advanced authentication integrations include e-mail, Wi-Fi, and VPN with the ability to automatically distribute the certificates to devices as part of enrollment. Deploying certificates to devices can provide second factor authentication to your corporate resources for added security or allowing corporate-owned mobile devices to access internal networks allowing for more efficient workflows for your users.

The following Certificate Authorities are some of those available for integration with AirWatch:

- Microsoft AD CS
- Symantec/VeriSign Managed PKI
- OpenTrust CMS mobile
- Entrust
- RSA Certificate Manager
- Generic SCEP

E-mail

Integration with your corporate e-mail infrastructure is available with multiple options for integration and deployment. AirWatch allows you to easily configure and deploy an e-mail to users' devices with security in mind. E-mail integration will be covered in more detail in *Chapter 7, Mobile E-mail Management*. The following e-mail infrastructures are some that are available for integration with AirWatch:

- Microsoft Exchange
- Microsoft Office 365
- Novell GroupWise
- Lotus Notes
- Google Apps

System Information and Event Management

AirWatch provides the ability to integrate with external **System Information and Event Management** (**SIEM**) solutions, allowing enhanced security and to be compliant with any regulations and/or corporate policies. AirWatch has the flexibility of exporting both device and console events to your enterprise SIEM. The following SIEM systems are some that are available for integration with AirWatch:

- Splunk
- RSA enVision
- ArcSight
- Tivoli
- Q1 Labs

Content repositories

Integrating with your content repositories allows you to manage and provide your corporate documents to your users securely via their mobile devices. Content repositories are provided to the users with AirWatch's SCL. Content repositories will be covered in more detail in *Chapter 8, Mobile Content Management*. The following content repositories are some of those that are supported with AirWatch:

- Network and file shares
- WebDAV
- SharePoint on-premise and online
- OneDrive
- Google Drive
- CMIS

Corporate networks

Integrating with your corporate networks allows you to provide an additional layer of security with your mobile devices and provides more visibility over mobile devices within your network. With corporate networks integration, you can better manage which networks users can access, enforce secure connections to your corporate resources using VPN, and provide automation to access your Wi-Fi networks. The following list provides some of the corporate network integrations available:

- Cisco
- Juniper Networks
- F5

- Dell
- Aruba Networks
- PPTP, WPA/WPA2, WEP, and VPN

APIs

AirWatch APIs allow you to integrate with existing IT infrastructure and third-party applications. The ability to integrate with open APIs allows easy integration and communication between systems without the need for additional programming, customization, and programs. An example of this is the ability to integrate your peripheral devices with AirWatch to allow communication and commands between devices and the AirWatch console. The following are the currently supported APIs:

- SOAP
- REST

Core enterprise integrations

For those of you who have been customers for a while, you are most likely to set up your integrations with **Enterprise Integration Service (EIS)**. EIS provides the ability to securely integrate with enterprise systems through one service whether you are an on-premise or SaaS customer. EIS has now been divided into two different products to allow improved integration. ACC and MAG are the most current enterprise integration from AirWatch around which we will focus our attention. EIS is still fully supported by AirWatch but they do recommend upgrading to ACC and MAG to receive the latest integration capabilities.

In order to integrate with what I consider the core enterprise components (directory services, certificate services, e-mail integration, and logging), you are required to set up the ACC service. ACC is an additional service that needs to be installed on Windows Server on your network to provide secure communication between the enterprise systems and AirWatch. The ACC installation is required on your network irrespective of whether you are a SaaS or on-premise customer.

The following enterprise integrations are available with ACC:

- Directory Services (LDAP/AD)
- Certificate Services:
  - Microsoft Certificate Services
  - Simple Certificate Enrollment Protocol (SCEP)
  - Other third-party Certificate Services

- Email Management Exchange 2010 (PowerShell)
- Blackberry Enterprise Server (BES)
- E-mail Relay (SMTP)
- Syslog (Events)

AirWatch Cloud Connector

Next, we will look at **AirWatch Cloud Connector** (**ACC**) and how to deploy it into your AirWatch deployment. In this section, we will cover the deployment options for ACC, requirements, how to install it, and its configuration.

ACC deployment options

Depending on which deployment method you selected for your AirWatch environment, whether on-premise or SaaS, will depend on how ACC will be deployed into your environment. If you have a small organization and you deployed on-premise, you may have opted to consolidate components, which means that your ACC can be on the server with all of the other components. If you are an on-premise deployment and you opted to set up a hybrid or multiple server deployments, your ACC will most likely be on a separate server, which will require communication to the AWCM server within your environment. If you are a SaaS customer, you will be required to set up a new server to install the ACC service for integration. There is no difference between the SaaS and on-premise integrations of ACC.

> Deploying ACC with an on-premise AirWatch installation is optional but will save the need to open additional ports between Device Services servers (which will be in DMZ) and the internal infrastructure. Deploying ACC with an on-premise installation allows firewall traversal, thereby creating a more secure deployment.

The following diagram shows the architecture of ACC for a SaaS customer and an on-premise user with multiple roles:

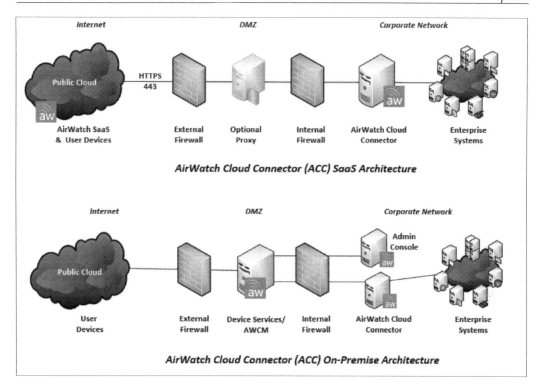

AirWatch Cloud Connector (ACC) SaaS Architecture

AirWatch Cloud Connector (ACC) On-Premise Architecture

ACC requirements

This section lists all the requirements for the ACC deployment. The hardware requirements for the ACC deployment are tabulated as follows:

Max number of users	Up to 10,000	10,000–50,000	50,000–100,000	100,000–200,000
Disk size	Standard OS requirements with 1 GB for ACC application and 5 GB for logging			
CPU cores	2	2 load-balanced servers with 2 CPU cores	2 to 3 load-balanced servers with 2 CPU cores	2 load-balanced servers with 4 CPU cores
RAM (GB)	4	4	8	16

Load balancing ACC varies depending on which version of AirWatch you are using. With version 5 of the AWCM services and 7.1 of AirWatch, you will be required to sit behind a load balancer. Prior to these versions, ACC is automatically load balanced.

The software requirements for the ACC deployment are listed as follows:

- Supported operating systems
  ◦ Windows Server 2008 R2
  ◦ Windows Server 2012
  ◦ Windows Server 2012 R2
- PowerShell (optional)
- .NET Framework 4.0

The general requirements for the ACC deployment are listed as follows:

- Remote access to ACC servers
- Notepad++ (recommended)
- Service accounts for authentication to enterprise systems

The network requirements for the ACC deployment are tabulated as follows:

Source component	Destination component	Protocol	Port
ACC server	AWCM for on-premise customers	HTTPS	2001
ACC server	AirWatch SaaS for AirWatch-hosted customers	HTTPS	443
ACC server	AirWatch Admin Console	HTTP or HTTPS	80 or 443
ACC server (optional)	Internal SMTP	SMTP	25
ACC server (optional)	Internal LDAP	LDAP or LDAPS	389, 636, 3268, or 3269
ACC server (optional)	Internal SCEP	HTTP or HTTPS	80 or 443
ACC server (optional)	Internal ADCS	DCOM	135, 1025–5000, 49152–65535
ACC server (optional)	Internal BES	HTTP or HTTPS	80 or 443
ACC server (optional)	Internal Exchange 2010 or higher	HTTP or HTTPS	80 or 443

The option of using an outbound proxy is available. The only requirement is the outbound connection from ACC must always be open and not terminate or reject connections.

Installing ACC

This section will cover the steps to install ACC. If you currently have EIS installed, you will need to go through a migration to set up ACC. The EIS to ACC migration can be found in *AirWatch Cloud Connector Guide for SaaS Customers* documentation or *AirWatch Cloud Connector Guide for On-Premise Customers* documentation in the myAirWatch portal.

To install ACC into your environment, you will need to complete the steps explained in the upcoming sections.

Installing Secure Channel Certificate on all AWCM servers

This is only required for on-premise deployments and may have already been complete as part of your AWCM installation. You will need to run through the following steps if this hasn't been completed to establish security between Admin Console and AWCM:

1. In the AirWatch console, navigate to **Groups & Settings | All Settings | System | Advanced | Secure Channel Certificate**.

2. Within the AirWatch **Cloud Messaging** section, click on **Download AWCM Secure Channel Installer**.

3. Copy the downloader to your AWCM server and run the installation.

4. Click on **Browse** to find the **Truststore** path, enter the password in the **Password** field, and then click on **OK** to verify that the certificate was successfully added.

Establishing communications with AWCM

The remaining steps will be applied to both SaaS and on-premise deployments. This allows you to configure the communication from AirWatch to use a specific AWCM server.

These settings may have already been configured for you if you are a SaaS customer, which means you won't see this section.

1. Navigate to **Groups & Settings | All Settings | System | Advanced | Site URLs** to access the AirWatch **Cloud Messaging** section.

2. Click on **Enable AWCM Server** and enter the values for **AWCM Server External URL**, **External Port** (443 for secure communication), and **AWCM Service Internal URL**, and then click on **Test Connection** to validate the configuration.

Enabling ACC from Admin Console

The next step is to enable ACC from Admin Console, generate the certificates, and select the enterprise integration services you would like to use:

1. Navigate to **Groups & Settings | All Settings | System | Enterprise Integration | Cloud Connector** and select **Enable Cloud Connector**.

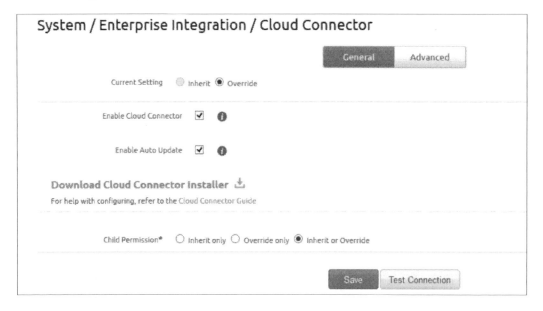

2. In the **General** section, select **Enable Cloud Connector** and **Enable Auto Updates** if you want ACC to automatically update when Admin Console is also updated.

3. Go to the **Advanced** section and click on the **Generate Certificates** option to generate the certificates for ACC and AirWatch.

> You can regenerate your certificates at any time to create a new thumbprint and expiration date. This can allow enhanced security in the event the certificate was to ever get compromised. If you do regenerate the certificate, you will need to perform the installation of ACC again.

4. Next, you can select all the enterprise services you would like to integrate with by putting a checkbox in each of them. For on-premise deployments, you will also need to select AirWatch services.

5. Click on **Save** and then navigate back to the **General** section and click on **Download Cloud Connector Installer**. Enter a password for the certificates (the password will be needed for the install). Click on **Download** and save the `Cloud Connector` setup file to the ACC server.

Installing the ACC software on the ACC server

Next, you will install the ACC software onto the ACC server to allow the enterprise integrations to occur:

1. Double-click on the installer from the ACC server.

2. Click on **Next** and accept the license agreement. Click on **Next** and then on **Change** if you would like to change the installation directory. Click on **Next**.

3. Enter the certificate password that was entered in Admin Console as part of the download and then click on **Next**.

4. If you would like to proxy your traffic through an outbound proxy, select the checkbox and enter the proxy information. Click on **Next**, then on **Install** and then on **Finish**.

Verifying that ACC is working

The last step is to verify that ACC is working and communication is successful between ACC and AWCM. To validate, log in to the console and perform the following steps:

1. Navigate to **Groups & Settings | All Settings | System | Enterprise Integration | Cloud Connector**.

2. Within the **General** section, click on **Test Connection**. If the connection is successful, you will see **Cloud Connector is active** and you are ready to setup your integrations.

Configuration of core enterprise integrations

Now that ACC is set up, you can start configuring integration with your enterprise systems. The first integration you should set up is your Directory Services so that you can start setting up access for your administrators and integrate the current user accounts, so you don't have to create separate accounts.

Directory Services

To set up integration with your current Directory Services, complete the following steps. If you are not too sure about your Directory information, it is highly recommended to include someone from the team that manages your directory services to ensure that everything is set up correctly:

1. Log in to Admin Console and navigate to **Groups & Settings | All Settings | System | Enterprise Integration | Directory Services | Select Server**.

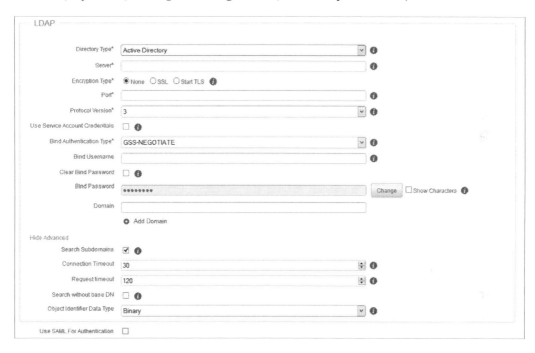

2. Enter the information based on your Directory:

   ° **Directory Type**: **Active Directory, Lotus Domino, Novell e-Directory** or **other LDAP**.

   ° **Server**: Here, you enter your directory server.

   ° **Encryption Type**: **None**, **SSL** or **TLS**.

   ° **Port**: Enter your port based on your encryption type (the default unencrypted is 389 and SaaS SSL can only use 636).

   ° **Protocol Version**: This is the LDAP version that is used. Active Directory uses LDAP Version 2 or 3. If you are unsure, start with Version 3.

° **Use Service Account Credentials**: This allows you to use credentials from the App pool on the MAG server that is used to authenticate with your directory services.

° **Bind Authentication Type**: Select the type of bind authentication. Start with **GSS-NEGOGIATE** if you are not sure.

° **Bind Username**: Here, enter the account used to authenticate with your directory services. It is recommended that you set up a separate read account and not use your own.

° **Clear Bind Password**: This clears the password used for the bind username from the database.

° **Bind Password**: This is the password for the username used to bind to your directory services.

° **Domain**: Here, enter the domain where your user accounts are located. You can add additional domains by clicking on **Add Domain**.

3. Click on **Show Advanced** to view the following fields:

° **Search Subdomains**: This allows you to search for users and groups in subdomains.

° **Connection Timeout**: This is the LDAP connection timeout in seconds.

° **Request Timeout**: This is the LDAP query request timeout in seconds.

° **Search without Base DN**: If using Global Catalog, a Base DN is not required to search for users and groups.

° **Object Identifier Base Type**: This is the unique identifier that will never be changed for a user and a group. This is typically in binary format.

° **Use SAML for Authentication**: Checking this option allows you to use SAML as the mode for authentication. Using SAML will bypass other authentication modes.

 For additional information on configuring SAML integration with your **Identity Provider (IdP)**, refer to the *SAML Integration Guide* in myAirWatch.

4. Click on **Save** once all of the information has been entered. Then, click on **Test Connection** to validate that you have successfully set up your directory integration.

The next step is to map Directory Users and User Groups in AirWatch:

- Mapping your Directory Users in AirWatch includes the following steps:

    1. Log in to Admin Console and navigate to **Groups & Settings | All Settings | System | Enterprise Integration | Directory Services | Select User**.

    2. Click on the **(i)** icon next to the **Base DN** field to display the Base DNs available. The Base DN you will want to use will be your top-level domain, for example, DC will be `mydomain` or `com`.

    3. Enter the value for **User Object Class**, which is most likely the user.

    4. Enter the value for **User Search Filter** to associate the user accounts with Directory accounts. The recommended format is `<LDAPUserIdentifier>={EnrollmentUser}` where `<LDAPUserIdentifier>` is the parameter used on Directory services to identify a specific user. For example, AD may look like `samAccountName={EnrollmentUser}` and other LDAP may look like `CN={EnrollmentUser}` or `UID={EnrollmentUser}`.

    5. Click on **Advanced** to select **Auto Merge** to allow user group updates to automatically merge with associated AirWatch accounts.

    6. Within **Advanced**, you can also select the option to automatically set disabled users to inactive. This will automatically unenroll users who have been disabled in your directory. Value for a disabled status allows you to identify in AirWatch how the directory lists the account as disabled.

    7. Lastly, you can enable **Custom Attributes** and review all mapping values used in AirWatch with your directory. These values can be modified to match your directory. Select **Sync Attributes** if any changes were made to **Mapping Value** or if any custom attributes were added.

    8. Click on **Save** and then on **Test Connection** to validate whether the settings are correct.

- Mapping your Directory Groups in AirWatch:

    1. Log in to Admin Console and navigate to **Groups & Settings | All Settings | System | Enterprise Integration | Directory Services | Select Group**.

    2. Click on the information icon next to the **Base DN** field to display the Base DNs available. The Base DN you will want to use will be your top-level domain, for example, DC=`mydomain`, DC=`com`.

3. Enter the value for **Group Object Class**, which is most likely the group and the **Organizational Unit Object Class**.

4. Click on **Advanced** to enter **Group Search Filter** to associate user groups with directory accounts. For example, if your **Group Object Class** is group, your **Group Search Filter** would be objectClass=group.

5. Select **Auto Sync Default** to automatically add or remove users in AirWatch based on their directory membership.

6. Within **Advanced**, you can also select **Auto Merge Default** to automatically apply sync changes without administrative approval and change the maximum allowable changes to be merged with AirWatch before administrators have to approve them.

7. Lastly, you can enable **Custom Attributes** and review all mapping values used in AirWatch with your directory. These values can be modified to match your directory. Select **Sync Attributes** if any changes were made to **Mapping Value** or if any custom attributes were added.

8. Click on **Save** and then on **Test Connection** to validate whether the settings are correct.

Now that everything has been configured, we can now add the directory users into AirWatch for administration and/or enrollment. First, let's look at the options of adding users from your directory to AirWatch. For user enrollment, there are three options to add your users:

- Batch upload using a CSV file

- Create users one at a time by searching for them in your directory from AirWatch

- Allow open enrollment, which automatically creates a user account when the user enrolls

 There is a lot more management required by managing users this way. The recommended method is to leverage existing directory groups to allow the use of the current directory structure and more efficient management of the user accounts.

To manage your user accounts most efficiently and effectively, you will need to utilize your directory groups to manage access for your administrators and allow your users to enroll. For the most part, you may already have groups that contain the users you would like synchronized. If not, you can simply create a new group in your enterprise directory that can be synchronized with AirWatch for management of users. Utilizing directory groups provides the following benefits:

- Better user management based on your directory by maintaining ownership of the user accounts

- The ability to apply groups to profiles and policies, allowing you to dictate what a user receives in AirWatch based on the directory group

- Improved security as AirWatch will automatically update groups based on the directory group membership

- More granular management of permissions within AirWatch based on the policies and profile assignments to only specific groups

- More efficient enrollment by allowing users to use their existing credentials and automatic assigning or organization groups

- Easy delegation to administrators without the need to create additional accounts for them to manage the environment

You can either batch import your groups or add them one at a time. To add your user groups, log in to Admin Console and navigate to **Accounts | Users | User Groups** and select **Add** to individually add your directory group, or click on **Batch Import** to add multiple directory groups. To add your admin groups, log in to Admin Console and navigate to **Accounts | Administrators | Admin Groups** and select **Add** (you can't use **Batch Import Admin Groups**). Now that your groups are imported, you can assign them to specific organization groups for enrollment and select who has permissions to manage them. There are also multiple other options within the group that can be configured to allow auto sync with the directory and auto adding members to the group.

Certificate services

It is critical that you understand how certificate services can provide additional protection to your mobile deployments. With ACC, AirWatch provides integration to multiple **Certificate Authorities (CAs)**. To integrate with a CA, log in to Admin Console and navigate to **Groups & Settings | All Settings | System | Enterprise Integration | Certificate Authorities**. Here, you have your certificate authorities and request templates. The first thing you will need to do is add your **Certificate Authorities**; click on **Add** within the **Certificate Authorities** section and fill in the information being requested.

Ensure that you work with the team that manages your certificate infrastructure to ensure that the integrations are set up correctly.

The available CA integrations are:

- Microsoft ADCS
- Generic SCEP
- Symantec/Verisign MPKI
- OpenTrust CMS Mobile
- Entrust
- RSA Certificate Manager

The **Add/Edit** window is shown in the following screenshot:

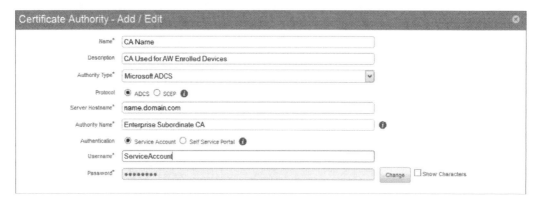

Once you have created the CA, you can create your request template by navigating to the **Request Template** section and clicking on **Add**. Enter the required information into the fields to build your certificate template then click on **Save**. You can now utilize your certificate template for any number of initiatives including:

- Certificate-based Email Authentication
- Certificate-based Wi-Fi Authentication
- Certificate-based VPN Authentication
- E-mail Encryption and Message Signing with S/MIME
- In-App Encryption and Authentication

Certificate services will be covered in more detail in *Chapter 4, Mobile Security.*

Logging

Logging of device and console events can be configured to send to external systems via Syslog integration. To configure Syslog integration, log in to Admin Console and navigate to **Groups & Settings** | **All Settings** | **System** | **Enterprise Integration** | **Syslog**. Enter the information based on your logging server and click on **Save** and then on **Test Connection** to verify the configuration.

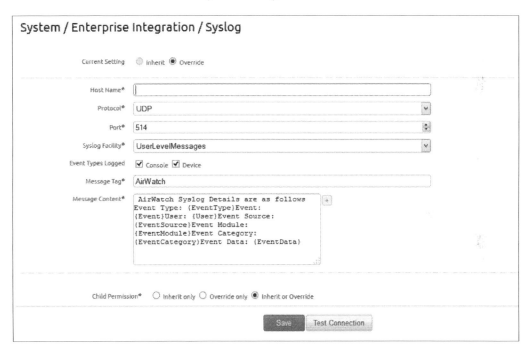

E-mail integration

The final core integration with ACC is e-mail integration. There are multiple e-mail integrations available with AirWatch. From simply accessing your enterprise e-mail with POP, IMAP, Exchange Web Services, or ActiveSync natively to utilizing the AirWatch Inbox and NitroDesk TouchDown are all options for your deployment. Deciding on which options to use will depend upon the enterprise systems you have in place and the security requirements in your organization. We will be covering e-mail integration in a lot more detail in *Chapter 7, Mobile E-mail Management.*

For your enterprise integrations with e-mail, ACC is required for Exchange PowerShell and SMTP integrations. Exchange PowerShell provides the ability to approve devices that are allowed to access e-mail via ActiveSync. The only step with ACC is to simply enable the feature by navigating to **Groups & Settings | All Settings | System | Enterprise Integration | Cloud Connector**. Click on **Advanced** and validate that there is a checkbox in Exchange PowerShell.

The other e-mail configuration available with ACC is Email (SMTP). Setting up SMTP allows you to integrate with your current e-mail environment to allow AirWatch to send e-mail notifications to users. To set up AirWatch and allow it to relay off your e-mail servers to send mail, navigate to **Groups & Settings | All Settings | System | Enterprise Integration | Email (SMTP)**. Within this page, configure the settings based on your e-mail environment. Click on **Save** and then on **Test Connection** to validate the configuration.

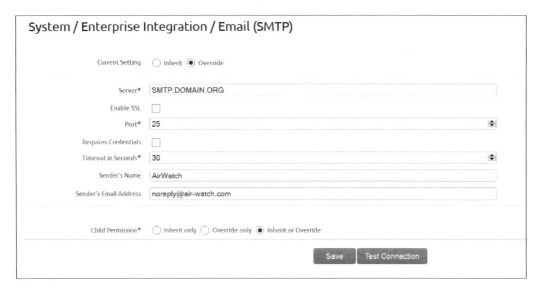

 You will want to work with the team that manages e-mail services to retrieve this information, and they may also need to configure the e-mail system to allow AirWatch to relay from it.

Blackberry Enterprise Server

The last option with ACC is to provide integration with your **Blackberry Enterprise Server** (**BES**). There are currently limited options on what you can manage with the BES devices but the capability is available. To allow Blackberry integration, go to **Groups & Settings** | **All Settings** | **System** | **Enterprise Integration** | **Cloud Connector**. Click on **Advanced** and validate that there is a checkbox in BES.

Mobile Access Gateway and Secure Email Gateway overview

In addition to ACC, AirWatch also has **Mobile Access Gateway** (**MAG**) and **Secure Email Gateway** (**SEG**) as part of the enterprise integrations.

Mobile Access Gateway

As mentioned earlier in the chapter, **Enterprise Integration Service** (**EIS**) was replaced with two technologies, ACC (which we have already covered) and MAG. MAG is a separate role that serves as a relay between your users' mobile devices and the enterprise systems on your corporate network. With MAG in place, you can provide secure access to the following resources:

- Internal document repositories with SCL on the user's mobile device
- Internal content with SCL on the user's mobile device
- Internal websites through AirWatch browser
- Internal web applications through AirWatch browser
- Utilize app tunneling through app wrapping
- Utilize app tunneling through per app VPN (iOS apps only)

Since MAG integrates primarily with the enterprise content management systems and applications, we will cover MAG in more detail in *Chapter 8, Mobile Content Management,* and *Chapter 9, Mobile Application and Mobile Browser Management.*

Secure E-mail Gateway

SEG is an additional role that serves as a proxy for all your ActiveSync traffic. This allows for much more security and control over the e-mails being delivered to mobile devices. The following are benefits of implementing SEG:

- Proxies all ActiveSync traffic for increased security
- Allows AirWatch to allow/block e-mail based on enrollment
- Allows whitelisting/blacklisting of devices
- Provides additional policies for increased control and security
- Provides attachment control to devices by forcing attachments open in SCL
- Provides control over how hyperlinks can be viewed
- Provides encryption for attachments and hyperlinks

Since SEG is a large component of e-mail, we will cover it in more detail in *Chapter 7, Mobile E-mail Management*.

Other enterprise integrations

Moving beyond the core integrations available with AirWatch, there are also other enterprise integrations that allow you to leverage your current investments and provide you with a more scalable and secure mobile deployment. AirWatch is currently partnered with multiple mobile technology providers and is currently growing these partnerships to create an ecosystem of mobile opportunity. To provide a central place of viewing the supported mobile technology providers and to view the opportunities available, AirWatch has created AirWatch Marketplace. AirWatch Marketplace provides a catalog of all the available integrated solutions by third-party providers. To view Marketplace and see the latest supported third-party integrations, visit `http://marketplace.air-watch.com/`. The amount of supported providers is constantly growing, allowing us to become creative and providing our customers with cutting-edge opportunities.

The following is a list of categories that is available within AirWatch Marketplace with multiple integration opportunities within each. There are too many provider integrations to cover in detail in this chapter, but you should get an idea from the categories and some of the listed providers of what can be implemented:

- **AirWatch Apps**: This will consist of Appcelerator, Breezy, Bria, Capriza, Catavolt, Troy Apps, FeedHenry, Formidable, HipaaChat, Kony, Laccon Mobile Security, Matrix42, MH Patient & MH Communicator, MicroStrategy, MobileDay, Myriad Mobile, Notability, OAB Studios, Oracle, PhoneGap, PrinterOn Mobile, Salesforce, SAP, Sencha Complete, Sitrion, Socialcast, Splashstop for AirWatch, StarMobile, Store Enabler, Telerik, TripLingo, Webalo, WillowTree Apps and Xamarin options

- **App Shield**: This will consist of Troy Apps Software, FeedHenry, Formidable, Ionic Mobile, and Crittercism options

- **Certificate Authorities**: This will consist of Certificate Management System (CMS), Comodo, Entrust, OpenTrust, and Symantec options

- **Device Manufacturers**: This will consist of Hypori, HTC, Intel, Kindle Fire, LG, Crittercism, Motorola, Nokia Lumia, Nook, Panasonic, Pidion, Spectralink, Samsung, Kyocera, Windows Phone, and Sony options

- **Enterprise Apps**: This will consist of Appcelerator, Appthority, Bamboo, FeedHenry, Jenkins, Kinvey, MediaTest, Crittercism, Veracode, FireEye, Notate, Palo Alto Networks, Pradeo, and Team City options

- **Mobile Retail**: This will consist of Ingenico, PAYware Mobile, Motorola, and Zebra Mobile Printers options

- **Mobile Security**: This will consist of EyeVerify, Lacoon Mobile Security, Blue Coat, Zscaler, F-Secure, Webroot, Symplified, Skycure, Websense, and Zimperium options

- **Network & NAC**: This will consist of Meru Networks, F5, Aruba Networks, CounterACT, Extreme Networks, Aerohive Networks, Cisco ISE, Junos Pulse, Bradford Networks, Impulse, SailPoint, SecureAuth, Xirrus, and ZoneDefense options

- **Printers**: This will consist of Breezy, PrinterOn Mobile, Datamax-O'Neil, Printonix, and Zebra Mobile Printers options

- **Software Platforms**: This will consist of Cloud Sherpas, MobiChord, and ServiceNow options

- **Telecom Expense Management**: This will consist of Asentinel, Wandera, MobileManager, MobilSense, MOBI Wireless Management, MDSL, Telesoft, Comview, and Wireless Analytics options

- **VPN**: This will consist of Cisco AnyConnect, F5 Edge Client, iSimplyConnect, Junos Pulse, and Aruba Networks VIA options

Summary

In this chapter, you learned about the enterprise integrations available within AirWatch and how important it is as an organization that we integrate with our current enterprise systems to provide additional efficiencies and security.

We first looked at the enterprise integrations at a high level to get an understanding of the features and capabilities. We then moved on to the core enterprise integrations available within AirWatch and what they included. To provide the core enterprise integrations, AirWatch provides ACC where we learned the requirements needed to deploy. Once this was set up, we went through the configurations of each of the core enterprise integrations, specifically the directory integration, as this provides the core to getting started with our deployments more efficiently with added security.

We then looked at MAG and SEG briefly to understand what enterprise integrations they provide. To finish the chapter, we looked at other enterprise integrations available within AirWatch and how AirWatch has created a market place to build on the mobile ecosystem. This allows us to move into the next chapter where we will look at how to best secure your EMM environment and provide the security controls to help better protect your corporate information.

4
Mobile Security

Before you get started with the deployment of your mobile devices, you need to fully understand the risks associated with Mobility and what you can do to best secure the devices for your users. With the ever-growing threat of cyber-crime and the continued increase of data leakage, we need to provide the best possible security available. At the same time, we also need to be conscious of the usability of the mobile solution. If we secure something to a level that makes the solution unusable, the users will circumvent the controls and find other ways to get what they need. This in turn creates more risk to the environment. With this, we need to ensure that the mobile solution being provided is secure, meets regulations, and is also a solution that allows the users to easily use and adopt.

We will first go into an overview of Mobile Security to better understand the vulnerabilities and risks associated with it. We will then take a look at the industry compliances that we need to adhere to today and what to use as technology professionals.

The following section will show us how AirWatch has put Security at the core of its solutions to help us meet the compliance and regulations we are faced with today. Moving beyond this, we will look at how to configure and enforce the security controls within your EMM deployment to better protect your corporate information and users.

The following will be covered in this chapter:

- Security overview
- Industry compliances
- Security with AirWatch
- Securing your devices

Security overview

We are living in a world where the consumer is driving the technology and the enterprises are trying to catch up with them. With the release of iPhone in 2007, there has been an incredible growth in the use of smart devices and this only continues to grow. The trend has also shifted to the adoption of tablet devices with the release of iPad in 2010. Since then, users are carrying around multiple different mobile devices. Because of this, users demand to be able to access and do everything from their smart devices. The big concern, as we all know, is how to provide this access to the users securely and ensure that the data isn't being leaked.

Over the years, the laptop and desktop markets have matured steadily with the growth of management tools to update the devices and the ability to enforce security policies and firewall rules and ensure that the antivirus is installed and up to date. With the rapid growth of mobile devices, we have been faced with the challenge of efficiently managing and securing these devices. Not only are we faced with managing and securing the devices owned by the enterprise, but also with providing the ability for users to access corporate information on personal mobile devices. This creates a whole new challenge for enterprises as there are multiple risks and challenges associated with this.

As we look to secure the mobile devices, we need to understand how the users are accessing the information and the risks associated with it. An everyday user may not fully understand the risks associated with the information they are accessing and may not realize how vulnerable their device is. To them, they are just doing their job as efficiently as possible. As technical experts, it is our job to understand the risks associated with using mobile devices and enforce the controls available as best as possible.

There are multiple ways in which data breaches can occur, some of the more common are:

- Intentional loss of data where a user steals data from within organization
- Cybercrime whether it be a virus, malware, hacking a device, physical theft by access and so on
- Accidental loss of data where a user unintentionally misplaces data for others to view or outside of the organization

As we look at each of the possible breaches, we need to be able to add controls as best as possible to secure the corporate data. The following is a list of some ways in which we should already be enforcing security within the corporate networks to help prevent data breach:

- Access Controls
    - Password/PIN enforcement, certificates, smart cards, biometric/retina

- Encryption
    - Data at rest and in transit, at disk level and file level

- Network
    - Firewalls, proxies, secure gateways, intrusion detection, VPNs

- Software
    - Virus/malware/spyware scanners, software and system updates/patches/fixes, firewalls, remote wipe/disable

- Auditing and logging
- Compliance and policies

As you deploy your enterprise mobile solution, you need to ensure that you enforce security controls you currently have in place onto your mobile devices and that you are at minimum meeting your policies and compliances. As you build the security requirements for your mobile devices, it is highly recommended that you work closely with your security and compliance teams. For example, I currently work in the health care industry and I have a good understanding of the compliances being enforced to our organization, but I'm not an expert and don't get to see the constant updates and changes to the requirements we need to meet. This is where your security and compliance teams will provide that added knowledge to help you fully understand and build a more secure mobile deployment.

It is important that you work to provide a secure environment for your users and your organization. There are more and more data breaches happening each day with data of millions of users/customers/patients getting into the wrong hands. The cost of this leakage is substantial to the organization, not only in the cost of dollars, but more importantly to the reputation of your organization. We live in a world where trust is critical, and if we can't maintain the trust with our customers because of data leakage, our business will struggle to survive. It is our job as technical professionals to understand and ensure that we are doing all we can to help protect the information within the organization.

Industry compliances

The following is a list of some of the larger industry segments that your organization most likely falls within:

- Health care
- Government
- Education
- Construction
- Technology
- Retail
- Financial
- Hospitality
- Transportation
- Energy/utilities/natural resources

In today's world with technology, your organization will most likely have to comply with some of the standards and regulations that fall within your industry. The compliance will also differ from each country, and it's important that you understand and comply with each of these compliances if they apply to your organization, as severe penalties will occur. As mentioned already, it is extremely important that you work closely with your security and compliance teams, as they will be educated with the latest and most up-to-date compliances that apply to your organization.

The following are some of the more common and known compliances you may be familiar with that can potentially affect your mobile deployment. We won't be able to list and describe all known compliances, but this will give you an idea of the security you will have to adhere to.

- **Payment Card Industry Security Standards Council (PCI)** establishes compliance to help protect customer information from debit/credit card usage. For more information, visit `https://www.pcisecuritystandards.org/`.
- **The Health Insurance Portability and Accountability Act (HIPAA)** enforces compliance to help protect the privacy of the patient's health information. For more information, visit `http://www.hhs.gov/ocr/privacy/`.
- **The Sarbanes-Oxley Act (SOX)** sets standards to help prevent corporate and accounting fraud. For more information, visit `http://www.sec.gov/about/laws.shtml#sox2002`.

- **The Gramm-Leach-Bliley Act (GLBA)** requires the protection of sensitive data and explanation of information sharing to customers of financial institutions. For more information, visit `http://www.business.ftc.gov/privacy-and-security`.

- **The Federal Information Security Management Act (FISMA)** helps strengthen the Federal Government information security. For more information, visit `http://csrc.nist.gov/groups/SMA/fisma/`.

 These compliances are those that fall within industries in the USA.

One point to note is that it shouldn't matter what industry you are in when looking at security controls and enforcement. If you don't have strict compliances to adhere to, you will have information in your organization that needs to be protected. Whether it is an employee's personal information or proprietary information for your organization, you should always look to enforce the best security controls possible to help prevent the leakage of information outside your organization.

 AirWatch has created white papers for multiple industries on how to become better compliant with the usage of VMware. To access these white papers, log in to `https://my.air-watch.com/` and go to resources; you will see a section with all the white papers.

Security with AirWatch

AirWatch has put security at the core of its Enterprise Mobility Management solution. From earlier discussions in the chapter, it is evident that security is not an option but rather a requirement. Your security controls should be fully enabled and in place before you start deploying your devices.

Although the focus of the security is built around the devices, we also need to ensure that Admin Console and the infrastructure used to provide your mobile deployment is also secure. For the most part, you are most likely to already have these controls in place as AirWatch will not be your first deployment of an application and infrastructure. As an overview though, here are the items that will help ensure that you are providing a better service with your AirWatch infrastructure and deployment:

- Physical access
    - ○ Ensure that your infrastructure is secure and contains limited access

- ○ Make sure that there is auditing and logging of who has access
- ○ Ensure that there are multiple layers of access to get to the infrastructure

- Network considerations
    - ○ Ensure that the infrastructure is behind firewalls, proxies, or **Intrusion Prevention Systems (IPS)**
    - ○ Use DMZ where applicable
    - ○ Ensure that network access is limited to the infrastructure via ACLs/VLANs
    - ○ Only allow access to ports/services that are required
    - ○ Plan and deploy redundancy for **High Availability (HA)**
    - ○ Plan and deploy scalability for reliability

- Application considerations
    - ○ Limit access to Admin Console to only those who need it
    - ○ Integrate with your current directory to provide better security controls around access
    - ○ Build roles and allow admin access to the needed function
    - ○ Limit Global Admin access to only a few users
    - ○ Keep application up to date with the latest patches/fixes
    - ○ Always enforce encryption for greater security
    - ○ Use certificates to provide secure access

- Logical considerations
    - ○ Enforce complex password policies
    - ○ Ensure that the server OS is always up to date with the latest patches
    - ○ Use server OS Firewall
    - ○ Ensure that the antivirus/anti-spam/anti-malware software is running and always up to date

- Compliance and policies
    - ○ Ensure that auditing and logging is enabled
    - ○ Ensure that you are meeting all compliance and policies and update any that are outdated
    - ○ User agreements during enrollment or for application usage

- Other considerations

    ° Build in High Availability and Disaster Recovery

    ° Back up and protect data

 Now that Admin Console and the infrastructure controls are in place, we can look at the security considerations for the mobile devices. With AirWatch, the following security controls are a focus with the mobile devices that will allow you to meet your security compliances and policies.

Device security

It is extremely important that we put all the controls available in place with the device as this is where all of the information will be accessed. If the device gets compromised or stolen and there is no security controls in place, all data that is accessible or stored on the device will be compromised. There are multiple controls in place to help protect the mobile devices being used to access your corporate information. With AirWatch, the following security controls can be enforced for the device:

- Use of the Mobile Device Management (MDM) agent to manage devices
- Device encryption enforcement to protect all data
- Device wipe or remote lock in the event a device is stolen
- PIN enforcement to prevent unauthorized access to the device
- Device restrictions on applications, device settings, browser usage and so on
- Enforce the minimum OS version in the event of vulnerabilities
- Enforce specific models for reduced management and vulnerabilities within specific devices
- Geofencing configuration to prevent information leaving specific boundaries
- Jailbroken/rooted detection to prevent access to corporate data
- Enforce installation of Security apps to detect viruses/malware on devices

Workspace security

Workspace provides you with the ability to deploy a virtualized encrypted work area to the user's devices. This is something that will most likely better fit your BYOD deployment as you don't need to manage the device using an MDM agent. AirWatch Workspace is deployed at the OS layer, which creates a lot more flexibility for your deployment. With AirWatch, the following security controls can be enforced using Workspace:

- AirWatch Workspace is secured with FIPS 140-2 compliant encryption mechanisms
- Workspace allows compromised detection to prevent access to corporate content
- Workspace allows enterprise-wipe of all corporate data not affecting personal content
- Enable **Data Loss Prevention (DLP)** policies such as copy/paste prevention
- Password protect Workspace and not the device

User security

In order to ensure the best user security, it is recommended that you integrate with your enterprise directory. This will allow you to provide the same level access to your users that you do today using the current policies and compliances you have in place with your current user accounts. You will also create a more secure environment by allowing your directory to own the enablement and termination of your users, preventing duplication of work and possible error of accounts not being correctly disabled in AirWatch. With AirWatch, the following security controls can be enforced for the users:

- Integration to your enterprise directory to provide the following security:
  - Current Directory policies should already be in compliant to meet security requirements
  - User accounts enabled and disabled will automatically allow enrollment/un-enrollment
  - Access can be provided based on user groups already in place

- Integration with certificate services can provide multifactor authentication
- Access to specific content/features can be limited based on the enrollment group

Content security

There are multiple controls available with AirWatch to ensure your content is secure and within compliance. Content can span an array of different entities including applications, e-mail, documents, images, and so forth. It is critical that the content on the user's devices is secure and access to it isn't gained by anyone who shouldn't. With AirWatch, the following security controls can be enforced to better help protect the content:

- AirWatch's SCL provides full security with FIPS-140 compliant 256-bit SSL encryption
- Access to content can be controlled based on location and time
- Policies can prevent content from leaving the SCL and being copied or moved to other locations

E-mail security

Protecting your e-mail and attachments is also a critical part of an organizations security policies. AirWatch provides multiple options to help secure your e-mail depending on how strict your policies and compliances are. With AirWatch, the following security controls can be enforced to better help protect your corporate e-mail:

- E-mail access can be limited based on enrollment of MDM or Workspace and polices enforced by them
- You can prevent copy/paste of an e-mail and e-mails from being forwarded
- E-mail can be deployed and managed via a native profile or a secure e-mail client
- Enterprise or device wipe can be performed to remove e-mail
- Only approved users can be configured to access e-mails
- Attachment control can be enforced with the use of SCL

Network security

You can integrate AirWatch with your existing network security policies by allowing and denying devices based on compliances from AirWatch. This allows you to only permit trusted and secure devices enrolled with AirWatch access to your internal network resources. If devices fall out of compliance with AirWatch, your network can detect and immediately remove access. With AirWatch and your network, the following security controls can be enforced to better help protect your organization:

- Integrate AirWatch to your Network Infrastructure devices via APIs to view device information
- Allow/deny access to Network based on compliances enforced in AirWatch
- Control access to Network based on enrollment of users
- Integrate with certificate authorities to approve and allow Network Access to internal resources
- Allow access to corporate network by use of an approved VPN
- Allow access to an internal application through the use of App Tunneling

Application security

There are multiple ways to ensure the protection of your apps to help meet your security requirements and compliances that have been put in place. For corporate-owned devices, you will be able to fully manage the application being accessed and used but there are some considerations with BYOD. Depending on the app and how it's being made available will depend on how much you can secure it. If vendors release an application that is available in the public app store, you will need to work with them to see what security controls they have in place with their app that can be integrated with AirWatch. With AirWatch, the following security controls can be enforced to better help protect your applications:

- Application installation can be granted or restricted using whitelisting or blacklisting
- Some native applications can be restricted on devices
- Applications can be deployed to only specific enrollment groups
- Access to applications can be disabled if devices don't meet your MDM or workspace policies
- Additional security features can be added to applications using the AirWatch **Software Development Kit (SDK)**
- Additional security features can be added to applications using AirWatch App Wrapping

Certificate security

There are a number of integrations available with certificates that will provide an additional layer of security to your mobile deployment. By leveraging certificates within AirWatch, you will be able to provide additional security to the following initiatives:

- E-mail authentication with certificates

- Wi-Fi access and authentication with certificates

- Certificate Integration for VPN authentication

- Certificates to encrypt e-mails and message signing with S/SMIME

- In-app encryption and authentication with certificates

The compliance engine

AirWatch has an extremely powerful compliance engine that will help you enforce the policies and security required within your organization. Compliance engine allows you to continuously monitor and detect devices that are out of compliance. If devices are out of compliance, you are able to apply multiple different actions to ensure that the device is put back into compliance or to simply enterprise wipe or device wipe if needed. With AirWatch, the following compliances can be enforced to help protect your corporate information:

- Application List (contains or does not contain a specific identifier, contains blacklisted or whitelisted app(s), does not contain required apps or does not contain a specific version)

- Cell data usage meets or exceeds a specific percentage

- Cell message usage meets or exceeds a specific percentage

- Cell voice usage meets or exceeds a specific percentage

- Device is compromised or is not compromised

- Device last seen within a specific amount of hours or days

- Encryption is not enabled

- Expiry of the interactive certificate profile within a specific amount of days

- Laptop encryption is not enabled

- Last compromised scan not within a specific amount of hours or days

- MHD terms of use acceptance not within a specific amount of hours or days

- The model is or is not a specific version

- The OS version (is the same, is not the same, is greater than a specific version, is greater than or equal to a specific version, is less than or equal to a specific version)
- The passcode is not present
- The device is roaming
- The SIM card change has been detected

Securing your devices

Now that we have a better idea on the security available with AirWatch, you will need to configure your environment to enforce the security controls discussed within this chapter to your devices. During this section, we will navigate through where you can configure the components that have been reviewed to better secure the mobile devices being managed.

Passcode and encryption

One of the most important security settings for your devices is the passcode and encryption. For your MDM-enrolled devices, you are going to want to enforce a device-level password and encryption to protect the information on the device. Depending on the manufacturer, the enabling of encryption may be a little different. For the iOS and Android, you can configure the passcode and encryption in the following way:

- For iOS password and encryption enforcement, perform the following steps:
    1. Log in to the Admin Console.
    2. Navigate to **Devices | Profiles | List View**.
    3. Click on **Add** and then on **Apple iOS**.
    4. In the **General** section fill out all the information required and assign it to the smart groups the policy will apply to.

 We will go into the profile creation in more detail within *Chapter 5, Mobile Device Management*. This chapter will simply demonstrate where to configure the security features to better protect your devices.

    5. Click on **Passcode** and then on **Configure**. Enter the required passcode on the device.

6. Fill out the passcode requirements based on your security requirements.

7. Click on **Save & Publish** to enforce the policy.

Have a look at the following screenshot:

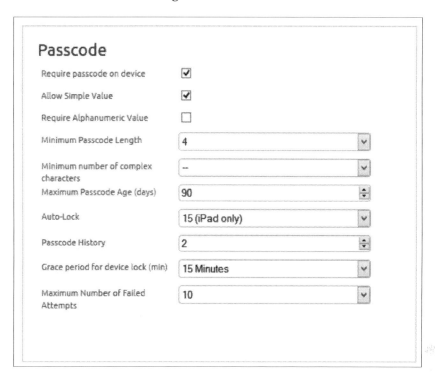

 iOS devices are encrypted by default, so you don't need to enforce encryption through the profile, but you will need to enforce a passcode in order to effectively prevent access to data on the device. Also, the **National Institute of Standards and Technology** (**NIST**) granted iOS 6 with the FIPS 140-2 certification. It is recommended that you configure your iOS profiles to require at least iOS 6 for additional security.

- For Android password and encryption enforcement, perform the following steps:

  1. Log in to the Admin Console.

  2. Click on **Devices | Profiles | List View**.

  3. Click on **Add** and then on **Android**.

4. In the **General** section, fill out all the information required and assign it to the smart groups the policy will apply to.

5. Click on **Passcode** and then on **Configure**.

6. Fill out the passcode requirements based on your security requirements and enable storage and SD card encryption.

7. Click on **Save & Publish** to enforce the policy.

Have a look at the following screenshot:

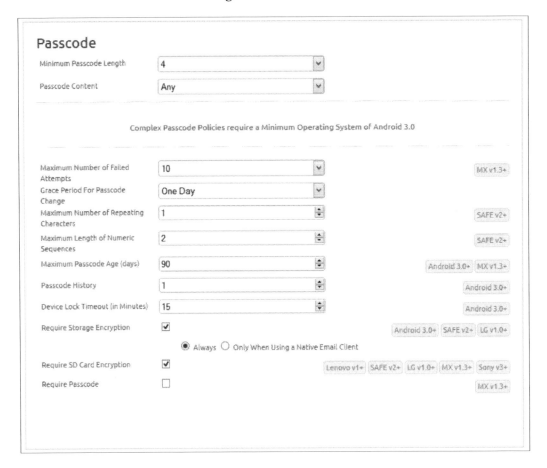

 As you can see with the Android profile, you need to enforce encryption on the devices as they don't have it enabled by default. This is similar on some of the other device types in which you will need to enforce and configure encryption.

Setting up a passcode for Windows 8 devices is very similar to setting up the iOS passcode profile.

If you aren't going to be using MDM for your deployment and you will be using workspace or apps that don't require MDM, you will want to require a passcode for access and ensure that encryption is enforced, which is by default on AirWatch native applications.

- Require Passcode on Workspace/Apps

    1. Log in to Admin Console.
    2. Click on **Groups & Settings** and then on **All Settings**.
    3. Click on **Apps | Settings And Policies | Security Polices**.
    4. Select the type of **Passcode Mode** to enable a passcode and fill out the passcode requirements based on your security requirements.
    5. Click on **Save** to save the settings.

Have a look at the following screenshot:

If you don't already have a password policy for mobile devices and workspace, you will need to work with your security and compliance team to create one. It is recommended that you don't simply use the current password policy you use for your enterprise directory for your mobile devices and workspace. Enforcing long complex passwords on a mobile device or workspace creates extreme difficulty and frustration and you have to evaluate the risk of possibly allowing a PIN. The PIN is only used for the mobile device and workspace and not used for any other enterprise access. The hacker would physically need access to the device in order to compromise and gain control, so the risk to use a PIN can be looked at as low. To add additional security to the device, configure a maximum number of failed attempts on the passcode to force a device wipe or enterprise-wipe on workspace after the specified number of incorrect attempts.

Certificate integration

To deploy certificates to your devices in AirWatch, you will need to ensure that you have set up your integration to your CA and configure the template AirWatch will use to deploy the certificates as covered in *Chapter 3, Enterprise Integration*. Once you have your CA and template set up, you can deploy certificates using AirWatch profiles. We will demonstrate how to configure a profile using the credentials payload (you can also configure SCEP) in AirWatch using the following instructions:

1. Log in to the Admin Console.
2. Click on **Devices | Profiles | List View**.
3. Click on **Add** and then on the platform to deploy the certificate (I will use iOS).
4. In the **General** section, fill out all of the information required and assign it to the smart groups the policy will apply to.
5. Click on **Credentials** and then on **Configure**.
6. Select one of the following credential sources:
   - **Upload** to import an individual certificate to the device
   - **Defined Certificate Authority** to select your integrated CA and certificate template
   - **User Certificate** for S/MIME
7. Click on **Save & Publish** to enforce the policy.

Have a look at the following screenshot:

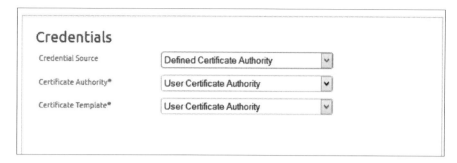

Now that you have configured the devices to use certificates, you can start leveraging them for multiple initiatives. One example I have just worked on is the integration of certificates with our enterprise Cisco ISE deployment. We are leveraging the AirWatch CA integration to install certificates from our internal CA with customized attributes in the certificate. ISE is then being configured to look for devices with the certificates we have deployed with the customized attributes. Once ISE has validated the device has the correct certificate, it will automatically onboard the device to the internal network to allow connection to all resources. This allows us to better manage our corporate assets as we have full control and management over them and what is installed.

For additional security, you can also manage, view, and revoke certificates from Admin Console. Simply navigate to **Devices** | **Certificates** | **List View** to see all deployed certificates in your environment.

There are way too many certificate integrations to cover in this book, let alone this chapter. To learn more on all the certificate options and integration in AirWatch, log in to the myAirWatch portal, go to Resources, click on **Home** on the left, and then click on **Certificate Management** to view all certificate management guides.

Enterprise and device wipe

Another great security feature within AirWatch is the ability to enterprise or device wipe an enrolled device. The difference between an enterprise-wipe and a device wipe is that an enterprise wipe will remove only the data that has been deployed as part of the enrollment. This will be most valuable in BYOD deployments, where you don't want to device wipe a user's personal device since legality issues may arise. A device wipe on the other hand is the ability to reset the device back to default and remove all data. This is most useful with corporate-owned assets and stolen devices.

The following steps demonstrate how to enterprise or device wipe an asset as an admin:

1. Log in to Admin Console.

2. Click on **Devices | List View**.

3. On the main screen, search for the device to be wiped.

4. Click on the device name under the **General Info** column.

5. In the top-right corner, click on More. Here, you will see the **Enterprise Wipe** and **Device Wipe** options.

6. Click on the action you would like to take with the device.

    Here is a screenshot for your reference:

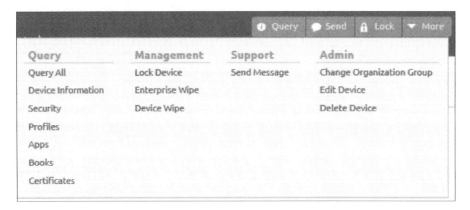

There is also a way for the user to enterprise or device wipe their device from AirWatch Self Service Portal. This allows the user to be more proactive and not have to wait for the IT group to wipe the device in the event it has been stolen. To wipe your own device, navigate to your environment's URL with /mydevice added to the end, for example, myenvironment.awmdm.com/mydevice. Log in with your e-mail or group ID, then click on **Next**, enter your username and password, and click on **Login**. Then, select your device and click on **Enterprise Wipe** or **Device Wipe** and then on click on **OK**.

> You may not see the option to device wipe because the device you are trying to wipe may be assigned to the employee-owned profile, which may be configured to not allow this. If you were requested to device wipe someone's device and it's on the employee-owned profile, you can simply change the device ownership to **Corporate-Dedicated** then device wipe.

Autodisable accounts

If you have integrated with your enterprise directory, which is recommended, you will want to ensure that the user accounts are being automatically disabled or removed from AirWatch based on the status within your enterprise directory. This allows one place to manage your accounts and allows the current process to continue without needing to manually disable the accounts in AirWatch. To ensure accounts are being automatically disabled and removed from groups, which will force un-enrollment in AirWatch and remove corporate data, you need to complete the following:

1. Log in to the Admin Console.

2. Click on **Groups & Settings** and then on **All Settings**.

3. Navigate to **System | Enterprise Integration | Directory Services**.

4. Click on **User** in the main screen and then on **Show Advanced**. Check **Automatically Set Disabled Users** to **Inactive** and then click on **Save**.

5. Click on **Group** on the main screen and then on **Show Advanced**. Check **Auto Sync Default** and **Auto Merge Default** and then click on **Save**.

> If you don't assign groups to your profiles, you don't need to have the groups auto sync and merge. You will just need to ensure that the account is set to automatically disable.

6. If you are leveraging groups in your profiles, you will also need to configure the group to automatically sync:

   1. Navigate to **Accounts | User Groups** and click on the group you would like to configure to auto sync.

   2. Check **Auto Sync with Directory** and **Auto Merge Changes** and then click on **Save**.

Geofencing and time schedules

Geofencing and time schedules allow you to better control where users can access your corporate information and apply time as to when they can access your corporate data. For Geofencing, you may need to require that your corporate information does not leave the state your organization resides in or the country you work in. With a Geofence profile, access to the corporate data will not be allowed if the device falls outside the scope of the defined area. For time schedules, this allows you to configure devices to only allow access during the specified time. For example, you may have employees who are working on an hourly basis and are not allowed to check their e-mail out of hours. You can prevent this by assigning a time schedule that will prevent them from accessing e-mail outside of work hours. To set up Geofencing and time schedules, you first need to define them:

1. Log in to Admin Console.

2. Navigate to **Devices | Profiles | Settings**.

3. Click on **Geofencing** to define the areas access is permitted.

4. Click on **Time Schedules** to create the time during which access is permitted.

Once you have defined the geofence area and time schedule, you can apply them to your profiles:

1. Log in to Admin Console.

2. Click on **Devices | Profiles | List View**.

3. Click **Add** and click on the platform to deploy geofence and time schedule (I will use iOS).

4. In the **General** section, fill out all the information required and assign it to the smart groups the policy will apply to.

5. Towards the bottom, click on **Enable Geofencing** and install only on devices inside selected areas. Select the created **Geofence** area.

6. Towards the bottom, click on **Enable Scheduling** and install only during selected time periods. Select the created **Time Schedule**.

7. Click on **Save & Publish** to enforce the policy.

Workspace security

There are multiple options to ensure that when you deploy workspace to the users, your corporate information is fully protected. You will want to ensure that there is a passcode enforced as described in the *Passcode and Encryption* section, **Compromised Detection** is enabled, and the **Data Loss Prevention** settings are configured. To enable or disable the configurations in workspace, complete the following:

1. Log in to Admin Console.
2. Click on **Groups & Settings** and then on All Settings.
3. Navigate to **Apps | Settings And Policies | Security Policies**.
4. Configure the security settings based on your corporate policy and then click on **Save**.

   Here is a screenshot for your reference:

Terms of use

For legal and compliance, you may be required to have users agree to the services that they are using. In AirWatch, you can force the users to agree to terms of use during enrollment, during an application installation, or for access to the console. If the user doesn't agree to the terms, they won't be able to use the service. To apply terms of use in your environment, complete the following steps:

1. Log in to Admin Console.
2. Navigate to **Accounts | Terms of Use | Add Terms Of Use**.
3. Select **Console**, **Enrollment**, or **Application**.
4. Fill out the options and add your terms and click on **Save**.

The compliance engine

Now that you have all the security configured in place, you need to ensure that the device is in compliance with your policies. AirWatch has an extremely powerful compliance engine that not only detects devices out of compliance, but allows you to take actions against the noncompliant devices. As seen earlier in the chapter, there are multiple rules that can be applied to your devices. The most notable ones you will want to enable first is **Compromised Status**, **Encryption**, and **Passcode detection**. There are too many rules to demonstrate within this chapter for all the configurations, so we will demonstrate one to give you an idea on how to configure the rest. We will configure **Compromised Status**, as this is the only way to detect jailbroken/rooted devices for MDM profiles. To configure your compliance policy, complete the following steps:

1. Log in to Admin Console.
2. Navigate to **Devices | Compliance Policies | List View** and then click on **Add**.
3. In the dropdown, select **Compromised Status** and click on **Compromised**.
4. Click the **+** sign to add additional rules or click on **Next**.
5. Next is the actions you choose; you have the following choices:
    ◦ Application to block/remove an app or all apps
    ◦ Command to enterprise wipe or request a check-in
    ◦ E-mail to block e-mail
    ◦ Notify to send an e-mail, an SMS, or a push notification to the device
    ◦ Profile to block/remove a profile or all profiles or install a compliance policy

6. For this example, we will notify the user by sending them an e-mail (you can create custom templates to use) that they have 24 hours to resolve the compliance issue or we will remove all profiles. Click on **Next**.

Here is a screenshot for your reference:

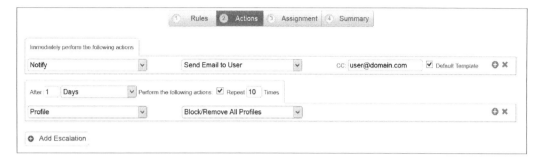

7. In the assignment screen, you will select the platform to apply the policy to. If you like, specify the **Model**, **Operating System** and **Ownership Type** then select **Managed By**. Select which smart groups to apply the policy to. Click on **Next**.

8. The **Summary** screen is where you specify the name and description of the policy and view how many devices are compliant and noncompliant to which the policy will apply. Click on **Finish And Activate** to apply the policy.

9. Build as many policies as you need to enforce compliance on the devices.

Other security controls

Other security controls within AirWatch include the ability to leverage third-party applications, more specifically, third-party applications that help with security to better protect your enrolled devices from viruses and malware. One example of this integration would be with Lacoon Mobile Security that helps protect your mobile devices from advanced mobile threats. With AirWatch, you can deploy the Lacoon mobile agent to your enrolled devices for added protection. In the event a user removes the agent, you can set up your compliance engine to remove AirWatch profiles to ensure safety of corporate information.

Additional security can be added to the devices through Restrictions. To add restrictions to your managed devices, log in to Admin Console and perform the following steps:

1. Navigate to **Devices | Profiles | List View.**
2. Click on **Add** and then on the platform to deploy restrictions.
3. In the **General** section, fill out all the information required and assign it to the smart groups the policy will apply to.
4. Click on **Restrictions** and deselect what shouldn't be available to the users.
5. Click on **Save & Publish** to enforce the policy.

Restrictions can include device, applications, security, media, and some others depending on the device type.

Outside of certificate integrations, you also need to secure your Admin Console access using an SSL. This would have been part of your deployment and should have already been complete. Other SSL usages will be with the MAG and the SEG, which will require you to use SSLs to encrypt all communication. The MAG and SEG configurations will be covered in more detail in *Chapter 7, Mobile E-mail Management,* and *Chapter 8, Mobile Content Management.*

Additional security controls within the profiles include configuring a Global HTTP Proxy, content filters, and VPN to allow access to internal resources (not all these options may be available for all device types). To configure these options, log in to Admin Console and perform the following steps:

1. Navigate to **Devices | Profiles | List View**.
2. Click on **Add** and then on the platform to deploy restrictions.
3. In the **General** section, fill out all the information required and assign it to the smart groups the policy will apply to.
4. Select the additional security controls (payloads) you would like to apply from the left-hand side of the screen.

It is extremely important that you maintain the AirWatch logs for auditing and logging purposes. It is recommended to export these logs to an external enterprise logging system to allow them to be centrally monitored along with all your other enterprise system logs. This will allow your Security team to monitor unauthorized access and any abnormal behavior within the AirWatch environment. To configure integration with your enterprise logging, log in to Admin Console.

1. Click on **Groups & Settings** and then on click on **All Settings**.
2. Navigate to **System | Enterprise Integration | Syslog** and configure your external logging server with AirWatch.

Summary

This chapter demonstrates the importance of security in the enterprise environment and how we must fully understand the risks associated with mobility. It is our job as professionals to ensure that we apply the required security controls to help us meet the organization's policies and regulations.

In this chapter, we first looked at mobile security at a high level to get a better understanding of the ways data can be breached and the ways in which we can help prevent the data from being breached. We then moved into looking at the different industries and listed some examples of industry compliances you may have to adhere to as part of your mobile strategy.

The next section showed us the security options available within AirWatch and how they can help us secure the mobile devices being enrolled. To finish the chapter, we demonstrated how to configure AirWatch to enforce the security controls and to ensure they aren't removed. Now that we have everything set up from the console to enterprise integrations, we can move to the next chapter, which will allow us to start building the profiles to allow mobile devices to be enrolled in to the environment.

Mobile Device Management

5

Now that you have been through the initial setup, configuration, integration, and security, you can set up your profiles and start enrolling your devices into the environment. Mobile Device Management will allow you to fully manage your mobile devices, allowing them to access your internal corporate resources securely. Once you have successfully enrolled your devices, you can deploy different profiles for different initiatives throughout the organization. Enrolling with MDM will allow you to enforce the same level of security and meet compliances like you do for your other user devices (laptops/desktops) in the environment.

In this chapter, we will give an overview of MDM and look at the different deployment options between BYOD and corporate-owned devices. We will then look at how to manage your deployments with Organization Groups and ensure that all the prerequisites are in place.

Following the prerequisites, you will create your first profile and explore the different options available within the profile. You will then publish the profile and before enrollment, we will ensure that everything is ready to enroll the first device. Once you enroll a device, we will look at Self Service Portal for users to self-manage devices. You will then finish off by un-enrolling the device from MDM.

The following topics will be covered in this chapter:

- Mobile Device Management overview
- Device ownership
- Organization and smart group
- Creating and publishing a profile
- Pre-enrollment
- Enrolling a device
- Self Service Portal
- Un-enrolling a device

Mobile Device Management overview

Mobile Device Management (MDM) is the fundamental of the **Enterprise Mobility Management (EMM)** platform and the beginning of a new era of device management for smart phones and tablets. Organizations are now challenged with ways to better manage and secure corporate or personally owned smart phones and tablets. MDM has helped bridge the gap between providing access to corporate information but at the same time maintain control over the information.

MDM allows you to manage, secure, and enforce compliance on mobile devices to ensure that they meet your organization's standards. You can compare MDM to that of your Corporate-owned laptops and PCs that are most likely managed and secured through Microsoft's **System Canter Configuration Manager (SCCM)** or something similar. There is no difference with the way you should treat mobile devices in your environment, they need to be managed, secured, and locked down just like your laptops and PCs.

With MDM in AirWatch by VMware, you simply enroll your mobile devices into the environment based on the enrollment URL, group ID, and permissions that have been granted. Once enrolled, your device will receive profiles that will allow your device to be configured to access corporate resources you have configured. Because the device has been enrolled, you can at any time publish additional profiles or remove profiles depending on the user's needs.

With MDM enrolled on your devices, you can enforce security policies to ensure that your devices are in compliance at all times. If devices fall out of compliance or your devices have been compromised or stolen, you are able to take an action against the device and force it to lock. In addition to locking the device, you can send a command to remove the corporate date or even wipe the device.

Some of the benefits of MDM with AirWatch include:

- Management of multiple mobile device manufacturers
- Simplified enrollment and un-enrollment
- Easy-to-use web-based management console
- Easily deploy access to corporate resources through profiles
- Enforce security and compliance policies
- Remote device management
- Secure mobile access to corporate resources
- Terms of use acceptance
- Real-time dashboards and reporting

Device ownership

As we reviewed in *Chapter 1*, *Getting Started*, AirWatch has set up its deployment based on three different ownership types:

- Corporate-dedicated
- Corporate-shared
- Employee owned

 There is also the unassigned ownership type used as a failover assignment in the event a device doesn't get an ownership assigned.

For the most part, you will most likely fall into two of these categories based on whether you are deploying a BYOD or corporate-owned deployment. Most likely, you will have a combination of both deployments and for BYOD, you will assign everything with employee-owned as the privacy given that the devices are someone else's ownership. For corporate-owned, you will most likely use corporate-dedicated for the most part, but there is the option of using corporate-shared as an alternative if there are any use cases for this.

Bring Your Own Device (BYOD)

BYOD, as the heading states, means users bringing their own devices to work and the organization provides access to corporate data on them. This appears to be the direction a lot of organizations are leaning towards now; they are moving away from supplying the users with corporate-owned devices. Part of this trend is most likely due to the growth of users being able to easily afford their own smartphone as the markets have continued to grow rapidly. It really makes no sense supplying the users a mobile device for work use and having them purchase a separate device for personal use. There are different approaches to how the organization can contribute to the costs of the personal device if they decide to, but the more common I've come across is the stipend approach. The organization contributes a static amount of funds into the employee's paycheck each month to pay towards the coast of the user's cell phone bill. This though causes a whole new dynamic in how we provide data to the user's personal device. Traditionally, a company could simply device wipe or remote lock a phone that it supplied to an employee to protect the data in the event it was lost/stolen or the employee was terminated. With BYOD, and as discussed in *Chapter 4*, *Mobile Security*, there's a lot to understand and take into consideration when deploying corporate information to an employee's personal devices.

One note to point out on the BYOD program is the ruling that just came out recently in California, part of it enforcing that organizations must contribute a fair amount of compensation towards an employee's personal device phone bill if it is used for work. I imagine that this will grow beyond California to other states and something that you will want to take seriously. For organizations in California, they will most likely need to rewrite their BYOD policies to meet the new law, and organizations outside of California may want to brush up on their policies to prevent any lawsuits against them and be prepared for any possible legal changes in the future.

> As you grow with your BYOD deployment, you will be challenged with questions from users with regard to MDM and the concerns of privacy. If MDM is your BYOD solution, you will need to ensure that you have policies and documentation in place that show users exactly what the MDM agent is collecting from the device to create a sense of comfort. For BYOD, you will also want to look at containerization as an option, which allows you to better differentiate work content from personal content. We will cover this more in *Chapter 6, Workspace Management*.

Corporate-owned devices

Traditionally, corporate-owned mobile devices are those that were supplied to users for phone usage and e-mail access along with organizations using rugged devices for corporate initiatives.

> Rugged Device Management is moving into a new era as we are seeing the opportunity to leverage these devices with the latest Android OS, allowing for more usability and flexibility over the traditional Windows mobile OS. As of Version 7.3, there is a full new section within **Devices | Products for Rugged Device Management**.

Most of you at some point were probably supplied a Blackberry, Palm Treo, or some other form of older smart device that was fairly limited in what it could do compared to the devices nowadays. These devices were provided by the organization, paid for by the organization, and traditionally limited to minimum data usage with e-mail access. Because these devices were paid for by the organization, they were probably limited to a smaller group, decreasing the footprint of allowing remote access to your corporate information. As mentioned earlier, this type of corporate-owned initiative appears to be moving more toward the BYOD program.

At the same time, along with the transition to BYOD, another form of corporate-owned device has taken off. With the release of iPad in 2010 and the increase of other tablets appearing on the market, we are seeing a sprawl in tablet purchases and usage. The ability for organizations to change and improve on processes and workflows and the ability for developers to create custom-built apps to meet the organization's needs is all possible with the tablets available today. Because of this, initiatives within the organizations are now limitless and tablets are being purchased for every available opportunity. The initial issue with this was the ability for organizations to manage and secure these devices like they have traditionally accomplished with their desktop and laptop fleet with tools such as Microsoft's SCCM. This is where AirWatch has been able to bridge the gap by allowing efficient management and securing of these tablets using MDM.

Whether you are deploying your devices with BYOD or corporate-owned profiles, MDM with AirWatch will allow you to deploy your corporate initiatives to these devices securely and allow you to meet security policies and compliance regulations.

Organization and smart groups

In this section, you will set up your organization and smart groups that allow you to define your infrastructure based on your deployment and to ensure that only those users that have been authorized are able to enroll successfully.

Organization groups

As discussed in *Chapter 2, Administration*, it is extremely important that you set up your organization group structure correctly from day one. This structure is what defines your deployment, and the better organized it is, the easier it will be to manage your deployments moving forward. Once you decide how to organize your organization groups, whether it be based on location for dispersed organizations, BYOD or corporate-owned, or even one that simply matches your directory infrastructure for consistency, we can start building the structure in AirWatch.

For demonstration, I'm going to build out the structure based on the geographic location, which will allow the ability to become more granular with the management to delegate out access to other locations.

In my current role, we have a centralized team that owns AirWatch with multiple locations throughout different states. We tried a couple of approaches, but the approach we have currently deployed is to simplify the structure by breaking it down into BYOD and corporate-owned assets. Within the BYOD organization group, we created organization groups based on the device type and MDM or containerization. For the corporate-owned organization group, we create organization groups based on the initiative, for example, a mobile video deployment group. The reason for this approach is that we keep everything standard for all our sites and users, so it didn't make sense to create organization groups based on sites and then duplicate the organization groups for each initiative. The only downfall is the granularity of security. When you delegate security, you won't be able to assign permissions based on the location to your admins within Administrator Console. If you have a good auditing policy in place, this shouldn't be a concern though.

To build out your Organization Group, please follow these steps:

1. Log in to Admin Console.
2. Navigate to **Groups & Settings | Groups**.
3. Then click on **Organization Groups | Organization Group Details**.
4. Here you will see your top-level organization group, as shown in the following screenshot. Complete or change the required fields, the details to be completed are as follows:

    ° The name should be your organization's name and the group ID will most likely be blank, as your devices should be enrolling with your child groups.

If you are a SaaS customer, you will see customer by default in the type box, and everything should already be configured for you.

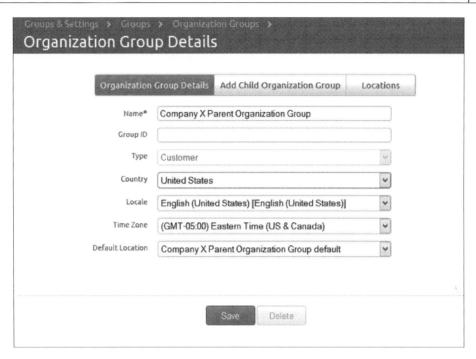

Now that we are at the parent Organization Group, we can start creating our child Organization Groups. To create your child Organization Groups, complete the following steps:

1. Within the parent **Organization Group Details**, click on **Add Child Organization Group**, as shown in the next screenshot.

2. Enter the new child **Organization Group Name**; we will use North America.

3. Enter the **Group ID**. Users will enter as part of enrollment (if you are creating additional child groups for the users to enroll, you need not add a group ID here).

4. Select the **Organization Group Type**; I have selected **Region** based on the group name.

5. Select the **Country** and the **Locale**.

6.   Ensure that **Add Default Location** is selected; this will automatically add the organization group as a location and add it to the **Locations** section where you can add additional information on the location.

7.   Click on **Save** to save the child Organization Group.

Now you can continue to build out the remainder of your organization groups in preparation for your deployments. The next screenshot is an example of how the structure will start looking as you build out your deployments.

1.   Go to **Groups & Settings | Groups | Organization Groups**.

2.   Click on **List View**.

Groups & Settings > Groups > Organization Groups >

List View

Organization Group	Active Devices	Inactive Devices
▼ Company X Parent Organization Group	0	0
Asia	0	0
Europe	0	0
▼ North America	0	0
California Office	0	0
▼ Florida Office	0	0
Florida BYOD MDM	0	0
Florida Corporate Owned	0	0

 You will need to ensure that you have selected the organization group that you would like to create a child group for before you create it. The next screenshot show how to change organization groups.

Smart groups

Next, we will create our smart groups. Smart groups are dynamic groups that determine what end users, device-specific criteria, and platforms receive as part of enrollment. Once a smart group is created, you can apply it to receive an application, book, compliance policy, device profile, or product provision. Smart groups allow you to only have to define the parameters once and apply them when needed multiple times without always having to redefine the criteria for deploying content, profiles, policies, and so on.

To create your smart groups, you need to complete the following steps:

1. Log in to Admin Console.

2. Select the organization group your smart group will apply against; I have selected **Florida BYOD MDM** as my group to set up first (to do this, click on the drop-down arrow in the header of the console and select the desired group you would like to manage), as shown in the following screenshot:

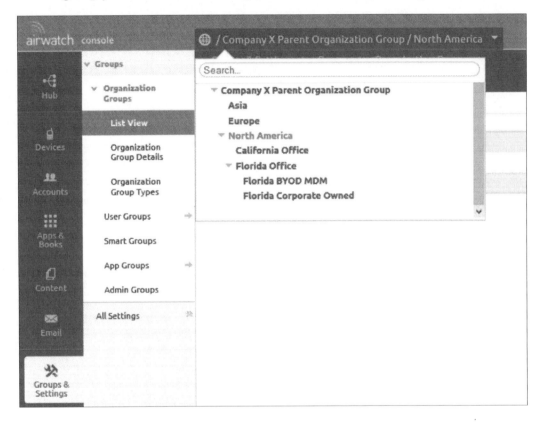

3. Click on **Groups & Settings** and then expand **Groups**.

4. Click on **Smart Groups** and click on **Add Smart Group**. Enter a name for the smart group in the top right then choose **Select Criteria** or select **Devices or Users**.

Using **Select Criteria** will be much more efficient with larger groups and specifically if you have integrated with your directory services for dynamic addition/removal based on group membership. Selecting **Devices or Users** will work better for smaller numbers and allow you to be more specific on device or user enrollment if needed.

5. We will use **Select Criteria** for our example. Within **Select Criteria**, configure the parameters of who will be included in the smart group based on the following options:

   ○ **Organization Group**: This shows which organization group the smart group will apply to.

   ○ **User Group**: This is the user group that the smart group will apply to. With directory integration, this will manage itself based on your directory management.

   ○ **Ownership**: This is the ownership of the device that applies to the **Corporate**, **Employee**, **Shared** or **Unknown** categories.

   ○ **Tags**: This shows any custom tags that may have been applied to a device.

   ○ **Platform**: This is the device platform the group is applied to.

   ○ **Model**: This is the model of the device the group will apply to.

   ○ **Operating System**: This is where you will apply an operating system maximum, minimum, or is equals to.

   ○ **Enterprise OEM Version**: This is where you can specify the OEM maximum, minimum, equals to, and so on.

   ○ **Additions**: Here you can add individual users or devices to be part of Smart Group.

   ○ **Exclusions**: This is where you can exclude specific users or devices.

6. Click on **Save** once you have configured your criteria, as shown in the following screenshot:

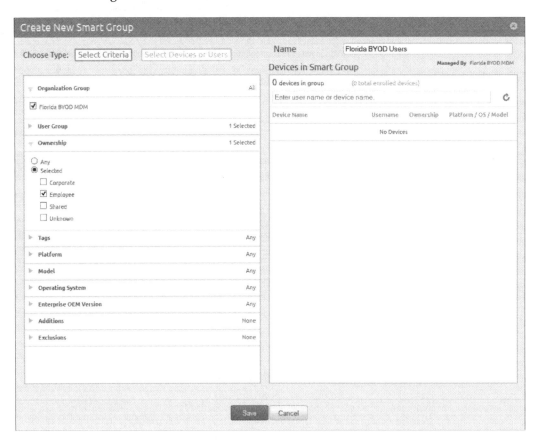

You can edit, delete, or view smart group assignments at any time by selecting the organization group the smart group is a part of, navigating to the **Smart Groups** page, and clicking on the options available for the smart group, as shown in the following screenshot:

Creating and publishing a profile

Now that our organization and smart groups have been created, we can create our profiles that will allow you to manage your devices and provide the desired settings and configurations to the users.

When you configure your profiles for your devices, you will configure what is known as payloads within profiles. **Payloads** are the specific settings within each profile that you configure, for example, the passcode, e-mail profile, or Wi-Fi settings.

> It is recommended to only configure a single payload per profile. This will allow you to make changes to that specific payload and publish it without having to re-push the profile for all payloads within that profile that may not need to be updated, for example, if you configured a passcode, Wi-Fi, and e-mail payload within one profile and only needed to change the passcode. When you change the passcode and publish the profile, all payload configurations will be reconfigured on the device causing the e-mail to be downloaded again and the Wi-Fi settings to be re-added.

To create your profile, complete the following steps:

1. Log in to Admin Console.

2. Go to **Devices | Profiles | List View** and then click on **Add**.

3. You will be presented with all the supported platforms, as shown in the following screenshot. Click on a platform to begin creating the profile. The available platforms are shown in the following screenshot

4. You will then be presented with the **General** payload screen and you will see all other payloads available. You are required to complete the **General** section that will determine who will receive the profile, and you will be required to configure at least one payload.

[Some of the payloads and options will be different for each of the platforms.]

5. In the **General** section, complete the following, as shown in the next screenshot:

   ○ **Name**: The name for the profile that identifies what it's for.

   ○ **Version**: This states the version of the profile.

   ○ **Description**: This is the description of the profile.

   ○ **Deployment**: Select **Managed** to automatically remove the profile with un-enrollment or **Manual** to allow the profile to remain on the device until the user removes it.

   ○ **Assignment Type**: This shows how the profile will be deployed to the enrolled devices:

       ○ Select **Auto** to automatically install the profile.

       ○ Select **Optional** to allow the users to install the profile from SSP.

       ○ Select **Interactive** to allow the users to install the profile from SSP that allows interaction with external systems to generate data to send to the device (this needs to be enabled before using).

       ○ Select **Compliance** to deploy the profile to devices that violates a compliance policy.

   ○ **Allow Removal**: This is to decide whether a user can remove the profile or not:

       ○ Select **Always** to allow the user to manually remove the profile.

       ○ Select **With Authorization** to allow the profile to be removed with administrator approval.

       ○ Select **Never** to prevent the user from being able to remove the profile.

   ○ **Managed By**: This specifies which organization group can administer the profile.

○ **Assigned Smart Groups**: The smart group that will receive the configured profile. If you still haven't created a smart group for this profile, you can select **Create New Smart Group** once you select the option.

○ **Exclusions**: This allows you to exclude smart groups from the profile by selecting **Yes**.

○ **View Device Assignment**: This shows which devices the profile will be assigned to.

○ **Additional Assignment Criteria**: Here you have the option to enable geofencing or enable schedules for when the profiles can be accessed.

○ **Removal Date**: This allows you to specify a date that the profile will be removed from the device.

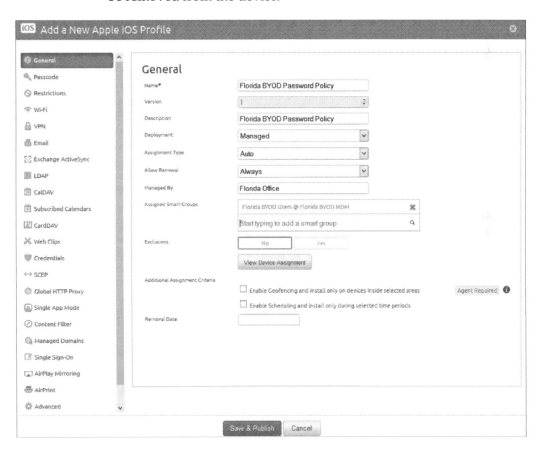

6. Next, you will need to configure your specific payload. For this example, we will configure the **Passcode** payload, which will most likely be the first you configure to comply with your access policies.

7. Select **Passcode** payload and configure the settings based on your security policies, as shown in the following screenshot:

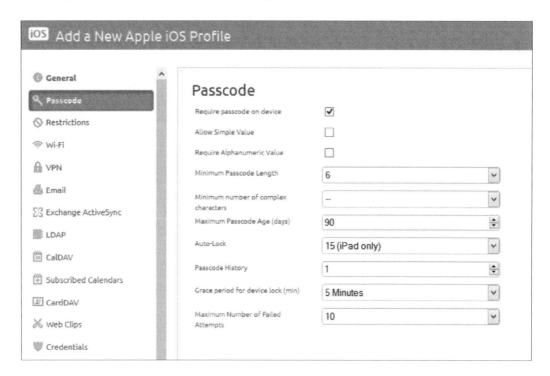

8. Click on **Save & Publish** once you are finished.

Since you can add multiple organization groups to a smart group, you can reduce the number of profiles you need to create for certain items. For example, if you have a standard password policy for all of your organization, you can apply the same profile to all your organization groups.

You will start to see the list shown in the following screenshot as you build your profiles with your different payloads for your different platforms. Over time, this list will continue to grow, so it will be important to plan and set up your smart groups efficiently to ensure you aren't creating multiple profiles for the same purpose.

The **List View** shown in the preceding screenshot is where you will manage all of your device profiles. From this page, you can toggle filters, edit, publish, view XML, and delete, copy, and view devices of all the profiles.

When you open a profile to edit, you will need to click on the **Add Version** option in order to make any changes and republish the profile.

Now that you have built out your first profile, you can start building out additional profiles that will be deployed to the devices as part of the enrollment, which is covered later in this chapter. For more details on the available payloads and how to configure them, log in to the myairwatch portal and click on **AirWatch Resources**. Then, click on **Platform** and open the **Platform Guide** for the specific platform you would like to configure.

Pre-enrollment

Before we do start enrolling devices, let's ensure that we have all our prerequisites and any other items in place that will ensure the deployment is efficient and secure:

- All security settings are in place based on the recommendations from *Chapter 4, Mobile Security*. For enrollment, you will want to ensure that the following specific configurations are set up:

    ◦ **Compliance Policies** (this is set up by navigating to **Devices | Compliance Policies | List View**)

- ○ **Privacy** settings based on ownership type (this is set up by navigating to **Groups & Settings | All Settings | Device & Users | General | Privacy**)

- ○ **Terms of Use** (this is set up by navigating to **Accounts | Users | Settings | Terms of Use**)

- How to set up and configure enterprise integrations as explained in *Chapter 3, Enterprise Integration*. For enrollment, you have multiple options for your users to authenticate:

    - ○ **Basic Authentication**: This allows manual creation of accounts in AirWatch

    - ○ **AD/LDAP Authentication direct or with ACC**: This integrates with the current directory for consistent credentials

    - ○ **Authentication Proxy**: This allows authentication via a reverse proxy or web server

    - ○ **SAML 2.0 Authentication**: This integrates via **Single Sign On (SSO)** through federation of SAML identity provider

    - ○ **Token-based Authentication**: Token-generated enrollment via **Simple Mail Transfer Protocol (SMTP)** or **Short Message Services (SMS)**

- Ensure that your **Apple Push Notification Service (APNs)** certificate is set up for iOS devices by performing the following steps:

    - ○ Navigate to **Groups & Settings | All Settings | Device & Users | Apple | APNs for MDM** to validate

 For more information on managing the APNs, log into `https://secure.air-watch.com/` and read *Generating and Renewing an APNS Certificate* located within **Resources | Documentation | Device Management**

- You are able to brand the console to match your organization's look and feel. To do this, complete the following steps:

    1. Navigate to **Groups & Settings | All Settings | System | Branding** to change the branding.

    2. You can change the logo and login page image, customize SSP, enable branding on reports, change the colors of the theme, and even use custom CCS.

- Message templates can be set up for communication by e-mail, SMS, or Push. To do this, complete the following steps:

    1. Navigate to **Devices | Settings | General | Message Templates** to set up and configure your templates.

    2. The category option for the **Message Templates** include **Enrollment**, **Application**, **Compliance**, **Terms of Use**, **Administrator**, **Content** and **Device Lifecycle**.

- There are additional enrollment configurations that can be configured per organization group. Navigate to **Devices | Device Settings | General | Enrollment** to view the additional options. Within this section, you will be presented with the following enrollment options:

 Ensure that you change your organization group to the one your are configuring for enrollment before making any changes. To make changes within the organization group, click on the **Override** option to allow the changes to be made.

  ° **Authentication**: Here you can configure auto-discovery enrollment based on the user's e-mail address, your authentication mode, device enrollment modes, and whether agent enrollment for iOS and OS X is required.

○ **Terms of Use**: This is where you can enable the terms of use for enrollment.

○ **Grouping**: This is where you can specify how group IDs are assigned to users for enrollment. The three options available are **Default**, in which an administrator provides the group ID to the user, **Prompt User To Select Group ID**, which allows the user to select which group ID to enroll with, and **Automatically Select Based on User Group**, which allows automatic assignment based on directory groups. Here you can also enforce the **Default Device Ownership**, **Default Role**, and **Default Action For Inactive Users**. For example, for your BYOD users, they will receive the **Employee Owned** device ownership, which you can enforce as part of enrollment and prevent them from having to select, as shown in the following screenshot:

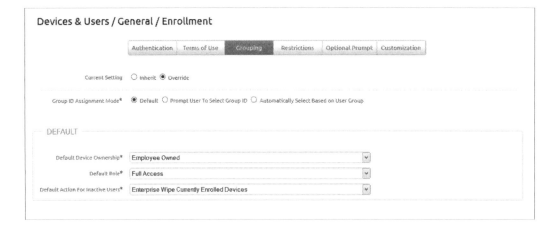

○ **Restrictions**: This is where you can limit your enrollment to known users or known groups, add a policy that allows specific ownership types, enrollment types, device types (platform, model, OS), and limit the amount of devices that can be enrolled.

○ **Optional Prompt**: Here you have additional options that you can make available during the enrollment process, as shown in the following screenshot:

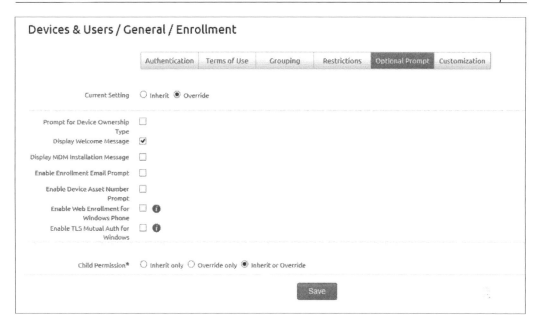

Devices & Users / General / Enrollment

| Authentication | Terms of Use | Grouping | Restrictions | Optional Prompt | Customization |

Current Setting ○ Inherit ● Override

Prompt for Device Ownership Type ☐
Display Welcome Message ☑
Display MDM Installation Message ☐
Enable Enrollment Email Prompt ☐
Enable Device Asset Number Prompt ☐
Enable Web Enrollment for Windows Phone ☐ ⓘ
Enable TLS Mutual Auth for Windows ☐ ⓘ

Child Permission* ○ Inherit only ○ Override only ● Inherit or Override

Save

- ° **Customization**: Here you can provide contact information to end users in the event they are unable to enroll their devices.

- There are multiple options for how the user enrolls and some of these will depend on how you have configured your environment for authentication:

  - ° **Manual**: The user manually enters the provided environment URL and group ID and enters the credentials whether they are basic or integrated.

  - ° **Notification**: The user receives an e-mail and/or SMS that they can click on to enter the group ID and credentials.

  - ° **Auto-discovery**: The user enters their e-mail address, which automaps them to the configured organization group for enrollment, and then the user will enter their username and password. This is configured within the **Authentication** section of the **Enrollment** options as mentioned earlier.

If users are required to enroll into multiple organization groups because of multiple devices or child organization groups below the enrollment organization group, they will be required to manually enter the group ID to ensure that they are enrolled into the correct organization group.

- ◦ **QR Code**: You can set up enrollment to allow your users to scan a QR code that contains the environment URL and group ID. Once scanned, the user will enter their username and password:

  - ◦ Use this URL to create your QR code: `airwatch://enroll?ServerURL=ENVIRONMENT URL&ActivationCode=GROUPID`
  - ◦ Here is an example website to generate your QR code: `http://www.qrstuff.com/`

- ◦ **Token Generated**: The user receives a single-use generated token along with the enrollment URL. This can be configured as a single click to authenticate or dual-factor can be added to require the user to enter their username and password.

- ◦ **Self-Registration**: The user can log in to SSP and register their own device to receive an e-mail with an enrollment URL.

- ◦ **Single-User Device Staging**: The administrator enrolls the device for the user or group of users.

- ◦ **Multi-User Device Staging**: The administrator will enroll the device that will allow multiple users to use the device. This will be covered in more detail in *Chapter 10, Multiuser and Laptop Management*.

> There are multiple ways to set up authentication and enrollment. Once you have a better understanding of the different options available, you will be able to better set up your environment to meet your organization's needs.

Enrolling a device

Now that you have set up the group ID and profile and completed all prerequisites, you can begin to enroll your devices. As we covered in *Chapter 1, Getting Started*, there are multiple platforms that are supported by AirWatch. For demonstration, we will look at the steps to enroll an iOS device and an Android device, as they are currently the most popular within the environments within the USA.

> Device enrollment will differ between the different types of OS types and sometimes versions. The following section will serve as a guide to the enrollment but you may see slight differences based on the OS type, version, and even the configuration of your profiles.

As a reminder, there are multiple ways that authentication and enrollment can be set up for the user as already discussed. For the demonstration in this book, we will look at steps to enroll using a QR code on one device and using your e-mail address on the other device. We will enroll the devices into **Florida BYOD MDM** test policy we created earlier, which has **Password** policy currently configured.

If you were to choose to manually enter the enrollment information, you would need the enrollment URL and group ID along with your credentials:

- **The Enrollment URL**: Your AirWatch environment URL
- **The Group ID**: For this use `FLBYODMDM`

iOS

For the iOS enrollment, you will enroll using your e-mail address. For this enrollment, you will need:

- Your e-mail address
- Credentials (this can be any of the authentication methods discusses in the *Pre-enrollment* section)

To enroll your iOS device, perform the following steps:

1. Navigate to `https://awagent.com/` from Safari and download and install the AirWatch MDM Agent app, or navigate to the App Store and search for AirWatch MDM Agent and download and install it.

2. Open the app once it has downloaded.
3. Enter your e-mail address and click on **Continue**, then again click on **Continue**.

4. Enter your credentials depending on how you set up authentication and then click on **Continue**.

 If you have the **Prompt** option for **Device Ownership Type** selected, you would need to select the type here.

5. Click on **Accept** to accept your terms of use.

6. Click on **Install** to install the profile and then on **Install Now**.

7. Enter your device password if you have one and click on **Done**.

8. Click on **Install** and then on **Done**. You will be redirected to a success page once complete.

9. You will then be auto-redirected to the homepage of the MDM App screen with the current status, as shown in the following screenshot:

 If you have SSO enabled, you will be required to setup a PIN to access the AirWatch MDM application.

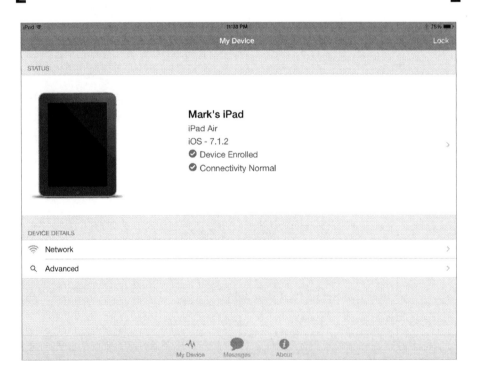

10. You will now begin to receive your configured profiles. In this instance, you will receive the passcode profile and you will be required to set up a passcode or meet the minimum requirements of the passcode configured in the profile. You can view the profiles by navigating to **Settings | General | Devices Management**.

> Depending on how you have configured your enrollment options within the management console will depend on the options seen during enrollment. For example, the preceding enrollment has been set up to automatically enroll the device as an employee-owned device, so you won't get the prompt to select device ownership.

Android

For the Android enrollment, you will enroll using a QR code. For this enrollment, you will need:

- The QR code (check the *Pre-enrollment* section for more information)
- Credentials (this can be any of the authentication methods discusses in the *Pre-enrollment* section)

To enroll your Android device, perform the following steps:

1. Navigate to `https://awagent.com/` from the Chrome browser and download and install the AirWatch MDM Agent app, or navigate to the Google Play Store and search for AirWatch MDM Agent and download and install it.

2. Open the app once it is downloaded.

3. Click on the QR code and scan it. Click on **Continue**.

 If you wanted to enter the information manually, you can click on **Server Details**, enter your server URL and group ID, and then click on **Continue**.

4. Enter your credentials depending on how you set up authentication. Click on **Continue**.

5. Click on **Accept** to accept your terms of use and then on **Continue**.

6. Click on **Install** to install the profile and then on **Install Now**.

7. Click on **Get Started**, then on **Continue** and on **Activate**.

8. Click on **Device Settings** and put a check in **Unknown Sources**. Click on **OK**.

9. Launch AirWatch App again and click on **Continue**.

10. Click on **Next** to install the device service. Click on **Next** two times. Then, click on **Install** and on **Accept** and then on **Activate**.

11. Create your Single Sign-On passcode for when you access AirWatch apps. Click on **Submit**.

 If you don't have SSO enabled, you will not be required to set up a PIN to access the AirWatch MDM application.

12. Click on **Continue**, then on **Continue** and on **Exit**.

13. You will then be auto-redirected to the homepage of the MDM App screen with the current status, as shown in the following screenshot:

14. You will now begin to receive your configured profiles. In this instance, you will receive the passcode profile, and you will be required to set up a passcode, or meet the minimum requirements of the passcode configured in the profile. You can view the profiles by opening the AirWatch Agent and selecting **Profiles**.

These instructions were completed with a Samsung device. There will be differences with the different Android manufacturers along with each manufacturer having its own device driver as part of the enrollment.

If you selected to encrypt your device as part of the payload, you will be required to run through encrypting your Android before continuing with any other settings. Android's Lollipop is beginning to encrypt Android devices by default just like iOS devices.

We will cover the enrollment of a Mac system and a PC in *Chapter 10, Multiuser and Laptop Management*.

Self Service Portal

Users are able to manage their enrolled devices via AirWatch **Self Service Portal** (**SSP**). SSP allows you to view device information and perform multiple remote actions from the console.

To access SSP, open up a web browser and navigate to `https://yourenvironmemnturl/mydevice`. To log in, you will need the group ID and your authentication information (if you configured e-mail registration, you can use your e-mail address as part of the login).

To simplify access to the users, you can create a customized SSP web clip or Bookmark that will allow the users to access SSP without needing to remember all the required information.

Once you are logged in to SSP, you can complete the following, as shown in the screenshot:

- View all enrolled devices
- View device information including a summary, security, compliance, profiles, apps, content, certificates, GPS and event log
- Manually add a device for enrollment
- You can perform actions such as: clear the passcode, delete a device, delete registration, device query, device wipe, download agent, enterprise wipe, find a lost device and many more

These actions are determined by permissions and not all of them may be visible to all users.

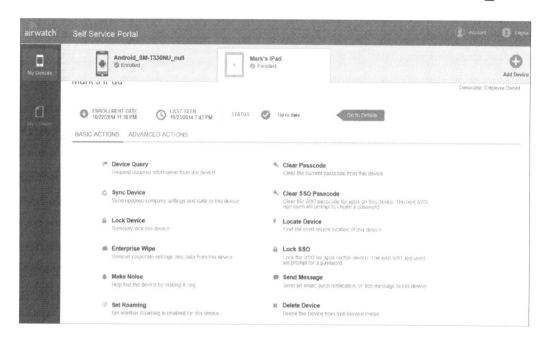

Un-enrolling a device

There are multiple ways a device can be un-enrolled from AirWatch. The following are some of the ways both the administrator and/or user can un-enroll a device from AirWatch:

- From the device a user can un-enroll by completing the following steps:
    - **iOS**: Open AirWatch App and click on your device. Then, click on **Device Enrolled** and on **Re-Enroll Device**.
    - **Android**: Open AirWatch Agent and click on the more option (the three dots) in the top-right corner. Then, click on **Un-enroll**.

 Un-enrollment may be slightly different on some devices, but this is possible within AirWatch MDM App unless AirWatch Admin Console has been configured to restrict it.

- From Self Service Portal a user can un-enroll by completing the following steps:

  ◦ Once you are logged in, select the device, and then select **Enterprise Wipe**.

- From Admin Console an admin can un-enroll by completing the following steps:

  ◦ As an administrator, log in into the console and navigate to **Devices | List View**. Then, search for the device and select it. Click on **More** in the top-right corner and then on **Enterprise Wipe**.

- Others can un-enroll using the following steps:

  ◦ Removing users from AirWatch or removing users from groups will un-enroll the users if these options were set up and configured to take this action as part of your initial setup and configuration.

 All devices can be managed navigating to **Devices | List View** of AirWatch Admin Console.

 To gain the most benefit out of your iOS deployment, Apple has a couple of additional tools available to you:

- The Apple **Device Enrollment Program** (**DEP**) enables the ability to prevent users from removing profiles, provision devices in the supervised mode, customize the enrollment process, and more. For additional information, AirWatch has created AirWatch Guide for the DEP document.
- Apple Configurator enables administrators to effectively deploy a large number of iOS devices a lot more efficiently, stage devices for pre-enrollment, and more. For additional information, AirWatch has created *AirWatch Integration with Configurator* document.

Summary

In this chapter, we covered how to manage mobile devices with MDM. MDM is extremely powerful and there are multiple opportunities available with it. This chapter gives you a broad understanding and the knowledge needed to set up and use MDM, but there is a lot more detail involved with the different options available. As you start building out your MDM profiles and configurations, you will realize and learn all the different options available for your deployment that will allow you to deploy a more robust deployment.

In this chapter, we looked at MDM at a high level to understand what is involved. We then looked at the different types of ownerships available for enrollment along with setting up your organization groups and smart groups in preparation for enrollment. We then saw how to build and publish a profile for your devices.

Moving on, we looked at all the pre-enrollment settings that are needed and/or recommended before continuing on to the enrollment of devices. Once enrolled, we looked at Self Service Portal that allows users to manage their own devices and finished off the chapter with how to un-enroll the devices. This allows us to move onto *Chapter 6*, *Workspace Management*, which will show you how to set up, configure, and deploy AirWatch Workspace, a virtualized, encrypted container that has been created to better suit the BYOD needs.

6
Workspace Management

In this chapter, we will look at the latest technology available for Bring Your Own Device deployments provided by AirWatch by VMware. As demonstrated in *Chapter 5, Mobile Device Management*, BYOD is fully supported with this deployment. However, moving forward, the management of personal devices needs to be better differentiated, allowing a clear distinction between personal-owned information and corporate-owned information. This is where workspace management comes in. workspace management allows you to deploy a virtualized encrypted container to a device, which then allows you to deploy and contain your corporate resources within the organization's control.

First, we will give an overview of workspace management and look at BYOD in more detail and how workspace management fits into this deployment. We will then set up and configure the organization and smart groups needed for enrolling into workspace.

Before enrolling a device into workspace, we will ensure that everything is in place for a secure and efficient deployment. Once enrolled, we will look at workspace on your device and how to manage it along with using SSP to allow self-management of the devices to the users. To finish off the chapter, we will demonstrate how to un-enroll your device from AirWatch Workspace.

The following topics will be covered in this chapter:

- Workspace management overview
- Bring Your Own Device
- Organization and smart groups
- Configuring workspace options
- Pre-enrollment
- Enrolling a device

- Managing workspace on your device
- Self Service Portal
- Un-enrolling a device

Workspace management overview

As MDM and BYOD matured and grew, there was a realization and an expectation that organizations are able to more efficiently provide access to corporate data on mobile devices. With MDM, there is a fine line between providing access to corporate resources and the manageability of a user's personal device and what information can be seen on that user's device. With MDM, a profile is needed on the device in order to manage and push profiles to that device. What an administrator can and can't see on that device is all dependent on the privacy settings that have been configured for the device ownership. Yes, it is important to ensure that the privacy for personal-owned devices is set up not to collect any personal information and that it is documented and communicated to the users, but there is always a possibility that this could be changed, or someone could easily change the ownership of a personal device that allows access to GPS information. As stated before, it is critical that auditing and logging is put in place to help prevent these changes from occurring, but if these changes occur, the boundaries of personal invasion have potentially been breached and you could become liable as an organization.

This is where workspace management has found its place in the EMM world. Workspace management is helping define BYOD deployments by allowing organizations to deploy access to its corporate data through containerization. Containerization allows you to deploy a virtualized encrypted container to a mobile device that is password protected at the application layer and the requirement to manage at the device level has been eliminated. This also eliminates the need to have a minimum hardware requirement, which is extremely challenging with Android devices as there are multiple manufacturers in the market. Deploying containerization to a device also better defines the boundaries between the user's personal information and the corporate information being provided for access. This eliminates concerns over what is being accessed on the device with MDM.

The following table will give you a better understanding of the differences between Workspace and MDM:

MDM	Workspace
MDM manages and controls the device through profiles allowing for more control at the device and Operating System level. The following can be performed using MDM: • Device level password • Rooted/jailbroken detection • Enforce data and device encryption • Remotely reset the device password • Remotely lock the device • Enable device restrictions • Control app usage • Enterprise or device wipe ability • Device location services • Send push notifications • Configure roaming restrictions	Workspace uses containerization for enrollment and access to corporate resources. Containerization is an encrypted secure area that is independent from the device. The container sits on top of the Operating System allowing for a defined distinction between personal and work data. The following can be performed using Workspace: • Managed space on device • Password protection for container • Single Sign-On functionality for apps • Encryption at the container level • Enterprise wipe the container only • Password reset for container only • Remotely lock container only • Application deployment to the container

Enrollment into workspace is very similar to the MDM enrollment process. You simply enroll workspace container into the environment based on an enrollment URL, group ID, and permissions that have been granted. Once enrolled, your workspace will deploy access to corporate resources that have been configured. Because workspace has been enrolled, you can at any time publish additional or remove configurations depending on the user's needs.

With workspace container, you can enforce security policies to ensure that the device and workspace is in compliance at all times. If the device or workspace falls out of compliance, has been compromised, or stolen, you are able to take actions against Workspace. As an admin or user, you are able to send an enterprise wipe to the device, which will only remove the corporate information deployed within Workspace, eliminating any impact on the user's personal information.

Some of the benefits of workspace management with AirWatch include the following:

- No MDM required
- Deployment is based on the minimum OS, allowing for more flexibility
- Passcode and encryption is enforced at the container level
- Full enterprise security and Data Loss Prevention enforcement
- The ability to truly separate personal information from corporate information
- AirWatch container include solutions for e-mail, applications, content, and browsing

 E-mail, applications, content, and browsing will be covered in more detail in *Chapter 7, Mobile Email Management, Chapter 8, Mobile Content Management,* and *Chapter 9, Mobile Application and Mobile Browser Management.*

- Easy-to-use web-based management console
- Terms of use acceptance
- Real-time dashboards and reporting

Bring Your Own Device (BYOD)

We briefly touched on BYOD in *Chapter 5, Mobile Device Management* as it does have its opportunities within MDM and is currently being used heavily for MDM deployments. We will continue this discussion in this chapter, as the workspace management deployment will most likely become the preferred method for BYOD in the future.

Using BYOD with MDM provides users with more native experience and deployment, but at the cost of needing to manage the device. As you continue to grow your BYOD strategy and deployment, you may still find a need to provide MDM for those users who truly prefer that native experience, and with AirWatch, you have the flexibility of providing the option. However, moving forward with BYOD and with the continued growth of more users purchasing their own smartphones and requiring access to more corporate information on their personal devices, containerization makes most sense.

From conversations with many organizations, it appears the trend is to move away from corporate-supplied smart devices. There is truly no need to supply a worker with a smart device when they most likely already have their own. Carrying around two smart devices really doesn't make a whole lot of sense. You can easily enhance productivity of users by providing them access to corporate information from their personal devices. By doing this, you will also create a more efficient environment for the users as they now only have to use one device to access both personal and corporate information. I personally find that I'm able to easily filter through e-mail and clean up my inbox while travelling or in meetings with it being provided on my personal device. This saves me a lot of time that would normally be spent at my desk working through e-mails.

As BYOD programs continue to grow for organizations, it is critical to understand that BYOD has grown beyond e-mail delivery and you need to strategize and plan for the bigger picture. The realization is that users are expecting to be able to access everything from their personal devices with BYOD. The main concern is to be able to provide access to that information securely and to ensure that the data is safe. As technical professionals, it is our responsibility to fully understand the risk associated with providing access to the corporate information and ensure that it is secure. In the event a user leaves or is terminated, we need to guarantee that the corporate information is safely removed from the user's device, leaving all personal information as is.

As you work on your deployments and learn the different components of EMM, you will realize and better understand that workspace management will most likely make most sense for your BYOD deployments. The ability to more efficiently deploy and define your corporate information without needing to invade the user's privacy will be critical for your BYOD deployments.

The following are several benefits of deploying a BYOD program:

- Potential cost savings on devices/plans
- Lower number of devices for users to manage and carry
- Allows users to select the preferred device and provider
- Increase in user productivity

Organization and smart groups

Before we enroll any devices, you will need to create your organization and smart groups for your workspace management deployment. Since the primary organization structure was already created in *Chapter 5, Mobile Device Management*, we only need to simply add an additional organization group for enrollment.

Organization groups

To add your new organization group for your workspace management devices, complete the following steps:

1. Log in to Admin Console.

2. Navigate to **Groups & Settings | Expand Groups**.

3. Expand **Organization Groups | Organization Group Details**.

4. Change your organization group to the **Florida Office** group as this is where you will continue to build on your structure, as shown in the following screenshot:

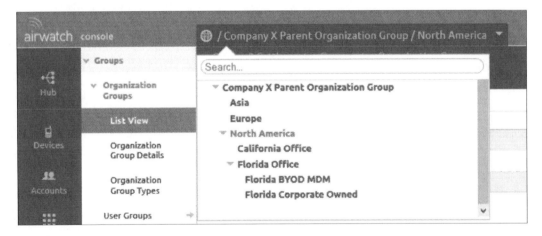

5. Within the **Florida Office** organization group details, click on **Add Child Organization Group**:

   1. Enter **Child Group Name**; we will use Florida BYOD Workspace.

   2. Enter the **Group ID** users will enter as part of enrollment; for this group, we will use FLBYODWORKSPACE.

The group ID is not case sensitive.

3. Select **Container** for **Organization Group Type**.

4. Select **Country** and **Locale**.

5. Ensure that **Add Default Location** is selected; this will automatically add organization group as a location and add it to the **Location** section where you can add additional information on the location.

6. Click on **Save** to save the child organization group.

Now you have created your workspace container organization group. You can view it within **List View** to see how your structure is building out as your deployments grows. To view the latest organization group structure, complete the following:

1. Change your **Organization Group** to **Parent Organization Group**.

2. Click on **Groups & Settings** and expand **Groups**.

3. Expand **Organization Groups** and click on **List View**.

4. Expand each of the arrows to view all child groups.

id="nav" />

Organization Group	Active Devices	Inactive Devices
▼ **Company X Parent Organization Group**	1	1
Asia	0	0
Europe	0	0
▼ **North America**	1	1
California Office	0	0
▼ **Florida Office**	1	1
Florida BYOD MDM	1	1
Florida BYOD Workspace	0	0
Florida Corporate Owned	0	0

Groups & Settings > Groups > Organization Groups >

List View

Notice that the two devices currently enrolled are within **Florida BYOD MDM** from *Chapter 5, Mobile Device Management*.

Smart groups

Next we will create smart group to define which users are eligible to enroll into organization group. There are a couple of ways this can be accomplished:

- If you created one group that includes users for both MDM and the workspace management deployment, you can simply modify the existing smart group being used for the MDM deployment and apply it to the newly created organization group for workspace management.

You can only modify the smart group to include the additional organization groups if the smart group was configured for management at a higher-level organization group. For example, if the smart group we are referring to in this example was created at **Florida Office Organization Group**, you can include the new organization group within the smart group. If the smart group was created within the **Florida BYOD MDM Organization Group**, which it was in the previous chapter's instructions, you will not be able to use the smart group for **Florida BYOD Workspace**.

- If you have configured separate user groups for each enrollment and you want to keep everything separate, you can simply create a new smart group that will apply to the new organization group for workspace management.

 As a reminder, how you configure your structure and the ability for your users to enroll and technicians to manage AirWatch all depends on how you set up your initial organization groups for management and smart groups for enrollment. You will want to go through a few test configurations to become fully familiar with the deployment options.

For this example, we will create a new smart group at the **Florida BYOD Workspace** organization group level as the smart group created previously will not allow us to add additional organization groups at the same level. To create your new smart group for the workspace management organization group, complete the following steps:

1. Log in to Admin Console.
2. Change your **Organization Group** to **Florida BYOD Workspace**.
3. Click on **Groups & Settings** and expand **Groups**.
4. Click on **Smart Groups** and then on **Add Smart Group**.
   1. Enter a name for the smart group in the top-right corner; we will use `Florida BYOD Users Workspace` for this group.
   2. Choose **Select Criteria** for this example and then select the following options:
      - **Organization Group**: Select **Florida BYOD Workspace**
      - **User Group**: Select the user group you would like the smart group to apply to; for this example, I created a `Florida BYOD Users` group

 If you don't see the user group you would like to apply to the smart group, you may need to add the organization group to the user group for assignment. To do this, click on **Accounts** then expand **Users**. Click on **User Groups** and then select the user group you would like to assign to a organization group. Click on **Permissions**, and click on **Add** to add additional organization groups for assignment if needed. Then, click on **Save**.

      - **Ownership**: Since this will be for BYOD and personally owned devices, I will only select **Employee** as the ownership for the devices
      - I will leave all other settings as default within the new smart group

5. Click on **Save** once you have configured your criteria. Here is a screenshot for your reference:

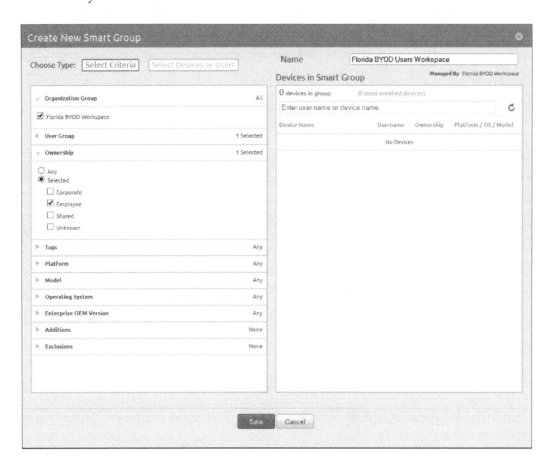

You can edit, delete, or view smart group assignments at any time by selecting the organization group the smart group is a part of, then navigating to the **Smart Groups** page, and clicking on the options available for the smart group.

Configuring workspace options

Now that the organization and smart groups have been created for your workspace deployment, we can configure the workspace management options that will provide the desired settings and configurations to the users workspace once enrolled.

In order to utilize the workspace deployment, you must meet the following minimum requirements:

- **Supported devices**: Currently, AirWatch workspace is supported on Android Gingerbread 2.3 or greater and iOS 5.0 or greater

- **Software requirements**: AirWatch workspace requires Version 6.5 or higher of Admin Console

- **Other requirements**: In order for AirWatch workspace to function correctly on iOS devices, AirWatch App Catalog must be enabled

 App Catalog will be covered in more detail in *Chapter 9, Mobile Application and Mobile Browser Management.*

There are multiple automatic features that are included within workspace once it has been downloaded to the user's device. They are as follows:

- **Encryption**: Workspace is secured with the FIPS 140-2 encryption at the application level and all data within the app is encrypted

 Full device or SD card encryption cannot be enforced at the device level with workspace.

- **App Tracking**: All enterprise-only apps that are installed using workspace are tracked

- **App Security**: Application security and compliance is enforced for apps that have been enabled to use with workspace

- **AirWatch Secure Content Locker**: Full content management is supported with the use of the AirWatch SCL

 SCL will be covered in more detail in *Chapter 8, Mobile Content Management.*

- **Asset Tracking**: The only data that is gathered from the device is the device platform, model and operating system

- **Location**: There is no location data being tracked by the workspace

- **Notifications**: Admins have the ability to push notifications to workspace from Admin Console

Next, we will configure the workspace settings the users will receive once they enroll their devices with AirWatch workspace. To configure the workspace settings, complete the following steps:

1. Log in to Admin Console.

2. Change your **Organization Group** to **Florida BYOD Workspace**.

 It is important that you change the organization group to the correct group to receive the correct settings. The settings being modified could affect other deployments if they are configured at a different organization group within the console.

3. Navigate to **Groups & Settings | All Settings | Apps | Settings And Policies | Security Policies**.

4. Select **Override** so that you can configure the setting for **Florida BYOD Workspace** organization group:

5. For **Security Policies**, configure the settings for your enrolled devices:

   ○ **Authentication Type**: This is where you can configure your password requirements for workspace to meet your security policies for authentication. The password configured will only apply to the workspace app, other AirWatch apps, application wrapped, and SDK-enabled apps and not the device. The configurable options are **Passcode** or **Username and Password** or **Disabled**.

   ○ **Single Sign On**: This configuration allows you to enable **Single Sign On (SSO)** for all AirWatch apps, application wrapped, and SDK-enabled apps that will use the password configured in **Authentication Type**. If this isn't enabled, the user will be required to enter their login credentials for each application every time they need to access it.

   ○ **Integrated Authentication**: Configuring this to **Enabled** allows the ability to access corporate resources through AirWatch Workspace or AirWatch MDM Agent using the AirWatch SSO credentials. **Integrated Authentication** works in AirWatch Browser and app-wrapped applications.

 We will cover more about **Integrated Authentication** in *Chapter 9, Mobile Application and Mobile Browser Management*.

   ○ **Offline Access**: Enabling this allows access to applications when the device is offline using SSO.

   ○ **Compromised Detection**: Enabling compromised detection prevents users from enrolling compromised devices or will un-enroll a device compromised after enrollment.

   ○ **AirWatch App Tunnel**: This is where you configure the ability for applications to communicate through a VPN or reverse proxy.

 We will cover more about AirWatch App Tunnel in *Chapter 8, Mobile Content Management*.

   ○ **Content Filtering**: If enabled, all AirWatch browser traffic that doesn't go through AirWatch App Tunnel can be configured to pass through a content filter.

- ◦ **Geofencing**: A geographic location can be applied to only allow Workspace to be used within the specified area. This is currently only supported on iOS devices.

- ◦ **Data Loss Prevention**: Here you can configure what can and can't be used on the device with workspace:

  - ◦ **Enable Copy and Paste**
  - ◦ **Enable Printing**
  - ◦ **Enable Camera**
  - ◦ **Enable Composing Email**
  - ◦ **Enable Data Backup**
  - ◦ **Enable Location Services**
  - ◦ **Enable Bluetooth**
  - ◦ **Enable Screenshot**
  - ◦ **Enable Watermark**
  - ◦ **Limit Documents to Open Only in Approved Apps**

- ◦ **Network Access Control**: This allows you to specify how workspace can access cellular and Wi-Fi connections. This is currently only supported for wrapped apps in workspace.

6. Click on **Save** once you have made the desired changes.

> The settings configured here may not apply to all device platforms and features. For more information on what settings apply to each platform and feature, log in to https://secure.air-watch.com/ and click on **AirWatch Resources**. Click on **Device Management** and open the *AirWatch Workspace Guide for Administrators*. Refer to *Appendix: SDK Profiles, Policies and Settings Compatibility*.

7. Next, we will configure the settings for workspace. To do this, navigate to **Groups & Settings | All Settings | Apps | Settings And Policies | Settings**.

8. Select **Override** so that you can configure the setting for **Florida BYOD Workspace** organization group:

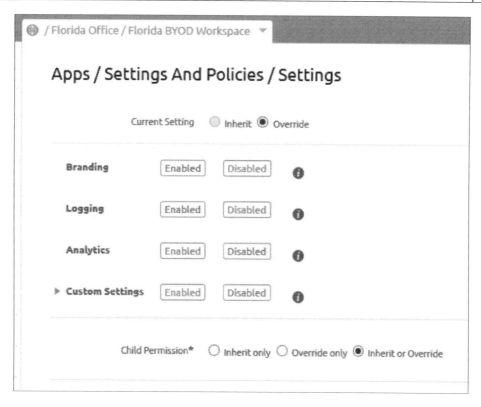

9. For **Settings**, configure the following for your enrolled devices:
    ◦   **Branding**: Here you can customize your application images and colors to match your organization's brand
    ◦   **Logging**: This is where you can enable logging for workspace and applications
    ◦   **Analytics**: You can enable this to allow apps to report analytics
    ◦   **Custom Settings**: You can define custom settings for the apps in this section

10. Click on **Save** once you have made the desired changes.

Pre-enrollment

Before we start enrolling devices, let's ensure that we have all our prerequisites and any other items in place that will ensure that the deployment is efficient and secure:

- All security settings are in place based on the recommendations from *Chapter 4, Mobile Security*. For enrollment, you will want to ensure that the following specific configurations are set up:

    - **Compliance Policies** (to check this, navigate to **Devices | Compliance Policies | List View**)

    - **Terms of Use** (to check this, navigate to **Accounts | Users | Settings | Terms of Use**)

    - Workspace security policies and settings as described in the previous section

- All enterprise integrations are set up and configured based on *Chapter 3, Enterprise Integration*. For enrollment, you have multiple options for your users to authenticate:

    - **Basic Authentication**: This allows manual creation of accounts in AirWatch

    - **AD/LDAP Authentication direct or with ACC**: This integrates with the current directory for consistent credentials

    - **Authentication Proxy**: This allows authentication via a reverse proxy or web server

    - **SAML 2.0 Authentication**: This integrates via SSO through federation of SAML identity provider

- You are able to brand the console to match your Organization's look and feel. To do this complete the following steps:

    1. Navigate to **Groups & Settings | All Settings | System | Branding** to change the branding.

    2. You can change the logo and login page image, customize the SSP, enable branding on reports, change the colors of the theme, and even use custom CCS.

- Message templates can be set up for communication by e-mail, SMS, and Push. To do this complete the following steps:

    1. Navigate to **Devices | Settings | General | Message Templates** to set up and configure your templates.

    2. The category option for **Message Templates** include **Enrollment**, **Application**, **Compliance**, **Terms of Use**, **Administrator**, **Content**, and **Device Lifecycle**.

- There are additional enrollment configurations that can be configured on each organization group. Navigate to **Devices | Settings | General | Enrollment** to view the additional options. Within this section, you will be presented with the following enrollment options:

 Ensure that you change your organization group to the one you are configuring for enrollment before making any changes. To make changes within the organization group, click on the **Override** option to allow the changes to be made.

- ○ **Authentication**: Here you can configure auto-discovery enrollment based on the user's e-mail address, your authentication mode, device enrollment modes, and whether agent enrollment is required for iOS and OS X.

- ○ **Terms of Use**: This is where you can enable the terms of use for enrollment.

- ○ **Grouping**: This is where you can specify how group IDs are assigned to users for enrollment. The three options available are **Default**, in which an administrator provides the group ID to the user, **Prompt User To Select Group ID**, which allows the user to select which group ID to enroll with, and **Automatically Select the Group ID**, which allows automatic assignment based on directory groups. Here you can also enforce default device ownership, default role, and default action for inactive users. For example, for my BYOD users, they will receive the employee-owned device ownership that I can enforce as part of enrollment and prevent them from having to select.

- ○ **Restrictions**: This is where you can limit your enrollment to know users or known groups, add a policy that allows specific ownership types, enrollment types, and device types (the platform, model, and OS), and limit the amount of devices that can be enrolled.

- ○ **Optional Prompt**: Here you have additional options that you can make available during the enrollment process.

- ○ **Customization**: Here you can provide contact information to the end users in the event they are unable to enroll their devices.

- There are multiple options for how the user enrolls and some of these will depend on how you have configured your environment for authentication:

  - ○ **Manual**: The user manually enters the provided environment URL, group ID, and credentials whether they are basic or integrated.

  - ○ **Auto-discovery**: The user enters their e-mail address that automaps them to the configured organization group for enrollment. Then, the user will enter their username and password. This is configured within the **Authentication** section of the **Enrollment** options as mentioned earlier.

> If users are required to enroll into multiple organization groups because of multiple devices or child organization groups below the enrollment organization group, they will be required to manually enter the group ID to ensure that they are enrolled into the correct organization group.

  - ○ **QR Code**: You can set up an enrollment to allow your users to scan a QR code that contains the environment URL and group ID. Once scanned, the user will enter their username and password to authenticate for enrollment:

    - ○ Use the `airwatch://enroll?ServerURL=ENVIRONMENT URL&ActivationCode=GROUPID` URL to create your QR code. Here is an example website to generate your QR code: `http://www.qrstuff.com/`

> If you send a registration e-mail to the user from AirWatch, the QR code is automatically generated in this e-mail. The preceding option allows you to create your own if you aren't sending a registration e-mail to the users.

Enrolling a device

Now that you have set up the group ID and the profile and completed all prerequisites, you can begin to enroll your devices. As mentioned earlier in this chapter, only iOS and Android devices are currently supported for the workspace deployment. Because of this, we will only look at the steps to enroll iOS and Android devices.

As a reminder, there are multiple ways in which authentication and enrollment can be set up for the user as already discussed. For the demonstration in this book, we will look at the steps to enroll using a username and password on one device and using your e-mail address on the other device. We will enroll the devices into the **Florida BYOD Workspace** test policy, which we configured earlier.

When enrolling manually, you will need the enrollment URL and group ID along with your credentials:

- **Enrollment URL**: Your AirWatch environment URL
- **Group ID**: For this use FLBYODWORKSPACE

iOS

For the iOS enrollment, you will enroll using your e-mail address. For this enrollment, you will need:

- Your e-mail address
- Credentials can be any of the authentication methods discussed in the *Pre-enrollment* section.

To enroll your iOS device, complete the following steps:

1. Open up the App Store.
2. Search for AirWatch Workspace and install the app.

3. Open the Workspace app once downloaded.

4. Select **Enroll** with your work e-mail.

5. Enter your work e-mail address and click on **Continue** and then again on **Continue** if required.

6. Enter your credentials depending on how you set up authentication. Click on **Continue**.

7. If you didn't preconfigure the device ownership, select **Employee Owned** or **Corporate-dedicated** depending on the device and then click on **Continue**

8. Click on **Accept** then again on **Accept** to accept the terms of use.

9. You will receive a notification page that your device has been successfully enrolled.

10. If you set up a password, you will be required to enter it based on the requirements configured. If SSO is also configured, this will be the password used to access the other installed apps. Click on **Continue** once the password has been entered and confirmed.

11. You will then be redirected to the Workspace app and your enrollment will be complete.

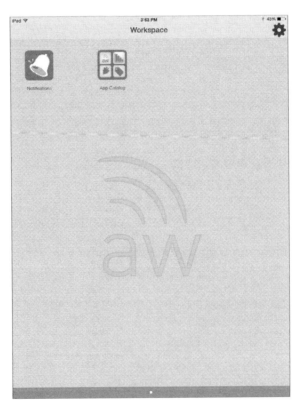

Android

For the Android enrollment, you will enroll using a username and password. For this enrollment, you will need the following:

- The enrollment URL and Group ID
- Credentials can be any of the authentication methods discussed in the *Pre-enrollment* section.

To enroll your Android device, complete the following steps:

1. Open up Play Store.
2. Search for AirWatch Workspace and install the app.

3. Open the Workspace app once downloaded.
4. Select **Enroll** with your group ID.
5. Enter your enrollment URL in the **Server** field and your group ID in the **Group ID** field. Click on **Continue** and then again on **Continue** if required.

> If you wanted to enroll with a QR code, you can select the **QR code** option and then scan the QR code.

6. Enter your credentials depending on how you set up authentication. Click on **Continue**.
7. If you didn't preconfigure the device ownership, select **Employee Owned** or **Corporate-dedicated** depending on the device and then click on **Continue**.
8. Click on **Accept** to accept the terms of use.
9. If you set up a password, you will be required to enter it based on the requirements configured. If SSO is also configured, this will be the password used to access the other installed apps. Click on **OK** once the password has been entered and confirmed.

10. If you would like to configure Workspace as the default launcher, leave the checkbox selected and click on Select **Default Launcher**. If not, uncheck the checkbox and select **Continue**.

11. You will be presented with a **Getting Started** screen; select Don't show again and click on **Done**.

12. You will then be redirected to the Workspace app and your enrollment will be complete.

 Now that you have enrolled your devices into Workspace, you can configure and publish AirWatch apps, such as AirWatch Inbox, AirWatch SCL, and AirWatch Browser, internal applications, public/ purchased applications, and web applications. All of these will be covered in the remaining chapters.

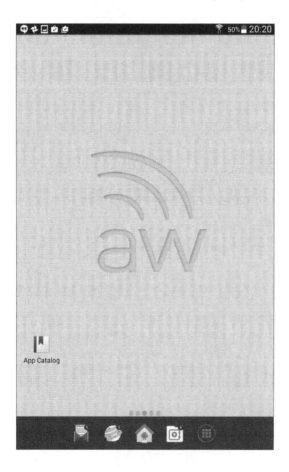

Managing Workspace on your device

To manage Workspace settings on an iOS device, complete the following steps:

1. Open up the Workspace app.
2. Log in with your password.
3. Click on the icon that looks like a gear in the top-right corner.
4. You will be presented with the following options:

To manage the Workspace settings on an Android device, complete the following steps:

1. Open up the Workspace app.
2. Log in with your password.
3. Click on Apps icon in the bottom-right corner.
4. Click on the **Settings** option.

5. You will be presented with the following options:

Self Service Portal

As demonstrated in *Chapter 5, Mobile Device Management*, users are able to manage their enrolled devices with Workspace via the AirWatch SSP the same way users manage their devices enrolled with MDM.

To access the SSP, open up a web browser and navigate to `https://yourenvironmemnturl/mydevice`. To log in, you will need the group ID and your authentication information (if you configured e-mail registration, you can use your e-mail address as part of the login).

 The following options will be different depending on the OS being used and the permissions assigned to the users.

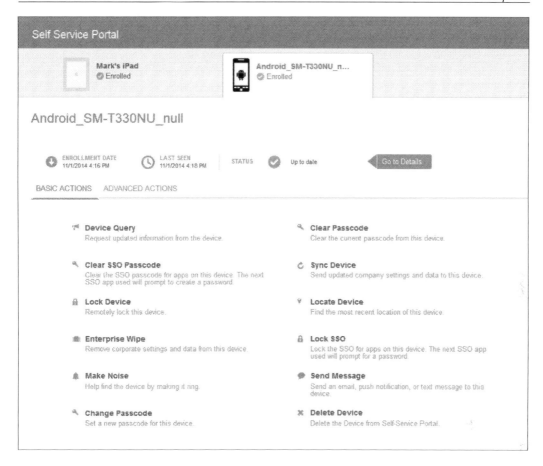

Un-enrolling a device

There are multiple ways a device can be un-enrolled from AirWatch. The following are some of the ways both the administrator and/or user can un-enroll a device from AirWatch:

- From the device a user can un-enroll by completing the following steps:
    - **iOS**: Open the AirWatch Workspace app. Log in with your password. Click on the icon that looks like a gear in the top-right corner and then on **Un-enroll**.
    - **Android**: Open the AirWatch Workspace app. Log in with your password. Click on Apps icon in the bottom-right corner and then on the **Settings** option, click on **Un-enroll**.

- From the Self-Service Portal:

  - Once logged in, select device and then Enterprise Wipe.

- From the Admin Console:

  - As an administrator, log in to the console. Navigate to **Devices** | **List View**. Search for the device and select it. Click on **More** in the top-right corner and click on **Enterprise Wipe**.

- Other:

  - Removing users from AirWatch or removing users from groups will un-enroll the users if these options were set up and configured to take this action as part of your initial setup and configuration.

 All devices can be managed within the **List View** section of **Devices** of AirWatch Admin Console.

Summary

In this chapter, you learned how to deploy AirWatch Workspace to mobile devices. AirWatch Workspace is the latest technology that allows us to better fulfill the BYOD deployment to users. With AirWatch Workspace, you are able to deploy a virtualized encrypted container at the operating system layer and not the device layer, which can be considered invasive on user's personal devices.

Throughout this chapter, we looked at workspace management at a high level to understand where it fits within EMM. We then looked at BYOD in more detail and why workspace management makes the most sense with BYOD before setting up your organization groups and smart groups in preparation for enrollment. Next, you learned where to configure AirWatch Workspace and the options available for configuration.

Moving on, we looked at all the pre-enrollment settings that are needed and/or recommended before continuing on to the enrollment of devices. Once enrolled, we looked at the settings available within AirWatch Workspace on the devices and then saw how users can self-manage their devices using Self Service Portal. We then finished off the chapter with how to un-enroll the devices from AirWatch Workspace. Now that we have completed the enrollment of devices with both MDM and workspace options, we can start focusing on the deployment of corporate resources to the devices. We will start with how to configure and deploy an e-mail to devices in the next chapter as e-mails have traditionally been the scope of corporate resources deployed to mobile devices.

7
Mobile E-mail Management

Now that we have enrolled the devices for management whether it is MDM or Workspace, we can start deploying corporate data to the enrolled devices. The first form of corporate data we will look at deploying to the devices is e-mail. E-mail has traditionally been one of the driving factors for providing mobile devices to users or provisioning content to user's personal devices. There are multiple opportunities available with deploying e-mails to devices with AirWatch by VMware. These opportunities span multiple e-mail vendors, the option between native and a container for delivery, and the option of providing full security including DLP if needed.

In this chapter, we will take a high-level overview of MEM and look at the reasons as to why we should be protecting e-mail service. We will then look at all the supported deployments available with AirWatch including the supported e-mail platforms. Moving on, we will look at how to set up SEG, Direct PowerShell, and Google Apps for Business for your deployments.

Once the e-mail infrastructure and/or configurations are set up and in place within the environment, we will look at the security options and where to configure e-mail security. We will then set up and configure the profiles to deploy e-mail before finishing off with how to manage e-mail on the enrolled devices and how to remove it from the devices.

The following topics will be covered in this chapter:

- Mobile E-mail Management overview
- Protecting e-mail
- Supported deployments
- Secure E-mail Gateway
- Direct PowerShell
- Google Apps for business

- E-mail security configurations
- Profile setup and configuration
- Managing and removing e-mail

Mobile E-mail Management overview

Mobile E-mail Management (MEM) is the vertical within EMM that represents all the opportunities available for e-mail deployment. Traditionally, e-mail was most likely deployed on a corporate-owned device that was provided to you by the organization that leveraged some of the first technologies available to deploy e-mail securely. Now that mobility has grown with the expectation that e-mail is to be provided on personal devices, we need MEM to provide e-mail to the user's devices. Most importantly though, we need to ensure that the e-mail is deployed securely and the information is contained within a secure environment.

As we are all aware, e-mail is a huge piece of how we communicate today and most likely one of the most common communication methods in an organization. Users rely extremely heavily on e-mail and the ability to have access to e-mail at anytime from anywhere is a reality a lot of us live in. I'd imagine that most of your deployments are somewhat still scoped to e-mail delivery to devices and your center of focus is to continue to provide that functionality, preferably in a BYOD fashion to user's personal devices. As discussed in previous chapters, there are considerations to take when deploying e-mail to devices. There may be laws that require you to reimburse users or prevent users from being able to access corporate resources outside of working hours as they aren't being paid. All this falls within MEM with AirWatch and is only a component of today's EMM.

If you've already provided e-mail to users' devices as part of your deployments, you'll realize how beneficial it is to users to be able to access e-mail conveniently from their mobile devices. As a technical professional, I receive hundreds of e-mails daily for different reasons including system notifications. Always having access to my e-mail allows for that extra convenience of being more proactive on receiving alerts (as long as e-mail is still working) with the ability to manage e-mail anywhere.

With MEM, there are multiple different deployment methods available with AirWatch to meet your organizations security needs. With AirWatch's MEM, you can expect the following as part of your deployment:

- Deployment of e-mail to multiple types of devices manufactures or operating systems
- The ability to deploy e-mail using native device e-mail, an AirWatch e-mail container, or a supported third-party application

- Support of multiple e-mail providers

- Enforce security with deployment of MDM or workspace

- Allow auto-configuration of e-mail with deployment

- Enforcement of SSL security

- DLP enforcement

- Compliance policies to prevent access to e-mail in the event a device is compromised or doesn't meet security needs

- The ability to deploy and remove e-mail without affecting the user's personal information

- Enhanced security with the Secure E-mail Gateway option

- The ability to auto provision access to e-mail for users

- Attachment control enablement

- Certificate integration for additional security

- The ability to apply geofencing to remove profiles outside of specified boundaries

- The ability to apply schedules to remove profiles outside of working hours if required

Protecting e-mail

As technical experts, it is critical to understand the importance of protecting corporate e-mail within your environments. All types of information are guaranteed to be traveling within the e-mail systems. I have personally seen information from usernames and passwords, social security numbers, confidential business information, legal information, credit card information to name some examples. Working in health care, we have multiple compliances we have to obey. It is critical that we are able to protect PHI and PCI within our environment, e-mail being a high risk to this information leaking.

As an organization, you will most likely have policies in place that enforce what an employee should and shouldn't be doing when it comes to e-mail usage. Although this may be in place, it typically doesn't prevent the users from using the technology to help them get their job done more efficiently. Even though these policies are in place, you and I both know that users will do what they can to be as productive as possible.

For me, policies are only part of the overall controls around protecting your organization's information. As a user, you are going to use the technology provided to you without realizing the potential risk and e-mail creates a significant risk, especially with the increase and demand of users requesting access with their personal devices. When it comes to e-mail delivery on mobile devices, especially personal devices, we need to ensure that we fully understand the risk associated with the information within the e-mails and how easy it can be for that information to leak outside the organization.

When looking at providing e-mail to the users on their personal devices, it is critical that we are able to protect the information from leaving the boundaries of the organization and entering the user's personal world. If we don't enforce these controls as technical professionals, the users won't even realize that they are doing anything wrong when they work with e-mail on their devices. For example, if there is no control around the attachments within your corporate e-mail and a user accidentally downloads that attachment to their personal device, data loss has just occurred and that information could land anywhere.

For all organizations, allowing access to e-mails via native ActiveSync, POP, or IMAP should be considered a security risk. Even if you don't have any compliances within your organization, your company does maintain employee records and information. Even more importantly, there will be some form of confidential information within an e-mail from leadership containing new strategies, organization changes, or intellectual property that if leaked, could compromise your company. With that, you need to ensure that when you provide e-mail to your employee's personal devices, it is secure. Some of the more important security controls that you need to be aware of are as follows:

- Password-protected device or e-mail access
- Ensuring devices or e-mail applications are encrypted
- Preventing jailbroken or rooted devices
- DLP is in place to prevent copy and paste or screenshot functions
- Attachment control.

With AirWatch, you are able to protect your e-mail with multiple options available for your deployment. Whether you are a Microsoft, Google, Lotus, or Novell environment, or if you would like to deploy a native experience or provide e-mail through a container, allow access to e-mail on multiple devices including iOS, Android, and Windows, provide full DLP or just some security controls are all possible with AirWatch's flexible MEM solution. With the options available from AirWatch, you will be able to meet your organization's security requirements to ensure a secure and usable solution.

Supported deployments

There are multiple supported deployments with AirWatch depending on what e-mail infrastructure you have in place and how secure you would like to make your deployment.

The following mail infrastructure is supported with AirWatch:

- Microsoft Exchange 2003/2007/2010/2013/Office 365
- Google Apps for Business
- Lotus Domino with Lotus Notes
- Novell GroupWise
- Any e-mail infrastructure that supports Exchange ActiveSync
- Any e-mail infrastructure that supports a POP/IMAP/SMTP configuration.

The following profile configurations are available to deploy e-mail to your devices once enrolled within AirWatch:

- **Android Devices**: POP/IMAP/SMTP, Exchange ActiveSync, Native Mail Client, AirWatch Mail Client, Lotus Notes, and NitroDesk TouchDown
- **iOS Devices**: POP/IMAP/SMTP, Exchange ActiveSync, Native Mail Client, AirWatch Inbox, and NitroDesk TouchDown
- **Windows Phone 8 Devices**: POP/IMAP/SMTP, Exchange ActiveSync, and Native Mail Client
- **Windows Mobile Devices**: Exchange ActiveSync and Native Mail Client
- **Symbian Devices**: Exchange ActiveSync and Native Mail Client
- **Apple Mac OS X Devices**: POP/IMAP/SMTP, Exchange Web Services, Native Mail Client, and Microsoft Outlook
- **Windows PC Devices**: Exchange Web Services and Microsoft Outlook
- **Windows 8/RT Devices**: AirWatch Inbox using Exchange ActiveSync

With AirWatch, you can deploy e-mail in its basic form with minimum security in place by simply setting up the configurations in a profile to be deployed to users. For the additional granular security, AirWatch has the option of three additional models that can be used with your environment:

- **Basic Profile with limited Security**: This can be set up for most if not all e-mail providers

- **Secure E-mail Gateway using the Proxy Model**: Microsoft Exchange 2003/2007/2010/2013/Office 365, Microsoft Office 365, Lotus Domino with Lotus Notes, Novel GroupWise using Exchange ActiveSync, and Google Apps for Business

- **PowerShell using the Direct Model**: Microsoft Exchange 2010/2013/Office 365

- **Google using the Direct Model**: Google Apps for Business

From the preceding options, you will receive the greatest security by using the SEG Proxy option. The additional security with SEG over direct model is the ability to encrypt and control attachments and hyperlinks, preventing them from leaving the AirWatch environment. The basic profile is obviously the least secure with very minimum controls over e-mail.

To view the supported functionality between the models and supported platforms, log in to the myairwatch portal, navigate to **AirWatch Resources | E-mail Management**, open *Mobile E-mail Management Guide*, and go to *Appendix: E-mail Management Functionality*.

Secure E-mail Gateway (SEG)

Now that we know what options we have with the MEM deployments, we will look at how to set up and configure SEG and the benefits of using this model.

SEG overview

SEG serves as a proxy server that is installed in-line with your corporate e-mail infrastructure. Once installed, you will configure your client profiles to send all traffic through the SEG servers to allow for additional security and controls over e-mail being delivered to mobile devices.

With SEG, you can provide the following additional security controls:

- Attachment control
- Hyperlink Management
- Encryption Enforcement
- Device Approval/Blocking
- Whitelisting/Blacklisting of Devices/Users
- Apply Compliance Policies.

SEG deployment options

The SEG server can only be deployed within your data center whether you are an on-premise or SaaS-based customer. The recommended deployment for your SEG is to install it within your DMZ or behind a reverse proxy server. The following diagram shows the recommended architecture for your SEG deployment:

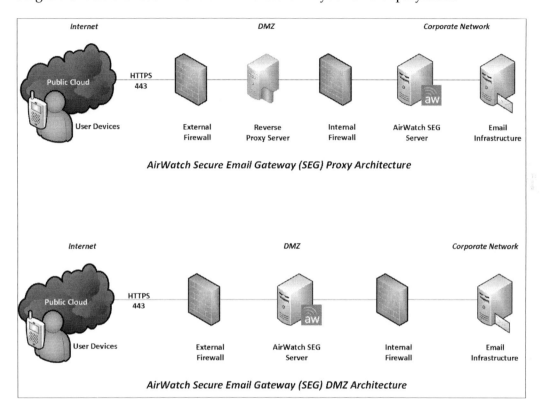

AirWatch Secure Email Gateway (SEG) Proxy Architecture

AirWatch Secure Email Gateway (SEG) DMZ Architecture

 This model can also be deployed with Microsoft Office 365 and Google Apps for Business.

SEG requirements

The next section lists all the requirements for the SEG deployment.

Prerequisites

Ensure that the SOAP API is enabled for the organization group SEG is being deployed for:

- Navigate to **Groups & Settings | All Settings | System | Advanced | API | SOAP API** and select **Generate Client Certificate**

Hardware requirements

VM or physical server	With attachment encryption, hyperlink security and tagging	Without attachment encryption, hyperlink security and tagging
Number of devices	1,200 Devices per 1 CPU Core and 2 GB RAM	2,000 Devices per 1 CPU Core and 2 GB RAM
Disk size	Standard OS requirements	
CPU cores	Minimum 1 and Maximum 8 CPUs	
RAM (GB)	Minimum 2 GB RAM	

 You can load balance the SEG servers for high availability.

Software requirements

The following lists all the software requirements for the SEG deployment:

- **Supported operating systems**: Windows Server 2008 R2, Windows Server 2012, or Windows Server 2012 R2

- **Server manager roles**: IIS 7.0 (Server 2008 R2), IIS 8.0 (Server 2012 or Server 2012 R2), or IIS 8.5 (Server 2012 R2 only)

- Server manager roles services

    - **Common HTTP features**: static content, default document, directory browsing, HTTP errors, HTTP redirection

    - **Application development**: ASP.NET, .NET Extensibility, ASP, ISAPI Extensions, ISAPI Filters, Server Side Includes

- ° **Management tools**: IIS Management Console, IIS 6 Metabase Compatibility

[ Ensure WebDAV is not installed.]

- Install **Application Request Routing (ARR)**
    - ° It is available at `http://www.iis.net/downloads/microsoft/application-request-routing`
- Enable the following server manager features
    - ° .NET Framework 3.5.1 Features (the full module)
    - ° Telnet Client
- .NET Framework 4.0
- Externally registered DNS
- SSL Certificate from a trusted third party with Subject or Subject Alternative Name of DNS
- IIS 443 binding with the same SSL certificate

General requirements

- Remote access to SEG servers
- Notepad ++ (recommended)
- Exchange ActiveSync test account

Network requirements

Source Component	Destination Component	Protocol	Port
Internet and Wi-Fi	SEG	HTTPS	443
SEG	AirWatch SOAP API	HTTP or HTTPS	80 or 443
SEG (optional)	Internal hostname or IP of other SEG servers for clustering	HTTP	8090
Device Services	SEG	HTTPS	443
SEG	Exchange	HTTP or HTTPS	80 or 443
SEG	Lotus Notes	HTTP or HTTPS	80 or 443
SEG	Google	HTTPS	443
SEG	Novell GroupWise	HTTP or HTTPS	80 or 443

Installation

Before we install SEG, we need to enable the SEG proxy in the AirWatch Admin Console. To do this, complete the following steps:

1. Log in to the AirWatch Admin Console.

2. Navigate to **E-mail | Settings** and click on **Configure**. You will be presented with the **Mobile Email Management Configuration** wizard:

3. Select the **Email Server Type** for your deployment. With Microsoft **Exchange 2010/2013/Office365** and Google Apps for Business, choose **With SEG Proxy**

4. On the MEM Deployment page, complete the required information:

    ○   **Friendly Name**: Add a name, as this is an easy way to identify usage.

    ○   **Secure E-mail Gateway URL**: This is the URL for your SEG to provision the policies.

    ○   **Ignore SSL errors between SEG and AirWatch server**: You can select this to ignore SSL errors.

    ○   **Use Basic Authentication**: It is recommended that you select this and enter a **Gateway Username** and **Gateway Password** to authenticate secure traffic. If this is not selected, anonymous authentication will be used.

    ○   Click on **Test Connection** to validate the connection to the SEG server.

> For Google Apps for Business, you will need the Google Apps domain, Google Apps admin username, and Google Apps admin password in addition to the information previously mentioned.

5. Click on **Next** to go to the **MEM Profile Deployment** option:

  ° For multiple SEG deployments, you will need to associate which profile will be used for each platform through the gateway being configured.

 Only one gateway can be configured per a device type and mail client type.

  ° Click on **Add** to add your profile deployments if required

6. Click on **Next** to view the **Summary** page and then click on **Save**.

Once you have saved the configuration, navigate back to the page to view the MEM configuration and additional options and perform the following steps:

- Navigate to to **E-mail | Settings** and then click on **Configuration**.
- You will see the profile you configured with the additional options:

  ° **Add**: This is to add additional SEG servers
  ° **Edit**: This is to edit current SEG settings

- ○ **Advanced**: This is to modify additional settings. By default, the **Use Recommended Settings** is selected

- ○ **Test Connection**: This validates that SEG settings are correct

- ○ **Export Settings**: You can export settings to XML and import them as an option during SEG installation

- At the bottom of the screen, you have options to disable or delete the configuration

Next, you will need to download the SEG installer from the Admin Console:

1. Navigate to **E-mail | Settings**.

2. On the main screen, click on **AirWatch Secure E-mail Gateway Installer** to download the installer file and copy the file to the SEG server.

 Disable **User Access Control** (**UAC**) to prevent any errors during installation.

On the SEG server, install the SEG:

1. Right-click on the installer file downloaded from the console and select **Run as Administrator**.

2. Click on **Next** on the **Welcome** screen.

3. Accept the **End User License Agreement** and click on **Next**.

4. Specify a destination to install the SEG or leave the installation path as default location (c:\AirWatch).

 The best practice is to install applications on a separate partition to the OS.

5. Validate that the default website is on the target site and click on **Next**.

6. Click on install then on **Finish** once the installation completes.

Configuration

Now that the SEG has been installed, we can configure the settings for it:

- The **Secure E-mail Gateway Setup** wizard should have auto-launched after installation. If not, click on the **AirWatch SEG Setup** shortcut on the desktop

- On the **Setup** page, configure the following:

  1. Enter the **API Hostname** which is typically the AirWatch API service URL. For example, it may look something like this for SaaS customers: `https://asxxx.awmdm.com`.

  2. Select **Ignore SSL errors between SEG and AirWatch** to ignore any SSL errors.

  3. Enter the SEG admin username and password.

 This is an AirWatch account that is needed to integrate with the API. If an admin account isn't set up in AirWatch, create a local admin account and assign it the allow remote access role resource in the AirWatch admin console. Ensure that this account is created at the same organization group level or above the organization group being configured with the SEG.

  4. If you have a proxy server, select the **Enable proxy for AirWatch** services communication checkbox and enter the proxy host, proxy port and authentication information.

 If you select **Advanced**, you could upload the XML file that was exported from the console, enter the password and API hostname, and then click on **Next**.

  5. Click on **Next**.

- Select the organization group the SEG will be used for, then select the specific MEM configuration you created for the SEG, and click on **Next**.

- On this page, configure the following:

  1. Select the **E-mail Server Type**. For Microsoft Exchange, select the version you are using.

  2. Enter the E-mail server hostname (your ActiveSync URL), then click on **Verify**, enter a mailbox username and password, and click on **Verify**.

   Google Apps for Business doesn't require a server hostname to be entered as you configured the information as part of the configuration within the Admin Console.

  3. If you selected **Exchange**, you also have the option of proxying web mail traffic through the gateway. Select the checkbox to route your webmail traffic through the proxy.

   For Microsoft Exchange webmail proxy and Lotus Notes, you will need to install the **Application Request Routing** (**ARR**) component, as stated in the requirements.

  4. The Secure E-mail Gateway settings will be prepopulated with the settings entered in the AirWatch admin console. You can make any changes that are needed that will update the AirWatch Admin Console.

  5. Click on **Next**.

- The next screen allows you to Enable SEG Clustering. If you have multiple SEG servers for High Availability or Load Balancing, select the option and add the following information:

  - Add the **Cluster Directory Name** information
  - Add the **Default Port** information
  - The node address

      °   To add the additional SEG servers to the cluster, select **Add Node**

      °   Click on **Next** once complete

- You will receive a **Finished** screen, and then you will be automatically redirected to the **Secure E-mail Gateway Service Settings** screen. You can navigate away from this page.

You have now completed the SEG installation and configuration and you are ready to set up your profile to deploy e-mail via the SEG.

      To upgrade the SEG, download the latest installer from the console (**E-mail** | **Settings**) after an upgrade and follow the simple upgrade instructions.

Direct PowerShell

Next we will look at how to set up the PowerShell integration method and the benefits of using this model.

PowerShell integration overview

Integrating PowerShell with AirWatch requires less infrastructure and is a much simpler deployment. With PowerShell integration, AirWatch issues PowerShell commands to Microsoft Exchange to allow or reject e-mail access with ActiveSync. This integration allows you to enforce access control by whitelisting/blacklisting user's devices. Using this will prevent you from leveraging the advanced features such as attachment encryption or hyperlink transformation.

PowerShell integration deployment options

The PowerShell integration model can be deployed using an AirWatch SaaS or on-premise deployment with an on-premise Exchange 2010/2013 or Office 365 infrastructure. The following diagram shows the recommended architecture for your PowerShell Integration deployment:

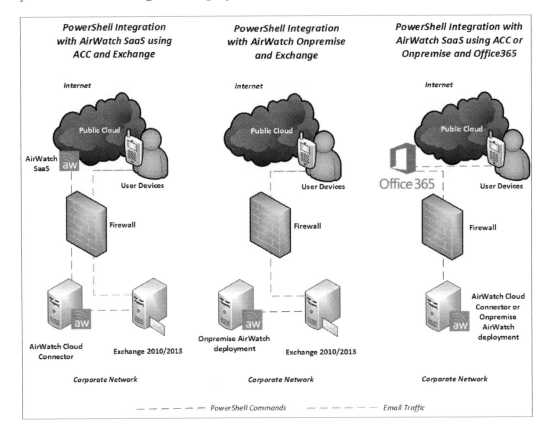

PowerShell integration requirements

The following section lists all the requirements for the PowerShell integration deployment:

- Service account with a mailbox that has remote PowerShell access to Microsoft Exchange Server
- The following roles are required for integration:
    - Organization Client Access role
    - Mail Recipients role

   ◦ Recipients Policies role (only needed for Windows Phone 7 and Blackberry devices)

- Access to the server-side session is required to execute `Exchange` commands
- Port 443 or 80 for communications
- Exchange ActiveSync profile
- ACC is required for SaaS deployments as covered in *Chapter 3, Enterprise Integration*

 You will need to work with your Microsoft Exchange administrators to successfully deploy PowerShell integration.

Configuring PowerShell integration

The following six steps are required to set up PowerShell integration with AirWatch:

1. Set up PowerShell admin user in Exchange 2010/2013

  1. Log in to Exchange Management console (Exchange Admin Center in Exchange 2013). Navigate to **Toolbox | Role Based Control User Editor** and log in as an Exchange administrator.

 This is the same as logging in to the **Exchange Control Panel** (**ECP**) directly and clicking on **Roles** and **Auditing**.

  2. Click on **New**, enter a name and description, and add these roles: Mail Recipients, Organization Client Access, and Recipient Policies. Click on **Save** to create the new role group.

2. Configure IIS on Exchange server

  1. Log in to your Exchange servers (or more specifically, your **Client Access Servers** (**CAS**)), open up IIS, and ensure that the PowerShell application within your default website is configured for Basic Authentication or Windows Authentication credentials.

  2. Open up Exchange Management Shell on each of the Exchange servers and run the following command:

```
Set-ExecutionPolicy RemoteSigned
```

3. Install and configure Windows PowerShell on AirWatch servers

    1. On AirWatch servers, verify that PowerShell is installed

    2. Open PowerShell on each of the AirWatch servers and run the following code/command:

```
Set-ExecutionPolicy RemoteSigned
```

4. Configure PowerShell integration in the AirWatch Admin Console

    1. Log in to the AirWatch Admin Console.

    2. Navigate to **E-mail | Settings** and click on **Configure**.

    3. You will be presented with the MEM configuration wizard.

    4. Select `Microsoft Exchange` for **E-mail Server Type** and select `Exchange 2010 / 2013 / Office 365`. Then, select `Exchange PowerShell` as the **Deployment Type** and click on **Next**.

    5. On the MEM deployment page, complete the following required information and then click on **Next**:

        ◦ **Friendly Name**: Add a name, as this is an easy way to identify usage

        ◦ **PowerShell URL**: Enter the Exchange PowerShell URL, for example, `https://e-mailserverurl/powershell`

        ◦ **Ignore SSL errors between AirWatch and AirWatch Server**: You can select this to ignore SSL errors

        ◦ **ACC Configuration for PowerShell integration**: This is only available for multiple MEM deployments and allows you to select which ACC server to integrate with

        ◦ **Use Service Account Credentials**: This allows you to leverage the AppPool service account on the ACC server

        ◦ **Authentication Type**: Select authentication to match the Exchange settings (**Basic**, **Negotiate**, or **Kerberos**)

        ◦ **Admin Username**: Enter the username for the PowerShell service account

        ◦ **Admin Password**: Enter the password for the PowerShell service account

        ◦ **Test Connection**: Click on **Test Connection** to validate configuration

> ○ **One-time sync after configuration**: This forces a sync after configuration has completed
>
> ○ **Limit sync results**: You can limit the sync to certain filtered groups

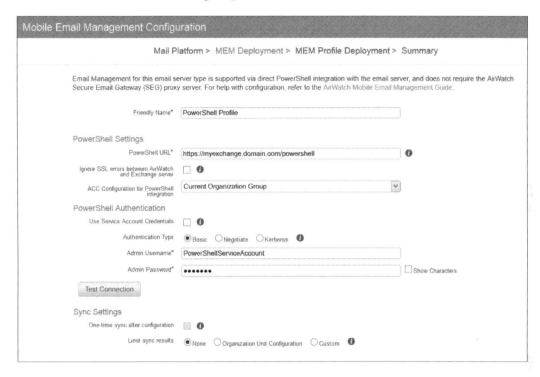

6. Click on **Next** to go to the **MEM Profile Deployment** option:

   ○ For multiple MEM deployments, you will need to associate which profile will be used for each platform through the gateway being configured.

 Only one can be configured per a device type and mail client type.

7. Click on **Add** to add your profile deployments if required.

8. Click on **Next** to view the **Summary** page and then click on **Save**.

9. Once you have saved the configuration, navigate back to the page to view the MEM configuration and additional options. Navigate to **E-mail | Settings** and then click on **Configuration**.

5. Start PowerShell integration by completing the following steps:

   1. Sync all mailboxes from AirWatch E-mail Dashboard with Exchange to import all devices with the EAS partnership.

   2. Allow devices to enroll and continue to sync daily to view devices as they convert from Unmanaged to Managed.

   3. Apply AirWatch E-mail Policy to block unmanaged devices when ready.

6. Configure Exchange to **quarantine** or **block new devices** by completing the following steps:

   1. To prevent anyone from configuring access directly to Exchange using ActiveSync, configure Exchange to quarantine or block any new devices upon configuration. Only devices enrolled in AirWatch will be able to access e-mail by issuing PowerShell commands to Exchange.

   2. Open up Exchange PowerShell on an Exchange server and run the following commands:

      ○ To quarantining devices:

      ```
      Set-ActiveSyncOrganizationSettings –
      DefaultAccessLevel quarantine
      ```

      ○ To block devices:

      ```
      Set-ActiveSyncOrganizationSettings –
      DefaultAccessLevel Block
      ```

You have now completed the PowerShell integration and configuration and you are ready to set up your profile to deploy e-mail to the devices.

Direct Google

The last integration option provided by AirWatch is Google Apps for Business integration.

An overview of Google Apps for Business integration

AirWatch has provided you with the opportunity to integrate Google Apps for Business with AirWatch for a secure deployment to the users. Google Apps for Business can be set up using AirWatch MEM with or without SEG. You will have the ability to deploy Exchange ActiveSync profiles to your devices once you have integrated Google Apps for Business with AirWatch. The benefits of integrating Google Apps for Business with AirWatch are as follows:

- Allows for a flexible configuration at the same time of maintaining controls
- Monitoring and management of e-mail
- Access control

Requirements for Google Apps for Business integration

The following are all the requirements for the Google Apps for Business integration deployment:

- Access to Google Apps for the Business API
- Google admin access with super admin privileges
- Access to Google services using Single Sign On
- AD/LDAP should not be synching passwords to a Google account
- The user should accept the Google end-user license agreement

Configuring Google Apps for Business integration

There are three different options of integration available from AirWatch with Google Apps for Business:

> If you choose not to use the super admin account, you will need to create an admin role with Admin Console privileges (read access to organization units , read and update users information, for example, rename users, move users, reset password, force password, add/remove aliases, suspend users) and Admin API privileges (same as Admin Console privileges). You will also need to enable the Google API (in the Google console, navigate to **Security** | **API Reference** and enable **API access**).

1. **Integration without SEG without password purge**: This consists of direct integration with Google Apps, and you have the ability to manage and monitor enrolled devices in the admin console. You are able to apply policies within the AirWatch admin console to determine whether devices are compliant or non-compliant. This method uses password switching to block non-compliant devices. Use the following steps to configure integration without SEG without password purge:

   1. Log in to the AirWatch Admin Console.
   2. Navigate to **E-mail | Settings** and click on **Configure**.
   3. You will be presented with the MEM configuration wizard.
   4. Select **Google Apps for Business** and **Without SEG Proxy** and click on **Next**.
   5. On the MEM deployment page, complete the required information:
      - **Friendly Name**: Add a name, this is an easy way to identify usage
      - **Google Apps Domain**: This is the URL for Google Apps
      - **Google Apps Admin Username**: Admin username that has access to the Google Apps API for password management
      - **Google Apps Admin Password**: Admin password that has access to the Google Apps API for password management
   6. Click on **Next** to go to the **MEM Profile Deployment** option:
      - For multiple MEM deployments, you will need to associate which profile will be used for each platform through the gateway being configured.

 Exchange ActiveSync profile is required for all Google integrations.

      - Click on **Add** to add your profile deployments if required.
   7. Click on **Next** to view the **Summary** and then click on **Save**.
   8. Once you have saved the configuration, navigate back to the page to view the MEM configuration and additional options: Navigate to **E-mail | Settings** and click on **Configuration**.

 When setting up your profile, enter m.google.com as the Exchange ActiveSync host.

2. **Integration without SEG with password purge**: This is the recommended approach from AirWatch. Using integration without SEG and with password purge, AirWatch communicates with Google Apps directly and doesn't store the password in the database. If a device is detected as non-compliant, AirWatch will remove the e-mail profile from the device until the device becomes compliant again. Once the device becomes compliant again, AirWatch will send a new password to the device with the e-mail profile. Use the following steps to configure integration without SEG with password purge:

   1. Follow the preceding steps in the integration without SEG without password purge section.

   2. Once you have browsed back to configuration, click on **Advanced** on the MEM profile you just created.

   3. Disable **Use Recommended Settings** and the **Retain Google Password** checkbox.

   4. You can also configure the following options:

      ° **Google Random Password Length**: You can enter a password length minimum of 8 up to a maximum of 100.

      ° **Password Retention Period**: This is the number of hours the password is temporarily saved for management reasons. The default value is set to 48 and it can be set between 1 and 100.

      ° **Auto-rotate Google Password**: Select this option to reset the password within the specified time; the minimum is 1 and the maximum is 90.

      ° **Auto-rotate Google Password Period**: This is the period specified to reset the Google password; the default is 30 days.

   5. Click on **Save**.

 For the integrations without SEG without password purge and with password purge, unmanaged devices are blocked by default.

3. **Integration with SEG Proxy**: Using the SEG proxy method, the SEG server sits in-line between AirWatch and Google Apps. The SEG server proxies all e-mail traffic from the devices and provides visibility of both managed and unmanaged devices within the admin console. The additional benefit is the ability to leverage the e-mail policies available within AirWatch. To set up Integration with SEG proxy, follow the configuration instructions within the *Secure E-mail Gateway (SEG)* section of this chapter. When you set up the configuration, select Google Apps for Business and With SEG proxy.

If you set up Google Apps for Business with E-mail Management through AirWatch, all passwords will change with all the preceding configurations. If you want to keep the passwords the same, do integrate with AirWatch, simply deploy the Exchange ActiveSync setting through a profile.

E-mail security configuration

Now that the infrastructure is in place, the next step before e-mail is deployed to the devices is to ensure that you enforce your security controls. To manage the security for your e-mail deployment, perform the following steps:

1. Log in to the AirWatch Admin Console.

2. Navigate to **E-mail | Compliance Policies**. You will be presented with the following options:

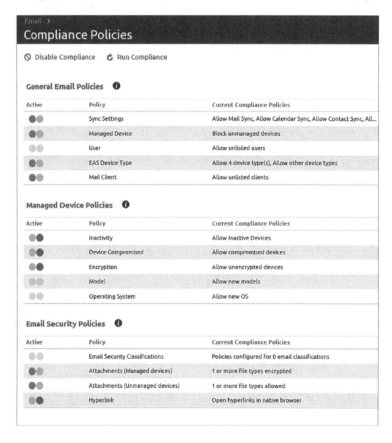

As you can see in the preceding screenshot, there are three main sections for configuration. The first section is **General E-mail Polices**, and in this section you can configure the following:

- **Sync Settings**: Configure the specific folder from syncing to the device. For example, you can block contacts from syncing.

- **Managed Device**: This allows e-mail to managed devices only.

- **Mail Client**: This specifies the mail clients that can be used to access e-mail.

- **User**: This allows you to specify which users can receive e-mail if enabled.

- **EAS Device Type**: Here you can whitelist or blacklist devices based on the Exchange ActiveSync type reported by the device.

The next section is **Managed Devices Policies** that enforces the configured policies on the managed devices accessing e-mail. The following can be configured:

- **Inactivity**: This allows you to specify in days how long a device is considered inactive to prevent it from accessing mail

- **Device Compromised**: This prevents access to e-mail for compromised devices

- **Encryption**: This prevents access to e-mail for unencrypted devices

- **Model**: This allows or blocks access to e-mail based on the device model and platform

- **Operating System**: This allows or blocks access to e-mail based on the operating system for specific platforms

The last section is the **E-mail Security Policies** that allows more control with attachments and hyperlinks. In order to use this section, you need to meet the following requirements:

- You need to use SEG for these configurations

- The users will need to install SCL

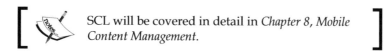

SCL will be covered in detail in *Chapter 8, Mobile Content Management*.

- Support is available for Microsoft Exchange 2003/2007/2010/2013/Office 365, Lotus Notes, Novell GroupWise, and Google Apps for Business

The following settings can be configured within **E-mail Security Policies**:

- **E-mail Security Classification**: Here you can configure policies for SEG to allow or block e-mails based on predefined or custom tags within the e-mail

- **Attachments (Managed devices)**: This allows, blocks, or forces encryption of attachments for selected file types, allowing them to only be opened in SCL on managed devices

- **Attachments (Unmanaged devices)**: This allows, blocks, or forces encryption of attachments for selected file types, allowing them to only be opened in SCL on unmanaged devices

- **Hyperlink**: This allows you to force hyperlinks to only be opened with a secure AirWatch application such as AirWatch Browser

 As stated earlier in the chapter, some of the e-mail policies will not apply to some of the e-mail deployment models.

The profile setup and configuration

Our last step is to set up and configure the profiles to deploy e-mail to the user's device. Depending on how you have decided to move forward with your e-mail deployment based on policy, security or functionality will dictate how you configure and deploy e-mail to your user's devices. As stated earlier in the chapter, there are multiple options to deploy e-mail to the user's devices and some of the options may be limited based on the manufacturer. In general, there are three client options available:

- **Native Client on the device**: The Native Client deployment allows for configuration of the built-in mail client on the user's device without the need for any third-party mail clients.

- **AirWatch Inbox**: This is a containerized e-mail client that provides the needed security and segregation from personal information on the device. AirWatch Inbox is best suited for BYOD deployments, as discussed in *Chapter 6, Workspace Management*.

- **NitroDesk Touchdown**: This is a third-party e-mail client that requires an additional license for its usage.

Based on the security requirements the e-mail provider being used in your environment will depend on which of the methods below you deploy.
The three options to deploy include the following:

- **Basic Profile**: Here you can configure the profile to configure access to your e-mail systems with minimum security in place

- **Direct Approach**: This approach allows more control over security controls and access to the corporate e-mail systems

- **SEG Proxy**: This is the most secure option that provides the most control with the added benefit of full attachment and hyperlink control

For demonstration purposes, we will set up a native profile on the iOS device with the SEG proxy method using MDM and AirWatch Inbox on the Android device using Workspace. Demonstrating all options of e-mail configurations alone could easily fill this book; the two methods we'll demonstrate will give you an idea on how to set up and deploy e-mail to the devices.

 Not all of the options will be the same for each of the mail clients and platforms within the profiles.

An iOS native profile with SEG proxy

Since we have already set up our MDM profile and enrolled our iOS device in *Chapter 5, Mobile Device Management*, all we need to do is set up the additional profile and apply it to the users who have already enrolled. To set up your e-mail profile and apply it to the iOS device enrolled in *Chapter 5, Mobile Device Management* and perform the following steps:

1. Log in to Admin Console.

2. Navigate to **Devices | Profiles | List View** and click on **Add**. Then, select **Apple iOS**.

3. In the **General** section, complete the information as you did to create a profile in the *Creating and Publishing a Profile* section of *Chapter 5, Mobile Device Management*. Ensure that you assign the profile to the correct smart group (whether you use an existing one or create a new one), and for the name, reference what the profile will be used for, for example, native e-mail iOS.

4. Next you will configure the e-mail settings by configuring the payload for the profile. Select Exchange ActiveSync and click on Configure:

- **Mail Client**: This is the mail client option available for iOS; select Native Mail Client

- **Account Name**: This is the name that will be displayed within the Mailboxes section of the device

- **Exchange ActiveSync Host**: Since we are using the SEG Proxy, this will be the address of your SEG proxy server

- **Use SSL**: Check to use SSL for incoming traffic

- **Use S/MIME**: Check to use S/MIME to use additional encryption certificates. To use this option, you will need to upload the needed certificates into the Credentials payload. The following three options will appear if you select **Use S/MIME**:

- **S/MIME Certificate**: Select this certificate to sign e-mail messages

- **S/MIME Encryption Certificate**: Select this certificate to sign and encrypt e-mail messages

- **Enable Per-Message Switch**: This allows users to select which messages to sign and encrypt

[Select **E-mail Payload** to configure **POP/IMAP** as an option.]

5. Next is the login information for the e-mail account. You can reference lookup values that are provided by AirWatch to pull the information directly from the user account record. You will need to verify that this information has been synched to the user's AirWatch account:

- **Domain**: Verify your e-mail domain name (the lookup value).

- **Username**: Verify the user login name (the lookup value).

- **E-mail Address**: Verify the user e-mail address (lookup value).

- **Password**: Leave this blank to have the user enter their credentials.

- **Payload Certificate**: Here you can define a certificate for certification-based authentication. To use this option, you will need to upload the needed certificates into the Credentials payload.

To learn more about certificate authentication, log in to the myairwatch portal, navigate to **AirWatch Resources | Documentation | Certificate Management**, and open the *Certificate Authentication for EAS with ADCS* guide.

6. The final section consists of the **Settings and Security** options:

    ° **Past Days of Mail to Sync**: This is the number of days to synchronize user's e-mail to device

    ° **Prevent Moving Messages**: This prevents moving messages to a different mailbox on the device

    ° **Prevent Use in 3rd Party Apps**: This prevents third-party apps from using the mailbox to send messages

    ° **Prevent Recent Address Syncing**: This disables suggestions for contacts

7. Once you have completed entering all the required information, click on **Save & Publish** and confirm the devices the profile is being applied to. Then, click on **Publish** to push the profile to the device and configure e-mail.

8. On the enrolled iOS device, open up the native e-mail app. If everything is applied correctly, you should be prompted for your e-mail password. Enter your password, and you should then see **Work E-mail** within your mailboxes and e-mail will start to sync to your device.

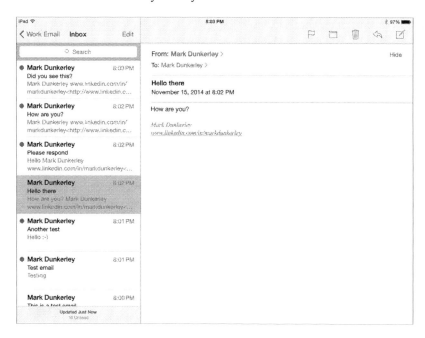

An Android AirWatch inbox profile with SEG proxy

Since we have already set up our Workspace profile and enrolled our Android device in *Chapter 6, Workspace Management*, all we need to do is set up the additional profile and apply it to the users who have already enrolled. To set up your e-mail profile and apply it to the Android device enrolled in *Chapter 6, Workspace Management*, complete the following steps:

1. Log in to the Admin Console.

2. Navigate to **Devices | Profiles | List View**, click on **Add**, select **Android**.

3. In the **General** section, complete the information as you did to create a profile in the *Creating and Publishing a Profile* section in *Chapter 5, Mobile Device Management*. Ensure that you assign the profile to the correct smart group (irrespective of whether you use an existing one or create a new one), and for the name, reference what the profile will be used for, for example, AirWatch Inbox Android.

4. Next you will configure the e-mail settings by configuring the payload for the profile. Select **Exchange ActiveSync** and click on **Configure**. You will then be provided with the following configuration options:

    ◦ **Mail Client**: This is the mail client option available for Android; select **AirWatch Mail Client**

     To learn more about AirWatch mail client and the supported operating systems/platforms, log in to the myairwatch portal, navigate to **AirWatch Resources | E-mail Management**, and open *AirWatch Inbox Admin Guide*.

    ◦ **Account Name**: This is the name that will be displayed for the mailbox on the device

    ◦ **Exchange ActiveSync Host**: Since we are using the SEG proxy, this will be the address of your SEG proxy server

    ◦ **Ignore SSL Errors**: Select this to ignore any SSL errors

    ◦ **Use SSL**: Check this option to use SSL for incoming traffic

    ◦ **Use S/MIME**: Check this option to use S/MIME to use additional encryption certificates. To use this option, you will need to upload the needed certificates into the credentials payload. The following two options will appear if you select **Use S/MIME**:

- ○ **S/MIME Certificate**: Select this certificate to sign e-mail messages
- ○ **S/MIME Encryption Certificate**: Select this certificate to sign and encrypt e-mail messages

> Select **E-mail Payload** to configure **POP/IMAP** as an option.

5. Next is the login information for the e-mail account. You can reference lookup values that are provided by AirWatch to pull the information directly from the user account record. You will need to verify that this information has been synched to the user's AirWatch account:

- ○ **Domain**: Verify the e-mail domain name (the lookup value).
- ○ **User**: Verify the user login name (the lookup value).
- ○ **E-mail Address**: Verify the user e-mail address (the lookup value).
- ○ **Password**: Leave this blank to have user enter credentials.
- ○ **Identity Certificate**: Here you can define a certificate for cert-based authentication. To use this option, you will need to upload the needed certificates into the credentials payload.

6. The next section is **Settings**:

- ○ **Past Days of Mail to Sync**: This is the number of days to synchronize a user's mail to device
- ○ **Sync Interval**: Here you can specify how often to sync mail to the device
- ○ **Past Days of Calendar to Sync**: This is the number of days to synchronize a user's calendar to a device
- ○ **E-mail Signature**: Optionally enter a signature for the users

7. Now, configure the **Contacts and Calendar** options:

- ○ **Contacts Application**: Select whether to sync the contacts with the native contacts application or the AirWatch Contacts application, or do not sync
- ○ **Allow Single Contact Export**: This allows a user to export a single contact

- ○ **Allow Bulk Contacts Export**: This allows a user to bulk export contacts
- ○ **Calendar Application**: Select whether to sync the calendar with the native calendar application or the AirWatch Calendar application, or do not sync

8. Configure the passcode if you would like your users to enter a passcode to the app. Since we have already configured Workspace to be password protected, we will not configure this for users. A good use case to configure this would be if you deployed AirWatch Inbox using the MDM approach and didn't password protect the device. You could simply password protect AirWatch Inbox to ensure that e-mail is protected.

9. The final section is **Restrictions**:
   - ○ **Restrict Copy-Paste**: Select this to prevent copying items outside of AirWatch
   - ○ **Allow Attachment**: Select this to allow attachments to be downloaded and then configure the maximum size
   - ○ **Restrict Attachments to be Opened in the Following Apps**: Select this to prevent the selected apps from opening attachments
   - ○ **Disable Screenshots**: Select this to prevent screenshots within the app
   - ○ **Restrict Domains**: Select this to whitelist or blacklist domains
   - ○ **Open all links in AirWatch Browser**: Select this to force links to be opened in AirWatch Browser

10. Once you have completed entering all the required information, click on **Save & Publish**, confirm the devices the profile is being applied to, and then click on **Publish** to push the profile to the device and configure e-mail.

11. On the enrolled Android device, log in to AirWatch Workspace and download and install AirWatch Inbox (Mail icon). Once installed, launch AirWatch Inbox (if it doesn't automatically configure, you may need to force a sync from the device by navigating to **All Apps | Settings | Troubleshoot | Sync**, or logging in to the Admin Console to push the profile).

 From experience, Android devices have a tendency to cause additional troubleshooting when re-enrolling, adding profiles sometimes because of the cache. It's recommended to clear the data and cache on the applications when re-pushing profiles or re-enrolling devices.

12. If everything is applied correctly, you should be prompted for your e-mail password. Enter your password to sync e-mail to your device. Here is a screenshot for your reference:

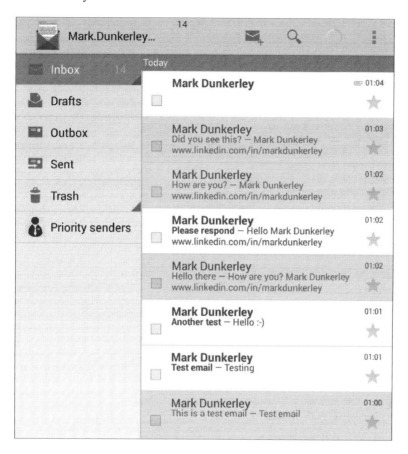

 AirWatch Inbox is part of the AirWatch applications catalog. The deployment of applications will be covered in more detail in *Chapter 9, Mobile Application and Mobile Browser Management.*

Managing and removing e-mail

It is critical that you are able to efficiently manage and remove e-mail from a user's device in the event that they leave the organization. The following section will cover where and how to manage e-mail within your deployment as well as remove e-mail from a user's device.

Managing e-mail

Once the devices have been enrolled for e-mail, you have the ability to manage and view the enrolled devices via the e-mail dashboard in the admin console. To access the dashboard, navigate to **E-mail | Dashboard**. Here you can gain a high-level view of your enrolled devices with e-mail access.

You also have the ability to view the user's devices that are being managed with MEM. To access the devices, navigate to **E-mail | List View**. Within this view, you can switch your search between the device or user. Within the views, you can search for devices to perform the following actions if desired:

- **Override**: Whitelist, Blacklist, or Default
- **Administration**: Dx Mode On, Dx Mode Off, Update Encryption Key, or Delete Unmanaged Device
- **Actions**: Run Compliance or Enable Test Mode

Removing e-mail

You can remove the e-mail configurations by following the instructions to un-enroll a device listed in *Chapter 5, Mobile Device Management, Un-enrolling a Device* section. If you want to remove only e-mail, you can remove the user from receiving the profile or the profile for all users to allow them to continue to be enrolled.

Summary

This chapter has covered everything to help you get deployed and started with MEM. MEM has traditionally been one of the biggest drivers with Mobility, and AirWatch continues to provide that opportunity with an extremely flexible deployment that will meet the needs for your organization whether you are looking to provide a simple enrollment for e-mail configuration, or you need to fully protect your e-mail down to the attachments.

This chapter provided an overview of MEM, and we looked at protecting corporate e-mail and some of the reasons as to why we should be protecting this information. We then looked at the supported deployments and platforms available within AirWatch before looking into setting up and configuring SEG, Direct PowerShell, and Direct Google options.

We then looked at the available security configurations within AirWatch before setting up and configuring the profiles to provide e-mail to the devices. Once e-mail is provided to the user's devices, we looked at where to manage e-mail on the devices before finishing off with how to remove e-mail from the devices.

Now that we have provided e-mail to the user's devices, we can start exploring additional opportunities with deploying corporate resources to the user's devices. In the next chapter, we will be looking at mobile content management and the options available for deploying corporate content to users' devices securely.

8
Mobile Content Management

Now that we have deployed what has traditionally been the basis of content delivery to users, we can move on to new opportunities starting with MCM. MCM opens the floodgates to much more than just e-mail delivery. With content management, we are able to provide access to much more internal corporate resources to the user's mobile devices securely. This content includes secure access to internal file shares, SharePoint farms, content repositories, and much more. Providing access to this content allows users to access, modify, and share their files all from their mobile devices, creating a more collaborative and productive environment.

In this chapter, we will review MCM at a high level. We will look at the reasons why we should be protecting corporate content and the importance of security with corporate content. We will then review MAG for proxy and content, the requirements, and how to install it. Once the MAG is set up, we will review and configure the security controls available within AirWatch by VMware for content delivery.

Once we have the security controls in place, we will look at all the available options to set up and configure the delivery of content to the users. The section following the setup of content will demonstrate how users will access the content before finishing off with how to manage and remove content from the devices.

The following topics will be covered in this chapter:

- Mobile Content Management overview
- Protecting content
- Mobile Access Gateway for proxy and content
- Content security configurations
- Configuring content management
- Accessing content
- Managing and removing content

Mobile Content Management overview

Users are requesting the ability to access more corporate information from their mobile devices. **Mobile Content Management (MCM)** is another piece of EMM that provides the ability to access more of the information that is expected to be available on our end users' mobile devices. Providing access to internal content such as file shares and SharePoint allows for a more collaborative and productive user experience. Providing access to these internal content repositories means to provide the ability to access data from anywhere and at any time. This is a shift in the way we've traditionally accessed content from PC and/or laptop devices.

As we start looking at providing MCM to the end users, we also have to take into consideration that MCM is part of a larger trend that has become available in the industry. **Enterprise File Sync and Share (EFSS)** is the ability to securely provide access to corporate content to a wide array of devices such as smart phones, tablets, PCs, laptops and more. As we move beyond MCM and EFSS, we have to now take into consideration where the user's content is being stored, as organizations are making a shift towards cloud opportunities. This provides additional challenges in that we need to be able to securely and efficiently provide access to all the possible different content touch points whether they are on-premise or in the cloud. Not only do we need to be able to access all these touch points, but we need to provide access to them all from one point of access. With AirWatch, we will demonstrate how to provide access securely to all these different content repositories from one place providing that full EFSS experience.

As you start deploying content to your users' mobile devices, you will start to realize how powerful MCM is. The opportunities to create or change work flows and processes are something that will naturally start to occur as your users adopt the technology more and more. In my current role, we set up MCM specifically for attachment control within our e-mail environment. As it was set up for attachment control, we are now able to start looking at new opportunities by providing access to internal file shares and SharePoint farms and even extending the access to Office 365 SharePoint, allowing a secure and central point of access to the users.

Within other industries, there are success stories such as in the field of education that allow teachers and students to share and collaborate more efficiently with projects and assignments and the ability to provide e-books. The airline industry is replacing the pilot's flights bags with electronic versions of their manuals and critical information. The legal industry is providing access securely to sensitive information on mobile devices. As you can see from the few examples provided, you can start to become as creative as you like with the opportunities.

To learn more on how others are deploying MCM, visit www.air-watch.com and navigate to **Resources | Case Studies**. On the left, select MCM in the **By Solution** dropdown.

With AirWatch's MCM, you can expect the following as part of your deployment:

- Securely deploy access to corporate content
- Access to multiple different content repositories including Network Shares, WebDAV, SharePoint on-premise and Office365, OneDrive, Google Drive, and CMIS
- Opportunities to re-create and build new processes
- Significant savings by implementing paperless work flows
- Industry standard encryption and Data Loss Prevention
- The ability to connect to cloud, on-premise, or hybrid repositories
- Secure access to internal resources using the Mobile Access Gateway
- Customization and branding with your deployment
- Analytics and reporting
- Deploy with MDM and AirWatch Workspace
- Access from multiple platforms through a single app
- Access is available through a mobile app, web portal, or a desktop client
- Content sharing, editing, and annotation for full collaboration
- Access and share content from Outlook
- Compliance policies to prevent access to e-mail in the event a device is compromised or doesn't meet security needs
- The ability to deploy and remove content without affecting users' personal information
- The ability to apply geofencing to remove a profile outside of the specified boundaries

Protecting content

As we've progressed through this book, we have demonstrated how critical it is to ensure that we can provide the required security controls to protect the corporate information being provided to the users' devices. The same applies to MCM and EFSS as you deploy these initiatives into your organization. Since we are expanding the user's ability to access content repositories, we need to ensure that we are able to control access to that content as well as data at rest and in transit. When we start looking at content, this could be anything from files, spreadsheets, videos, pictures and so on that will contain all kinds of information about your organization. Allowing any of this information to leave the control of your organization could create significant penalties and build a negative image for your company.

As we discussed in *Chapter 7, Mobile E-mail Management*, there will most likely be policies and regulations in place that enforce what a user should and shouldn't do with corporate content. Again, although these policies are in place, it doesn't mean the users will follow them. As technical professionals, this is where we need to understand the technology we have available to ensure that we configure and apply the security controls available using AirWatch.

As you start deploying your initiatives, you will need to understand the security controls available with MCM and how to ensure they are enforced through AirWatch. For corporate-owned initiatives, the security should be fairly simple as the organization owns the device. Simply password protecting the device, encrypting your data, and preventing access to unapproved apps, websites, and so on should provide the basic security requirements to meet your security needs. The biggest challenge, as always, is going to be with the personally-owned devices. We need to ensure that the organization's content stays within the control of the organization and doesn't cross over to the user's personal world. At the same time, we need to ensure that we can safely remove the corporate content from the user's personal device, without affecting their personal content. With AirWatch, this is all possible to accomplish as we will see in this chapter.

With AirWatch, the following security controls are available when deploying corporate content:

- **Multiple authentication methods for access**: AD/LDAP, Kerberos, token-based and certificate-based
- **Data Loss Prevention policies**: Disable copy and paste, disable printing, disable camera and Bluetooth, disable data backup, enable location services, enable watermark, control which Apps documents can open in, and Geofencing

- **Compromised detection**: Detect whether the user's device is jailbroken or rooted
- **Encryption**: Data in transit with MAG and SSL and Data at rest with AES 256-bit, FIPS 140-2 encryption

Mobile Access Gateway for proxy and content

Next we will look at **Mobile Access Gateway** (**MAG**), its purpose, and deployment for usage. The usage of MAG will also be covered in *Chapter 9, Mobile Application and Mobile Browser Management*, as it is also needed to provide initiatives with browser deployments securely.

MAG overview

MAG serves as a secure relay between your mobile users and your internal corporate content. This allows you to provide access securely and efficiently to users' devices once they have been enrolled with AirWatch. MAG is able to authenticate and encrypt all traffic to and from user devices to corporate systems where the data exists.

> As stated in *Chapter 3, Enterprise Integrations*, you may have installed the EIS as an old customer. The EIS has been replaced by ACC and MAG and you can only install EIS or ACC/MAG. Since ACC was installed in *Chapter 3, Enterprise Integrations*, the EIS should already be disabled and shouldn't cause any issues with the MAG installation.

With MAG, you are able to provide secure access to internal content repositories using SCL on the user device. Intranet and web applications can be accessed with AirWatch Browser and business applications using app tunneling and app wrapping. Additionally, App VPN can be set up for iOS devices to access internal corporate resources.

There are two deployments available for MAG depending on what you would like to integrate with. The following two options are available:

- **MAG for Windows**: This is the proxy and content component that provide access to internal resources via AirWatch Browser and SCL
- **MAG for Linux**: MAG for Linux is the tunnel component that provides per app VPN access to internal and public apps for iOS 7 and greater devices

Since MCM only requires MAG for Windows, we will focus on setting up MAG for Windows in this chapter. MAG for Linux will be covered in *Chapter 9, Mobile Application and Mobile Browser Management*, when we cover App VPN access.

MAG deployment options

MAG servers need to be deployed within your data center whether you are an on-premise or SaaS-based customer. There are multiple options available with the deployment of MAG. You have the option of deploying a simple installation where MAG will sit in your internal network, or for additional security, you can deploy as MAG relay that will sit in a DMZ network before connecting to a MAG installed in your internal network. With both of these deployments, the option to deploy multiple MAG is also available to provide high availability and load balancing. The following diagram shows the recommended architecture for your MAG deployment:

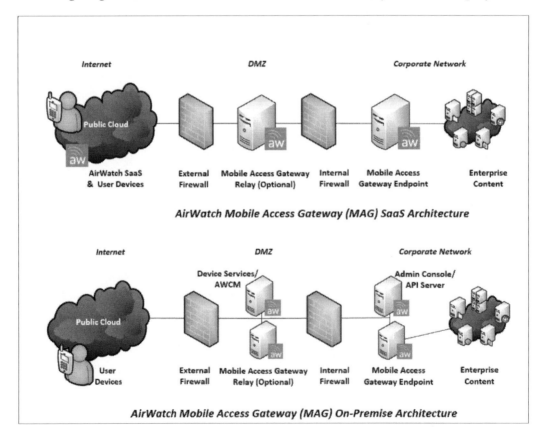

AirWatch Mobile Access Gateway (MAG) SaaS Architecture

AirWatch Mobile Access Gateway (MAG) On-Premise Architecture

MAG requirements

The following section lists all the requirements for MAG for Windows deployment for both SaaS and on-premise deployments.

Hardware requirements

The following table represents the hardware requirements for MAG:

Maximum number of users	Up to 5,000	5,000–50,000	50,000–100,000	100,000+
Disk size	Standard OS requirements with 5 GB disk space for installation			
CPU cores	1	4 CPUs or 2 load balanced servers with 2 CPU cores	4 CPUs or 2 load balanced servers with 2 CPU cores	2 load balanced servers with 4 CPU cores
RAM (GB)	4	4	8	16

> You can load balance MAG servers behind your enterprise load balancer for growth and High Availability.

Software requirements

The following are the software requirements for MAG:

- **Supported operating systems**: Windows Server 2008 R2, Windows Server 2012, or Windows Server 2012 R2

- **Server manager roles**: IIS 7.0 (Server 2008 R2), IIS 8.0 (Server 2012 or Server 2012 R2) or IIS 8.5 (Server 2012 R2 only)

- **Server manager features**: .NET Framework 3.5.1 features (full module) and Telnet Client

- .NET Framework 4.0

- Java Runtime Environment 7 and higher. This is available from `http://java.com/en/download/index.jsp`

- **Internally registered DNS**: DNS should point to MAG relay server if it has been deployed; if not, it should point to the MAG endpoint

- **Externally registered DNS**: DNS should point to MAG relay server if it has been deployed; if not, it should point to the MAG endpoint
- SSL certificate from trusted third party with subject or subject alternative name of DNS
- IIS 443 binding with the same SSL certificate
- Ensure that the AWCM SSL intermediate and root CA certificates are in Java CA keystore on MAG server. On MAG server, use the command line to enter the following:

```
keytool -list -v -keystore $JAVA_HOME\jre\lib\security\cacerts
```

General requirements

The general requirements for MAG are listed as follows:

- Remote access to SEG servers
- Notepad++ (recommended)

Network requirements

The network requirements for MAG are as follows:

Source component	Destination component	Protocol	Port
Devices from Internet and Wi-Fi	AirWatch MAG	HTTP	80 for Browser
		HTTPS	2020 for Browser
		HTTPS	443 for Content
Basic MAG deployment with no relay			
MAG endpoint	AirWatch Cloud Messaging server*	HTTPS for SaaS	443 for SaaS
		HTTP or HTTPS for on-premise	2001 for on-premise
MAG endpoint	The AirWatch REST API	HTTPS for SaaS	443 for SaaS
		HTTP or HTTPS for on-premise	80 or 443 for on-premise
MAG endpoint	Internal content repository	HTTP or HTTPS	80 or 443
MAG endpoint	Internal web server/app	HTTP or HTTPS	80 or 443
MAG endpoint	Internal system	ANY	ANY

Source component	Destination component	Protocol	Port
MAG - relay deployment			
MAG relay	AirWatch Cloud Messaging server	HTTPS for SaaS HTTP or HTTPS for on-premise	443 for SaaS 2001 for on-premise
MAG relay	The AirWatch REST API	HTTP or HTTPS	80 or 443
MAG relay	MAG endpoint	HTTP	2010 for browser
MAG relay	MAG endpoint	HTTPS	443 for content
MAG endpoint	Internal content repository	HTTP or HTTPS	80 or 443
MAG endpoint	Internal web server/ App	HTTP or HTTPS	80 or 443
MAG endpoint	Internal system	ANY	ANY
AirWatch device services	MAG relay	HTTP or HTTPS	80 or 443
AirWatch console	MAG relay	HTTP or HTTPS	80 or 443

*For SaaS customers, reference the AirWatch IP ranges for the most up-to-date IPs. To access the ranges, log in to the myairwatch portal, navigate to **Knowledge Base**, search for **What are the AirWatch IP ranges for SaaS data centers?**, and click on the link to view the ranges.

If you plan to connect to network file shares, your MAG must either be on the same Windows domain as the file share servers or there must be a trust between the domains.

Installation

Before we install MAG, we need to enable and configure the settings in AirWatch Admin Console. To do this, complete the following steps:

1. Log in to AirWatch Admin Console.

The next two main points are for on-premise deployments only.

2. Navigate to **Groups & Settings | All Settings | System | Advanced | Site URLs**.

3. Ensure that the following URLs are correct and then click on **Save**:

    ○   The REST API URL should be `https://<YourURL>/api`

    ○   The AWCM server external URL should be `server.domain.com` with no HTTPS in front of it

    ○   The AWCM service internal URL should be in the `https://server.domain.com:Port/awcm` format where the port is usually 2001

4. Next, navigate to **Groups & Settings | All Settings | System | Advanced | Device Roots Certificates** and validate whether the root certificates exist. If not, click the **Override** option and generate the root device certificates.

 If you don't see this option in your SaaS, continue to the next steps. This will already have been complete for your environment.

5. Navigate to **Groups & Settings | All Settings | System | Advanced | API | REST API** and click on the **Override** option. Check **Enable API Access** if not already checked and validate whether an API Key is shown and click on **Save**.

Next we will configure MAG for Windows-specific settings with the following steps:

1. In Admin Console, navigate to **Groups & Settings | All Settings | System | Enterprise Integration | Mobile Access Gateway** and click on **Configure**.

    1. Select **Configure MAG for Windows** and click on **Continue**.

    2. Select **Basic-Endpoint** or **Relay-Endpoint** depending on what you select for your deployment and click on **Next**.

 Setting up MAG relay will provide an additional layer of security.

2. In the **Details** section, enter the following information for a **Basic-Endpoint** deployment:

    ○   **Endpoint Host Name**: This is the name of MAG server (this will be the internal and external DNS records you set up).

    ○   **Default HTTP port**: This is the non-secure port that communicates with MAG, and the default is 2010.

    ○   **Default HTTPS port**: This is the secure port that communicates with the MAG, and the default is 2020.

    ○   **Use Kerberos proxy**: If checked, this allows access to Kerberos authentication. **Kerberos Constrained Delegation (KCD)** is currently not supported.

3. Enter the following information in addition to the Basic settings if you selected the **Relay-Endpoint** option:

    ○   **Endpoint Host Name**: This is the FQDN of the MAG server.

    ○   **Relay-Endpoint Port**: This is the port used for traffic between MAG relay and the MAG endpoint. Do not use port 80 as this is required for the binding of the MAG installation. The default is 8080.

4. Next you will complete the content configuration for a Basic setup:

    ○   **Content Repository URL**: The URL used to access MAG content repository, which is usually the same as the hostname field with `https://` added.

    ○   **Content repository port**: This the port used to communicate with the content repository. The default is set to 443.

5. Enter the following information in addition to the Basic settings if you selected the **Relay-Endpoint** option:

    ○   **Endpoint URL**: The name of the MAG endpoint with `https://` appended to it. You will need to ensure that the certificate contains the name used for configuration.

    ○   **Relay-Endpoint Port**: The port used to communicate with the content repository. The default is set to 443.

The following represents the configuration for a **Relay-Endpoint** configuration:

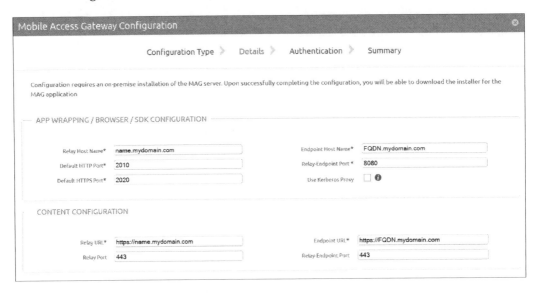

6. Click on **Next** to move to the **Authentication** section:

    1. Select the checkbox to use a public third-party SSL.

    2. Click on **Browse** to upload your certificate in the PFX or P12 format.

    3. Select **Ignore SSL Errors** to ignore any SSL errors.

7. Click on **Next** and review the configuration. Click on **Save**.

8. On the **Mobile Access Gateway** page, click on **Advanced** to configure the **Advanced** settings:

    1. First, we will configure the **Mobile Access Gateway** section:

    2. Select **Enable API and AWCN outbound calls via proxy** if the communication between MAG relay and the AirWatch API or AWCM is through an outbound proxy

    3. Select **Show detailed errors** to inform client applications that MAG has failed to authenticate a device

    4. Select the desired log level for MAG service

    5. The next section is the **Authentication** section:

    6. Select **Generate Certificate** to enable the MAG authentication

    7. If you plan to SSL offload the MAG server, export the MAG certificate and then import it onto the server that will offload the SSL

8. The last section is **Admin User Credentials**:

9. This is the username and password for authentication between the MAG relay and endpoint. In this section, use an AirWatch admin account by creating one in the Admin Console or leverage one that has already been created.

10. Click on **Save** once complete.

9. We will now download the software to be installed on servers:

1. Click on the **General** option and scroll to the bottom of the screen.

2. Click on the **Download Windows Installer** link (app wrapping, browser, content).

3. Enter and confirm a password for the certificate (minimum of six characters) and click on **Download**.

 If you make any settings after you have downloaded and installed MAG, you will need to redownload and reinstall MAG.

Now that all configurations are complete, we can move onto installing MAG. If you have a **Relay-Endpoint**, you will need to run the installer on both Relay and Endpoint servers. The same goes if you have multiple MAG servers for high availability. You will need to run the installer on all servers. For demonstration, we will run through the installation of MAG on both relay and endpoint servers:

 If you only have an endpoint server, the second section below, installing MAG onto the MAG endpoint, will be exactly the same for the installation.

1. Log in to your relay server and copy the downloaded executable to the server to begin the installation:

1. Right-click on the installer file copied from the console and select **Run as Administrator**.

2. Click on **Next** on the Welcome screen.

3. Accept the **End User License Agreement** and click on **Next**.

4. Specify a destination to install MAG or use the default (C:\AirWatch) and click on **Next**.

The best practice is to install applications on a separate partition to the OS.

5. Select the checkbox if you are offloading the SSL onto another server.

6. Select the **Relay** option to install the relay and click on **Next**.

7. Enter the password you entered for the certificate when you downloaded the installer and click on **Next**.

8. Select the target site where AirWatch should install (the default website will be listed as default) and click on **Next**.

9. If you are using Windows firewall (which you should), you will receive a notification that you will need to add the ports configured for MAG. Ensure that you add the ports specified in the configuration as allowed in the firewall. Click on **OK** to the notification if you received it.

10. Click on **Install** to install MAG and click on **Finish** once complete.

2. Next, we will install MAG onto the MAG Endpoint; copy the downloaded executable to the server. Complete the following steps to install the MAG:

3. Right-click on the installer file copied from the console and select **Run as Administrator**.

    1. Click on **Next** on the Welcome screen.

    2. Accept the **End User License Agreement** and click on **Next**.

    3. Specify a destination to install MAG or use the default (C:\AirWatch) and click on **Next**.

    4. Select the **Endpoint** option to install the Relay and click on **Next**.

    5. On the next screen, you can select to use a proxy server:

        1. Check **Will MAG use an outbound proxy?** if you are using a proxy server.

        2. Check the option to use a proxy auto-configuration (PAC), if needed.

        3. Enter the proxy host and proxy port number used for communication.

        4. If credentials are required, check the option next to **Does the proxy require authentication credentials?** and enter the credentials whether they are Basic or NTLM.

5. Click on **Next** to enter the PAC URL or upload the PAC file if this option was selected. Click on **Next**.

6. Enter the password you entered for the certificate when you downloaded the installer and click on **Next**.

7. Select the target site where AirWatch should install (the default website will be listed as default) and click on **Next**.

8. If you are using Windows firewall (which you should), you will receive a notification that you will need to add the ports configured for MAG. Ensure that you add the ports specified in the configuration as allowed in the firewall. Click on **OK** to the notification if you received it.

9. Click on **Install** to install the MAG and then on **Finish** once complete.

4. To verify that the installation was successful and MAG is functional, in the Admin Console, navigate to **Groups & Settings | All Settings | System | Enterprise Integration | Mobile Access Gateway** and click on **Test Connection** in the **General** section. You will be told whether the connection to MAG was successful or not.

> If you are upgrading MAG, the installer will autodetect that there is a previous installation and will offer to simply upgrade MAG. It is recommended to keep MAG up to date with the same version as that of the console.

Content security configurations

For the most part, your security configurations have most likely been configured already as part of *Chapter 6, Workspace Management*, as the security controls for content management are in the same place. You will just need to ensure that the configuration that was set up in *Chapter 6, Workspace Management*, is applied to the same organization group or groups that will be used in content management. To configure Security Policies for content management, navigate to **Groups & Settings | All Settings | Apps | Settings and Policies | Security Policies**.

This is where you will see your **Security Policies** for AirWatch apps including SCL, which will be used to access the content from mobile devices. These options were covered in *Chapter 6, Workspace Management*, within the **Configuring Workspace Options** section. I will point out the **Data Loss Prevention (DLP)** section as this is where you will want to ensure that you have your restrictions in place to prevent data leakage for SCL. Here is a screenshot for your reference:

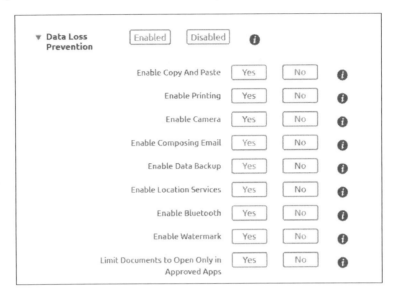

Ensure that the **Security Policies** have been applied to all organization groups receiving content. When setting up Workspace, you may have only applied the security settings to that specific organization group, which will not enforce **Security Policies** on the MDM organization group for content deployment.

Configuring content management

Now that the infrastructure is in place and the security controls have been configured, we can start configuring the system in preparation to deploy content to the users. There are a lot of different options and configurations available when it comes to configuring content management. We will not be able to cover them all in detail in this book. However, we will give you an overview of where each of the configurations are. This will allow you to become familiar with each of the available options.

Content options

With AirWatch, there are three primary forms of content available for configuration:

- **AirWatch Managed Content**: This is the content you upload manually to the Admin Console for the users to view. For example, you may have a company policy you want all users to be able to access and read.

- **Corporate File Servers**: Here you can integrate multiple different types of repositories for your users to access the content:

    ○ **Admin Repositories**: Corporate repositories that you configure are made available to users to access from their devices. For example, you could set up access to the organization's policies located on a SharePoint site for all users to access.

    ○ **User Repositories**: These are repositories set up that allow users to configure access to their own repositories. For example, you could set up access to a user's home directory on a file server. The following can be configured for user repositories:

        ○ **Automatic Templates**: This allows you to assign lookup values to the configuration to dynamically assign repositories.

        ○ **Manual Templates**: This allows users to assign their own repositories based on the template created by the admin.

- **Personal Content**: This creates a separate repository for the users to add and manage their files.

The following is an overview of the different storage options for SaaS and on-premise:

SaaS and on-premise	AirWatch Cloud/on-premise	Corporate server	Remote file storage	Network file storage (on-premise only)
AirWatch managed	X			X*
Corporate file servers		X		
Personal content	X		X*	X*

X* Additional configuration required that will not be covered in detail within this book.

You are provided with 5 GB storage from AirWatch with the AirWatch Cloud deployment for AirWatch managed and personal content. With AirWatch on-premise, the content is stored on your on-premise AirWatch server.

Recommended configurations

Now that you have an understanding of the different types of content and the different storage options, we will begin to configure the Admin Console in preparation to deploy content. Before we do deploy the content, there are some configurations that are recommended to look at first:

1. Log in to the AirWatch Admin Console.

2. Navigate to **Content | Categories** then complete the following steps:

    1. Click on **Add Category** to add a new category and enter the required information and click on **Save**.

    2. This will allow you to tag your documents to better organize your content and allow them to be easily searched for.

 You can also create subcategories to create an additional organization.

3. Navigate to **Content | All Settings | Advanced**:

    ° **File Types**: Here you can Whitelist, Blacklist, or Allow All file types.

    ° **Required Content**: Here you can configure AirWatch to prevent users from accessing anything deployed by AirWatch until the users have reviewed the specified materials.

 This is only available on iOS 7+, iOS SCL 2.4+, and devices that are in the supervised mode.

4. Navigate to **Content | Featured Content**:

    ° This is the content that you can add from the **List View** section by clicking on the drop-down arrow of the file. These files will be given priority within the SCL for easier access to the users.

Personal content repository

Now we can start to upload the content and configure the repositories for the users to access. First, we will enable **Personal Content** repository if you would like to make this available to the users:

1. Within Settings, navigate to **Content | Personal Content**. Select **Enabled** to enable **Personal Content** and to configure the additional options which are as follows:

    ° **Storage Allocation**: This is where you configure the allocated storage for the personal content along with user quotas

    ° **Shared Links**: If enabled, this will allow the users to share links

    ° **Shared Folders**: If enabled, this will allow the users to share folders

    ° **E-mail Notification**: If enabled, this will notify a user when a folder is shared with them

    ° **Data Loss Prevention**: This provides DLP against the personal content repository: Allow open in e-mail, allow open in third party apps and allow printing

2. Click on **Save** once finished. Here is a screenshot for your reference:

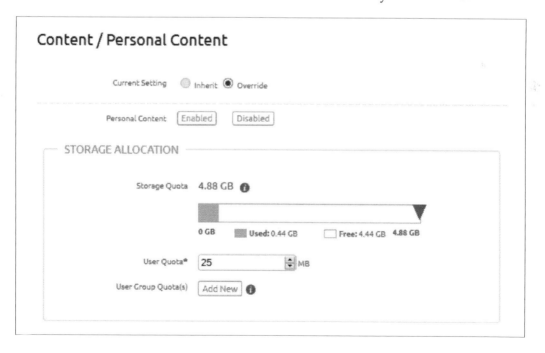

Based on the table with the different storage options, you can add additional storage for personal content and AirWatch managed.

The first option is **Remote File Storage (RFS)**, which can be configured both in a SaaS or an on-premise deployment for personal content only. To configure this, navigate to **Content | Settings | All Settings | Remote Storage** and click on **Configure**.

The second option is **Network File Storage (NFS)**, which can be configured for on-premise only for AirWatch managed and personal content. To configure, navigate to **Groups & Settings | All Settings | Installation | File Path** and select **File Storage Enabled**.

For additional information on the configuration, log in to the myairwatch portal, navigate to AirWatch **Resources | Documentation | Content Management**, open the *Mobile Content Management* guide, and go to the **File Storage** section.

AirWatch-managed content

Next we will look at where you can upload documents to make them available to the users using AirWatch managed content:

1. Navigate to **Content | List View** where you will see **AirWatch Managed** or **Corporate File Servers** options. Ensure that **AirWatch Managed** is selected:

   1. Navigate to **Add Content | Select Files** to go to the files you would like to make available and click on **Open** (or you can drag and drop these files).

Make sure that you are configuring for the correct organization group. I will configure my documents in this example to all devices in the Florida Office.

2. You will then be presented with all the options available for configuration as shown in the following screenshot:

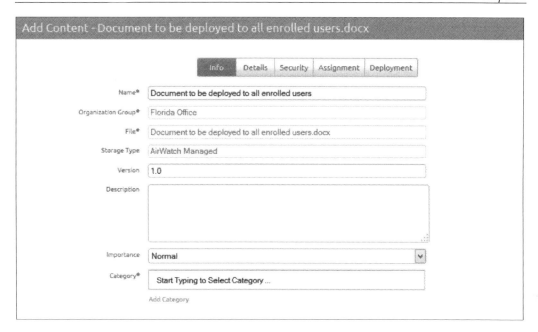

- ° **Info**: Here you can configure **Name, Organization Group** the document applies to, the **File** uploaded, **Storage Type** that should state **AirWatch Managed, Version, Description** (optional), **Importance** of the document, and **Category** you would like to apply based on what was configured earlier.

- ° **Details**: This is where you can configure **Author, Notes, Subject**, or any **Keywords**.

- ° **Security**: Within **Security**, you can configure whether the document is available for online or offline viewing, whether encryption should be enforced, allow open in e-mail or third-party apps, allow saving into other repositories, to add a watermark, and allow printing and editing.

- ° **Assignment**: Here you can specify what device ownership to deploy the documents to, which organization groups will receive the documents, and which user groups.

- ○ **Deployment**: This is where you can configure documents to only be downloaded with **Wi-Fi Only** or **Any** as a transfer method, prevent the document from being downloaded while roaming, whether the document will be automatically downloaded or on demand, whether the download is of high or low priority, whether the document is required to be reviewed, and select **Effective Date** and **Expiration Date** if required.

2. Click on **Save** once complete.

 You can bulk upload content quickly by navigating to **Content | Batch Status** and uploading a CSV file. Click on the information symbol to download a template.

Corporate file servers access

Next we will deploy access to corporate files servers to provide access to the current file and content repositories. First, we will set up an Admin Repository that will provide access to a content repository for the users:

1. Navigate to **Content | Repositories | Admin Repositories**, click on **Add**, and complete the following:
    - ○ **Name**: This the name of the repository
    - ○ **Type**: You have options such as **Unknown, Network Share, WebDAV, SharePoint, SharePoint WebDAV, SharePoint O365, SharePoint O365 ADFS, SharePoint Windows Auth, SharePoint ADFS, Google Drive, OneDrive, SharePoint - Personal (My Sites), OneDrive for Business, OneDrive for Business ADFS, CMIS and Box.**

 AirWatch is constantly expanding on the options listed here.

- ○ **Link**: This is the link to the repository
- ○ **Organization Group**: This is the organization group the repository will apply to

○ **Authentication Type**: Select a user to enter a service username and password to allow administrators to administer the content

○ **Access via EIS/ MAG**: This shows whether the repository is to be accessed via EIS or MAG server

○ **Allow Inheritance**: This allows child organization groups to access this repository

○ **Enable Sync**: This enables automatic synchronization of the repository. The current limit is 200 folders per repository

○ **Allow Write**: This allows users to create, edit, and upload files to the repository

 Some of the preceding options may not appear depending on the **Type** selected.

2. Click on **Test Connection** to verify that the repository has been set up correctly and then click on **Continue**. You will then be presented with additional configuration options:

○ **Security**: Within **Security**, you can configure whether the document is available for online or offline viewing, encryption should be enforced, allow open in e-mail or third-party apps, allow saving into other repositories, to add a watermark, allow printing and editing.

○ **Assignment**: Here you can specify what device ownership to deploy the documents to, which organization groups will receive the documents, and which user groups.

○ **Deployment**: This is where you can configure documents to only be downloaded with **Wi-Fi** or **Any** as a transfer method, prevent documents from being downloaded while roaming, whether the document will be automatically downloaded or on demand, whether the download is of high or low priority, whether the document is required to be reviewed, the effective date, and an expiration date if desired.

3. Click on **Save** once complete to make the repository available to the users enrolled in the organization group the repository was configured for.

The next option we have with corporate file servers is to provide access to a user repository that allows you to get more granular and provide access to users' home directories for example. Within the user repository, we can configure an automatic template that allows us to use lookup values to automatically provide access to the repository on the users' devices. Otherwise, we can configure manual repositories that allow the users to manually add their own repositories from **Self Service Portal** (**SSP**) based on the template set up by the administrator:

1. To set up a manual repository, navigate to **Content | Repositories | Templates | Manual** and click on **Add** and fill in the following information:

    ○   **Info**: Here you configure the name, user repository name the user will see, repository type (**Network Share, WebDAV, SharePoint, SharePoint O365, SharePoint Windows Auth**, and **SharePoint O365 ADFS**), link to the repository name, organization group the document applies to, whether the repository is accessible through EIS/MAG, **Allow Inheritance**, and **Allow Write**.

Click on the information icons to use lookup values in the user repository name and link.

    ○   **Security**: Within **Security**, you can configure whether the document is available for online or offline viewing, whether encryption should be enforced, allow open in e-mail or third-party apps, allow saving into other repositories, to add a watermark, and allow printing and editing.

    ○   **Assignment**: Here you can specify what device ownership to deploy the documents to, which organization groups will receive the documents and which user groups.

    ○   **Deployment**: This is where you can configure documents to only be downloaded with **Wi-Fi** or **Any** as a transfer method, prevent documents from being downloaded while roaming, and whether the document is required to be reviewed.

2. Click on **Save** once complete.

3. To set up an automatic repository, navigate to **Content | Repositories | Templates | Automatic** and click on **Add**. Complete the following fields within the template:

   ◦ **Info**: Here you configure the name, link to the repository and type (**Network Share, WebDAV, SharePoint, SharePoint O365, SharePoint Windows Auth**, and **SharePoint O365 ADFS**), organization group the document applies to, whether the repository is accessible through EIS/MAG, **Allow Inheritance** and **Allow Write**.

   ◦ **Security**: Within Security, you can configure whether the document is available for online or offline viewing, whether encryption should be enforced, allow open in e-mail or third-party apps, allow saving into other repositories, to add a watermark, allow printing and editing.

   ◦ **Assignment**: Here you can specify what device ownership to deploy the documents to, which organization groups will receive the documents, and which user groups.

   ◦ **Deployment**: This is where you can configure documents to only be downloaded with **Wi-Fi** or **Any** as a transfer method, prevent documents from being downloaded while roaming and whether the document is required to be reviewed.

4. Click on **Save** once complete.

Now we have completed the configurations and set up the repositories, the users will be able to access the content.

Accessing content

For the most part, you will use SCL to access your corporate content. For personal content, AirWatch has provided additional ways to access the content outside of SCL. To access personal content, you can access your files from the SSP as well as SCL sync as discussed later in this chapter.

Configuring SCL

To allow your devices to access the configured content, you will need to install the **Secure Content Locker (SCL)**. Before the users install SCL, you will need to configure the settings in the Admin Console. To configure the SCL settings, complete the following:

1. Navigate to **Content | Settings | All Settings | Applications | Secure Content Locker** and configure the settings for your users (ensure that you are in the correct organization group):

    ○   **Settings and Policies**: To use the default **Settings & Policies** defined within the security policies, select **Default** or **Custom** to select the iOS and Android profiles, **Authentication Method** (Single Sign On if configured for the applications), default authentication method if not using SSO, the option for the users to keep signed in, maximum number of failed attempts, authentication grace period, the ability to prevent compromised devices, allow offline login compliance and apply an iOS SDK profile.

    ○   **General**: This is where you can configure the number of days to keep the content, require MDM enrollment, enable editing/annotation (the license key needs to be entered at global level; this is the feature that upgrades to Yellow License Suite), the option to change the repository name, allow/disallow hyperlinks, where to open Internet links, whether to allow or disable local storage on the device and to enable or disable upload using Wi-Fi only.

    ○   **Terms of Use**: You can select the terms of use that the user is required to accept.

    ○   **Notifications**: Here you can assign notifications to SCL based on the platform, which application type, application name, bundle ID, and the badge count.

    ○   **SCL for Desktop**: This is where you can enable or disable the ability to download SCL for desktop from SSP.

2. Click on **Save** once you have configured the settings.

Installing SCL

Next we can download the SCL client on our devices to access the configured repositories. Since we have already enrolled our devices and configured the repositories for the organization groups configured in *Chapter 5, Mobile Device Management*, and *Chapter 6, Workspace Management*, we can simply install the SCL to receive the configured repositories on our iOS and Android devices:

1. SCL is currently available for iOS, Android, Windows Phone 8, and Windows 8/8.1/RT/XP/7. For iOS, open the App Store, search for AirWatch and look for the AirWatch - Secure Content Locker app, and click on **Get to install the App** and complete the following steps:

   ° Once installed, launch the SCL.

   ° Depending on how you configured your settings, you may be required to enter a username or password or just the PIN if you configured SSO.

   ° Once logged in, you will see AirWatch content that will contain the documents you uploaded for all enrolled users to view with managed content. You will also see the repositories that were configured in the admin templates and all the user repositories within User content that includes the personal content if configured, local storage if enabled, and any repositories configured using automatic user templates.

2. For Android, open the Play Store, search for AirWatch and look for the AirWatch - Secure Content Locker app, and click on it. Then, click on Install to the App

   ° Once installed, launch the SCL.

   ° Depending on how you configured your settings, you may be required to enter a username or password or just the PIN if you configured SSO.

○ Just like the iOS, you will see all configured repositories and files, as shown in the following table:

iOS	Android
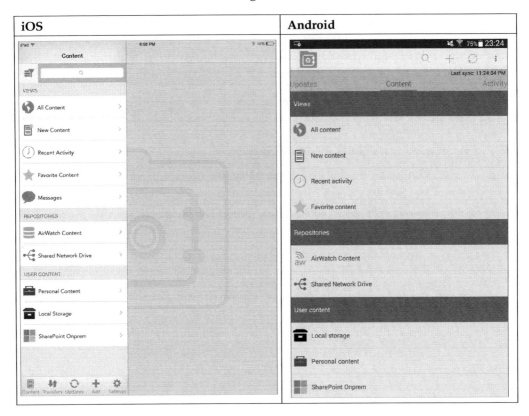	

 You can also deploy and make the SCL available to the users automatically as part of Mobile Application Management, which will be covered in *Chapter 9, Mobile Application and Mobile Browser Management*. In addition to deployment, you can also customize and brand SCL, as discussed in *Chapter 6, Workspace Management*.

Accessing Self Service Portal

To apply any manually configured user templates and to install the SCL on Windows XP/7 computers (Windows 8/8.1 can be installed from Windows App Store), you will need to log in to Self Service Portal. Accessing the SSP was covered in the *Self Service Portal* section in *Chapter 5*, *Mobile Device Management*:

1. Log in to the SSP and click on **My Content**. Here you can manage all your content and repositories.

    1. To add a repository from a manual user template, click on **My Repositories**. You will see the repositories already assigned.

    2. Click on **Add**, enter a name for the repository, select **Type** based on what the administrator has configured, enter the link to your repository, enter your username and password, and then click on **Test Connection** to validate the configuration. Click on **Save** once complete. The repository will appear within your SCL.

2. To install SCL on your Windows XP/7 machine, click on the SCL download link on the **My Content** page and complete the following steps:

    1. Once downloaded, install SCL.

    2. Once installed, launch SCL. Your information should autopopulate; if not, select **Change Server**, enter your server URL, Group ID, and username, and select the **Use Authorization Token**.

    3. To retrieve your token, navigate to **My Devices** in the SSP. Click on **Account** in the top-right corner, then on **Apps** and on **Generate Token**.

    4. Paste the token into the **Password** box and then click on **Next** to log in and access your content and repositories.

Additional options

In addition to SCL, there are a couple of additional end user tools that are available to supplement with content sharing and the EFSS experience. The first is SCL sync, which is a tool that allows you to add/remove content to a folder on your PC or Mac. The content is then synched with your personal content, allowing you to access the synched content from SCL sync, SCL, or the SSP. To configure the SCL, complete the following:

1. In the Admin Console, navigate to **Content | Settings | All Settings**.

2. Navigate to **Applications | SCL Sync** and select **Enabled**.

3. Select **Enabled** on **Client Download** to allow download and on **Enabled** to **Require MDM Enrollment** if desired. Add the terms of use and then click on **Save**.

To download SCL sync, access the SSP from the PC or Mac (32 or 64 bit Windows XP, Vista SP1+, 7, 8, or Mac OS X Lion+) you would like to install SCL sync on:

1. Log in to SSP and navigate to **My Content | Download SCL Sync** from the bottom-left corner.

2. Once downloaded, run the installer, click on **Next**, accept the agreement, and then click on **Next**. Click on **Next** again and then on **Install**.

3. Click on **Finish**. You should be able to access your personal content by opening the personal content shortcut and dragging files into the folder.

The next option available to the users, if enabled, is the Outlook add-in, which allows users to send secure files as a link from Outlook rather than sending the file. This allows the files to become more secure as the link will only be accessible to those who it was sent to and SCL will be required to access the file. This option can also help with file limits that are in place with e-mail systems, allowing you to send larger attachments than normal. To configure the Outlook plugin, complete the following:

1. In the Admin Console, navigate to **Content | Settings | All Settings**.

2. Click on **Applications | Outlook Add-in** and select **Enabled** next to **Client Download**.

3. If desired, select **Enabled** on **Automatically convert attachments to links** and **Recommend converting attachments to links** and add the size in MB. Then, click on **Save**.

4. Select **Enabled** on **Client Download** to allow download and enable require MDM enrollment if desired. Add the terms of use and then click on **Save**.

To download Outlook add-in, access the SSP from your PC (32 or 64 bit Windows 7 or 8 and 32 or 64 bit of Microsoft Outlook 2007+) that you would like to install Outlook add-in. To do this, complete the following steps:

 You will need to ensure that **Link Sharing** is enabled within personal content to use this feature (to do this, navigate to **Content | Settings | All Settings | Personal Content** to enable).

1. Log in to SSP, navigate to **My Content**, and download the Outlook add-in from the bottom-left corner.

2. Once downloaded, run the installer and install any prerequisites if needed. Click on **Next**, accept **Agreement**, and then click on **Next**. Click on **Next** again and then on **Install**.

3. Click on **Finish**. The secure content plug-in will be available in Outlook.

Managing and removing content

It is critical that you are able to efficiently manage and remove content from a user's device in the event that they leave the organization. The next section will cover where and how to manage content within your deployment as well as remove content from a user's device.

Managing content

Once you have configured and deployed the content to the users, there are multiple ways to view and manage the content. To view more information and manage the content deployed, complete the following steps:

1. In the Admin Console, navigate to **Content** and click on **Dashboard** to view the available reports.

2. Click on **List View** to view **AirWatch Managed** content and **Corporate File Server** content that has been deployed.

3. Navigate to **Repositories | User Repositories** to view who is using user repositories.

4. Click on **Settings | User Storage** to view the user's storage usage.

Removing content

You can remove content from users' devices by following the instructions to un-enroll a device listed in the *Un-enrolling a device* section in *Chapter 5, Mobile Device Management*.

As MCM grows and matures, there is a realization that this is all slowly becoming part of the bigger picture of collaboration. The ability to efficiently and effectively collaborate in the environment is becoming critical. AirWatch realized this and they have just expanded their solution to include chat (AirWatch Chat) and video (AirWatch TV). These products have just been released, which is why there is currently minimum information, but as MCM grows with collaboration, we should expect to see more integrated tools like these.

Summary

This chapter has covered how to set up and securely deploy corporate content to the workforce. MCM has allowed organizations to become much more creative in the way they utilize mobile technology, and it only continues to provide additional opportunities in the workplace today. Once the fundamentals are in place and you understand the concepts available, building a content collaboration experience for the users will only become easier.

This chapter provided an overview of MCM, and we looked at protecting content within the organization and why it's important to protect the content. We then set up and configured MAG for proxy and content to allow the delivery of internal content.

We then looked at the content security configurations available with AirWatch before configuring content for the users. Once configured, we looked at the available ways users can access the content. Lastly, we finished off with how to manage content and remove it from the user's devices.

Now that we have both the e-mail and content on the users' devices, we can start looking at expanding the deployment to application and browser management. In the next chapter, we will look at how to set up and configure Mobile Application Management and Mobile Browser Management and the opportunities available with both.

Mobile Application and Mobile Browser Management

9

The next opportunity that we will look at with AirWatch by VMware is application and browser management. With application management, you have a lot of different options available with your deployment. You can opt to simply deploy internal or public apps from AirWatch app catalog, or you have the option of advancing your application deployment with the AirWatch SDK and app wrapping. This allows you to provide a true user experience by providing access to internal resources using mobile apps with added customization, branding, and security. Mobile Browser Management allows you to provide a more secure and managed environment when it comes to browsing on mobile devices. The ability to manage what the users can and can't access on a browser and to provide access to internal resources will provide a more productive environment.

In this chapter, we will review MAM and look at the opportunities available within the enterprise. We will then set up and install MAG per app VPN before looking at the different application types and the options available within AirWatch. We will then move onto the options available with deploying the applications and finish off this section with application management.

The second subject in this chapter will cover MBM and what purpose it can serve within the organization. We will then end the chapter on the configuration and deployment of secure browser and the options available.

The following topics will be covered in this chapter:

- Mobile Application Management
  ◦ Mobile Application Management overview
  ◦ Mobile Application Gateway per app VPN
  ◦ Application types
  ◦ Application deployment
  ◦ Application management
- Mobile Browser Management
  ◦ Mobile Browser Management overview
  ◦ Mobile browser configuration and deployment

The first part of this chapter will cover MAM using AirWatch.

Mobile Application Management overview

Traditionally, organizations have managed and deployed applications to their corporate-owned desktops and laptops for several years, which has become an extremely mature process. With the sudden growth of demand for mobile devices in the workforce, the need to better manage and deploy applications has become a reality for organizations. This has been identified by AirWatch, and as part of their EMM suite, AirWatch has provided **Mobile Application Management** (**MAM**) as a way to allow enterprises to become much more efficient with its mobile application management and deployment. These capabilities are similar to that of desktop/laptop application deployment and management.

Now that we have e-mail and content delivery implemented and deployed, we can start to look at the opportunities with application deployment within AirWatch. There are currently an endless amount of applications available today that users use for multiple different opportunities. These applications allow users to become more productive in their everyday lives. The same applies to organizations. We are at a point in time where every application now has a mobile app. If there isn't a mobile app, the company providing the application will eventually become legacy with its customers looking for new and better opportunities.

As mobile applications are growing and becoming more demanding, it is critical that we are able to efficiently manage and deploy the applications to the users, especially with the growth of versions with bugs and new features. Applications are being updated at a faster pace than we have ever seen, which can be challenging to manage. This is where being able to provide a corporate application catalog is critical as part of your MAM deployment. As an organization, you will significantly simplify the user's workflow and experience by providing them an application catalog with the ability to install the latest apps available within the organization.

Although there are a significant amount of public applications available to use for your deployment, many organizations are also building home-grown apps to provide better workflows and efficiencies within the organization. This is where your development teams will be highly involved. It will be critical that they have the ability to efficiently deploy these home-grown apps to the users. As part of MAM with AirWatch, there are advanced tools that the development teams can leverage to ease the use and integration for the users using app wrapping and the SDK.

With MAM, you can expect the following with AirWatch:

- Application catalog to manage and deploy applications
- Internal, public, and purchased application management
- Integration with Apple VPP
- Software Development Kit
- App wrapping
- Application restrictions including whitelist, blacklist, and restrictions
- Compliance enforcement
- DLP enforcement
- Application reputation analysis
- Analytics, reporting, feedback, and ratings

Mobile Application Gateway per app VPN

Before we move into more detail on application management, we will go through the steps to install MAG for per pp VPN access. In *Chapter 8, Mobile Content Management*, we covered MAG in detail and completed MAG for Windows proxy and content installation. Now, we will complete MAG for the Linux component:

- **MAG for Linux**: MAG for Linux is the tunnel component that provides per app VPN access to internal and public apps for iOS 7 and greater devices.

MAG deployment options

MAG for Linux deployment is much simpler than MAG for Windows, as it doesn't support a relay deployment. The only option to deploy MAG for Linux is with an endpoint. As with MAG for Windows deployment, MAG Linux servers need to be deployed within your data center whether you are an on-premise or SaaS-based customer. The following diagram shows the recommended architecture for your MAG deployment:

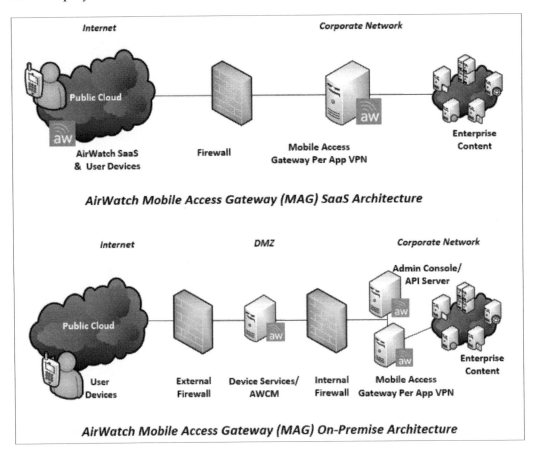

MAG requirements

This section lists all the requirements for MAG for Linux deployment for both SaaS and on-premise deployments.

The hardware requirements for MAG are as follows:

Max number of users	Up to 5,000	5,000 - 50,000	50,000 - 100,000	100,000+
Disk size	Standard OS requirements with 5 GB disk space for installation			
CPU cores	1	4 CPUs or 2 load balanced servers with 2 CPU cores	4 CPUs or 2 load balanced servers with 2 CPU cores	2 load balanced servers with 4 CPU cores
RAM (GB)	4	4	8	16

> You can load balance MAG servers behind your enterprise load balancer for growth and High Availability.

The software requirements for MAG are as follows:

- Supported operating system: CentOS 6.5, 64-bit only
- Recommended to use **Command Line Interface (CLI)** only

The network requirements for MAG are tabularized as follows:

Source component	Destination component	Protocol	Port
MAG endpoint	AirWatch Cloud Messaging server*	HTTPS for SaaS HTTP or HTTPS for on-premise	443 for SaaS 2001 for port you configure for on-premise
MAG endpoint	The AirWatch REST API	HTTPS for SaaS HTTP or HTTPS for on-premise	443 for SaaS 80 or 443 for on-premise
MAG endpoint	Internal resources	HTTP, HTTPS or TCP	80, 443, Any TCP
Devices	MAG endpoint	TCP	ANY

* For SaaS customers, reference the AirWatch IP ranges for the most up-to-date IPs. To access the ranges, log in to the myairwatch portal, go to Knowledge Base, search for **What are the AirWatch IP ranges for SaaS data centers?** and click on the link to view the ranges.

Installation

Before we install MAG, we need to enable and configure the settings in the AirWatch Admin Console. If you have already installed MAG for Windows, this has already been completed. If not, complete the first five steps within the Installation section of *Chapter 8, Mobile Content Management*.

Next, we will configure MAG for Linux-specific settings:

1. In the Admin Console, navigate to **Groups & Settings | All Settings | System | Enterprise Integration | Mobile Access Gateway** and click on **Configure** (you may need to click on override if you have already configured the MAG) and complete the following steps:

   1. Select **Configure AirWatch Tunnel for Linux**, click on **Continue** and then on **Next** (if presented with configuration type)

   2. Configure the **PER-APP TUNNELING CONFIGURATION** by completing the following information:

      ◦ **Host Name**: This the name of MAG server

      ◦ **Port**: This the secure port that communicates with MAG

   3. Click on **Next** to move to the **Authentication** section and to optionally configure the **Per-App VPN SSL Certificate** section:

   4. Select the checkbox to use a **Public third-party SSL**

   5. Click on **Browse** to upload your certificate in the PFX or P12 format

   6. Click on **Next**, review the configuration, and click on **Save**.

2. We will now download the software to be installed on servers:

   1. Click on the **General** option and scroll to the bottom of the screen.

   2. Click on the **Download Linux Installer (App Wrapping, Browser, Content, iOS 7+ Per-App Tunnel)** link.

   3. Enter and confirm a password for the certificate (minimum of 6 characters) and click on **Download**.

If you make any changes to the settings after you have downloaded and installed MAG, you will need to redownload and reinstall MAG.

Now all the configurations are complete, we can move onto installing MAG for Linux:

1. Copy the TAR file to MAG Linux server and log in to begin the installation:

    1. Navigate to the copied file and un-archive the file with the following command:

       ```
       tar -xvf VpnInstaller.tar
       ```

    2. Run the MAG install file with the following command (these will be extracted `Config.xml`, `MobileAccessGateway.bin`, and `Vpn_config.xml`):

       ```
       sudo sh MobileAccessGateway.bin
       ```

    3. Press *Enter* twice.

    4. Decide which features you would like to install:

       ○ AirWatch proxy for browser and the app wrapping component

       ○ AirWatch app tunnel for iOS app tunnel

    5. Enter 1 and 2 to install both features or just 1 or 2 for an individual feature. Press *Enter* and then again press *Enter* on summary screen.

    6. Enter the password you entered for the certificate when you downloaded the installer and press *Enter*.

    7. Validate everything on the summary screen and click on *Enter* to install MAG.

2. Once complete, run `sudo ps aux` and then `grep vpnserv` to validate that the VPN service installed and is running.

You are now ready to use the per app VPN for iOS 7 and greater devices.

 To upgrade MAG for Linux, complete the same steps listed earlier once AirWatch has been upgraded to the latest version.

Application types

With AirWatch, there are multiple different application types available for deployment. It is important that you understand each of them for when you get ready to deploy them to your users:

- **Internal applications**: These are the applications that have been built internally by your developers. These applications will most likely not be publicly available in the stores. You can still make them available to your users by uploading them onto AirWatch for deployment. The following are supported files for deployment using the Internal Application feature:
    - `.ipa` for Apple iOS
    - `.app` for Mac OS X
    - `.apk` for Android
    - `.sis` and `.sisx` for Symbian
    - `.xap` for Windows Phone 8
    - `.appx` for Windows 8.1/RT

- **Public applications**: These are applications that are available in the public stores (free or purchased) that are added to AirWatch and deployed to your users.

- **Purchased applications**: If you have a large deployment where you would like to deploy an application(s) to many users, you can utilize Apple **Volume Purchase Program** (**VPP**). Using VPP, you can deploy public applications available from the store or B2B applications received/purchased from a developer.

> Visit `https://www.apple.com/business/vpp/` to learn more about Apple VPP.

- **Web applications**: These applications are those that you have deployed using URLs and device profiles. Web applications can be deployed using the following:
    - Bookmarks on Android
    - Web clips on Apple iOS and Mac OS X

Application deployment

In this section, we will look at how you will deploy applications to your devices and users within your organization. There is an overwhelming amount of information available with MAM in AirWatch that we will not be able to cover in detail within this chapter. You will, however, get an understanding of where everything is located and configured to allow you to grow beyond what this book provides.

Prior to deploying applications to the users, there are some items that you will be required to configure depending on your deployment:

- **Google Play Integration**: For on-premise customers only, you will need to configure AirWatch to connect to Google Play Store. To configure integration, you will need to navigate to **Groups & Settings | All Settings | Device & Users | Android | Google Play Integration**.

- **Windows 8.1/RT Apps**: To deploy internal applications to Windows 8/RT devices, you will need a side-loading key and a code-signing certificate from Microsoft. To do this, complete the following steps:
    - Visit the Microsoft Developer site for more information on obtaining the two items at `http://msdn.microsoft.com/library/windows/apps/jj206719(v=vs.105).aspx`
    - To configure AirWatch to deploy Windows 8/RT applications, navigate to **Groups & Settings | All Settings | Device & Users | Windows | Windows 8/RT | Enterprise Apps**

- **Windows Phone 8 Apps**: To deploy internal applications to Windows Phone 8 devices, you will need to gain approval from Windows Phone Dev Center:
    - Visit the Microsoft Developer site for more information on gaining approval at `http://msdn.microsoft.com/library/windows/apps/jj206719(v=vs.105).aspx`
    - To configure AirWatch to deploy Windows Phone 8, navigate to **Groups & Settings | All Settings | Device & Users | Windows | Windows Phone 8 | Agent Settings**

Before you start assigning applications, you will need to ensure that you have set up your smart groups. Smart groups is how you will deploy your apps to your users and devices. Since I have already created my smart groups from previous chapters, I will continue to use the same groups for my application deployment. If you need to create additional Smart Groups, visit the *Smart Group* section in *Chapter 5, Mobile Device Management*.

AirWatch categorizes content as managed and unmanaged. Managed content is content that is automatically pushed to the devices or made available to the users to download, which allows AirWatch to remove the content. Unmanaged content is content that directs users to the App stores to download, which AirWatch cannot remove from the devices.

Application catalog

You can deploy an App Catalog to users' devices to allow easy access to all available corporate applications. The App Catalog may not serve as much of a need with corporate-owned devices, as you will most likely be managing and pushing the application to those devices. For personally owned devices, the App Catalog will provide a great deal of value as part of your mobile deployment. The App Catalog allows easier access to download applications made available from the organization without the need to search a public app store, or manually install internal applications. It also helps define to the user what are and aren't work-related applications.

The App Catalog is currently available for Android, Apple iOS, Apple Mac OS X, and Windows 8/RT. To deploy the App Catalog, you have two options. You can deploy it automatically, or you can deploy it using a device profile with a web clip or bookmark:

- For a more efficient deployment, deploy the App Catalog automatically. To deploy it automatically, complete the following steps:

    1. Log in to the Admin Console and navigate to **Groups & Settings | All Settings | Apps | Catalog | General**.

    2. Click on the **Authentication** tab. Here you can require authentication if desired and specify whether the user needs to re-authenticate and after how many days. Then, click on **Save** once finished.

    3. Click on the **Publishing** tab. In the **Catalog Title** field, enter a name that will be displayed to the users on their devices, select which platforms the App Catalog will be deployed to automatically, and upload a customized icon if desired. Click on **Save** once finished.

    4. Click on the **Customization** tab. This is where you can upload a logo to brand the catalog with your organizations logo, define the landing page for the App Catalog, specify how the apps are sorted, and highlight up to four selected categories. Click on **Save** once finished.

- If you wanted to publish the App Catalog manually, create a profile and publish it do the enrolled users and devices by completing the following steps:

  1. Create a profile as described in the *Creating and Publishing a Profile* section in *Chapter 5, Mobile Device Management*.

  2. Use the web clips payload for Apple iOS, Mac OS X, and Windows 8/RT or use the Bookmarks for Android.

  3. For the URL, enter `https://{Environment}/Catalog/ViewCatalog/{SecureDeviceUdid}/{DevicePlatform}`.

The App Catalog will then be deployed to your enrolled devices with applications that have been published:

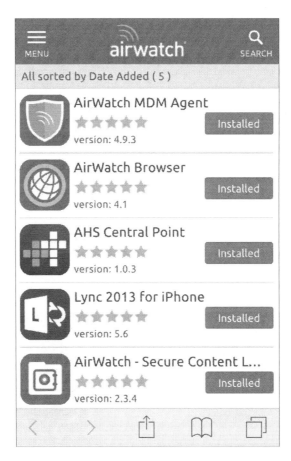

Before you start deploying applications, it is recommended that you create categories that better help the users find applications. To configure categories, navigate to **Apps & Books | Applications | Settings | App Categories**.

Deploying internal applications

Internal applications are those that may have been built internally and not available in the public App Store. To upload an internal application and make it available to the users, complete the following steps:

1. Once logged in to the Admin Console, navigate to **Apps & Books | Applications | List View**, click on **Internal** and then on **Add Application**. Then perform the following steps:

    1. Select which organization group will manage the application and click on **Upload**. Select **Local File** (**Browse** to upload) or **Link** (**Link** to external repository that is hosting the app) then click on **Save**.

    2. Click on **Continue** and configure the options for deployment:

        ○ **Details**: Here you will find the **Name** for the App, **Managed By**, **Application ID**, **Actual File Version**, **Build Version**, **Version**, **Is Beta**, **Change Log**, **Categories**, **Minimum OS**, **Supported Models**, and **Default Scheme**

        ○ **Description**: Here you can enter a **Description**, **Keywords**, **URL**, **Support Email**, **Support Phone**, **Internal ID**, **Copyright**, **Developer Information**, **Log Notification for App SDK**, and **Application Cost Information**

        ○ **Images**: Upload an image that the users will see in the App Catalog

        ○ **Terms of Use**: Select the required terms of use for the App

        ○ **Files**: Files needed to distribute internal apps through AirWatch

        ○ **Wrapping**: Select **Enable App Wrapping** to wrap the app

        ○ **Assignment**: Select the smart group for users and/or devices to deploy the app to

- ○ **Deployment**: Here you can configure the push mode (Auto prompts the users to install and on demand lets the user decide), **Effective Date**, **Expiration Date**, whether the app uses **AirWatch SDK, Remove on Unenroll, Prevent Application Backup, Use VPN, Send Application Configuration**, and any **Add Exceptions**
- ○ **Reputation**: Select the **Run Reputation Analysis** option to gather analysis on the app

3. Click on **Save & Publish** once complete.

 Every Apple device that uses an internal application must have the Apple iOS provisioning profile installed on it. For additional information, refer to Apple iOS developer enterprise program.

To help an organization with the workflow of internal applications and to ensure applications are thoroughly tested through a lifecycle, AirWatch has provided a feature to help. This feature includes four participants to work through the life cycle: a developer, reviewer, assigner, and publisher. To use this feature, you will need to configure the admin roles for the each of the participants, assign the roles, and then enable the workflow by navigating to **Groups & Settings | All Settings | App | Catalog | Application Workflow**, selecting **Enable Workflow for Applications**, and configuring the settings, and then clicking on **Save**.

Deploying public applications

With AirWatch, you can deploy public applications to your users and devices. To deploy a pubic application and make it available to the users, complete the following steps:

1. Once logged into the Admin Console, navigate to **Apps & Books | Applications | List View**.

2. Click on **Public**, and then click on **Add Application** and perform the following steps:

   1. Select which organization group will manage the application and select the platform for the app. Enter a search name in the **Name** field and select **Search App Store** (if you don't select this, the app is unmanaged). If requested, enter a URL for the Google Play Store.

2. Click on **Next** and select the App to be deployed. Configure the options for deployment:

   ° **Info**: Here you will find the **Name** for the App, **Application ID**, **URL**, **Managed By**, **Comments**, **Reimbursable**, **Rating**, **Categories**, **Supported Models** and **Default Scheme**

   ° **Assignment**: Select the smart group for users and/or devices to deploy the app to

   ° **Deployment**: Here you can configure the push mode (Autoprompts the users to install unless they are already signed into iTunes and on demand lets the user decide), **Remove on Unenroll**, **Prevent Application Backup**, **Use VPN**, **Send Application Configuration**, and any **Add Exceptions**

   ° **Terms of Use**: Select the required terms of use for the App

3. Click on **Save & Publish** once complete.

 For Corporate-owned iOS devices, you can prevent users from installing public apps from the iTunes App Store by navigating to **Groups & Settings | All Settings | Apps | Catalog | App Restrictions** and enable **Restricted Mode** for public iOS applications.

Deploying web applications

Web Applications consists of applications added using URLs and device profiles. You can deploy a web application using a Bookmark with Android or using a web clip with Apple iOS or Mac OS X. To deploy a web application and make it available to the users, complete the following.

iOS Web Clip

The steps are as follows:

1. Once logged into the Admin Console and browse to **Devices | Profiles | List View**.

2. Click on **Add** and select **iOS** to deploy a web clip to an iOS device:

   1. Configure the general settings as instructed in the *Creating and Publishing a Profile* section of *Chapter 5, Mobile Device Management*

   2. Select the **Web Clips Payload | Configure** and enter the following information:

      1. Enter a label for the web clip, enter the URL that will be displayed, put a check in **Removable** to allow users to remove, upload an icon, put a check in **Precomposed** icon to remove visual effects, put a check in **Full Screen** to open webpage in full screen mode and select **Show in App Catalog/Workspace** to list the app in the App Catalog.

      2. Click **Save & Publish** to deploy to the users.

Mac OS X Web Clip

1. Once logged into the Admin Console and browse to **Devices | Profiles | List View**. Click on **Add**, select **Apple Mac OS X** and then select user to deploy a web clip to an Mac OS X device:

   1. Configure the general settings as instructed in the *Creating and Publishing a Profile* section of *Chapter 5, Mobile Device Management*.

2. Select the **Web Clips Payload | Configure**:

    1. Enter a label for the web clip, enter the URL that will be displayed, upload an icon and select **Show in App Catalog** to list the app in the App Catalog.

    2. Click **Save & Publish** to deploy to the users.

Android Bookmark

1. Once you are logged in to the Admin Console, navigate to **Devices | Profiles | List View** and click on **Add**. Select **Android** to deploy a Bookmark to an Android device:

    1. Configure the general settings as instructed in the **Creating and Publishing a Profile** section of *Chapter 5, Mobile Device Management*.

    2. Select the **Bookmarks Payload** and click on **Configure**:

        1. Enter a label for the Bookmarks, enter the URLs that will be available to the users, upload an icon, put a check in **Add to Homescreen** to have Bookmarks appear on device's homescreen and select **Show in App Catalog/Workspace** to list the app in the App Catalog.

        2. Click on **Save and Publish** to deploy to the users.

Deploying purchased applications with Apple Volume Purchase Program

You can deploy public or business-to-business purchased applications to iOS devices with Apple **Volume Purchase Program (VPP)**. The two supported methods are redemption codes with iOS 5+ or managed distribution with service tokens with iOS 7+. To deploy purchased applications to the users, complete the following steps.

Before you deploy the apps, you will need to enroll in Apple's VPP at http://www.apple.com/business/vpp for business and http://www.apple.com/itunes/education for education institutions. Once enrolled, you can purchase the applications and books to be deployed at https://vpp.itunes.apple.com/us/store and sign in with your VPP Apple ID.

Content using redemption codes

Complete the following steps once you are logged into the Admin Console:

1. **Upload redemption codes**: Navigate to **Apps & Books | Applications | Orders** or **Apps & Books | Books | Orders**:

    1. Click on **Add**, select **Purchased Public App** or **Purchased Custom App** (for app only).

    2. Click on **Browse**, and select **CSV** or **XLS**. Click on **Save** and if presented with the **Product Selection Form**, locate the product and click on **Select** to complete upload.

2. **Assign redemption codes**: Navigate to **Apps & Books | Applications | Orders** or **Apps & Books | Books | Orders**:

    1. Locate the order to be redeemed. From the drop down menu, click on **Edit Assignment** and go to **Assignment**.

    2. In the **Redemption Codes On Hold** section, enter the number of redemption codes to place on hold for use later. Assign an organization group or smart group to **Add Assignment By** to allocate redemption codes. Verify the users, allocated and redeemed columns. Select the **Assignment Type** as **Auto** or **On-Demand**. Select **Remove On Unenroll** to remove from the device when unenrolled from AirWatch and optionally select to prevent backups of applications and the ability to use VPN for iOS 7 and greater.

    3. Click on **Save** once complete.

3. **Publish apps and books**: Navigate to **Apps & Books | Applications | List View | Purchased** or **Apps & Books | Books | List View | Purchased**. On the actions menu, click on **Publish**.

 To view and access redemption code information, navigate to **Apps & Books | Orders | Redemption Codes**.

Content using managed distribution

The first step is to download your sToken for your purchased app from the iTunes Store. Once downloaded, log in to the Admin Console:

1. **Upload sToken**: Navigate to **Apps & Books | Settings | Catalog | VPP Managed Distribution**:

   1. It is recommended to enter your VPP account ID into the **Description** field, select **Upload** to upload the sToken, then select the country you purchased the content. Select **Automatically Send Invites** to users of iOS 7.0.3+ to automatically send invite immediately and then select a Message Template to be sent to the users via e-mail (only applies to iOS 7.0.0-7.0.2 as iOS 7.0.3+ will automatically receive an invite command with the previous step).

   2. Click on **Save** once complete.

2. **Invite/reinvite users**: Navigate to **Apps & Books | Applications | List View | Purchased** or **Apps & Books | Books | List View | Purchased** and select **Manage Devices**.

3. **Syncing licenses**: Navigate to **Apps & Books | Applications | List View | Purchased** or **Apps & Books | Books | List View | Purchased** and complete the following steps:

   1. Select **Sync Licenses** and choose **Sync Recent Purchases Only** or **Resync All Apps**.

   2. You can also sync licenses by applications by clicking on the applications actions menu and selecting **Sync Licenses**.

4. **Assigning managed distribution content**: Navigate to **Apps & Books | Applications | List View | Purchased** or **Apps & Books | Books | List View | Purchased**:

   1. Find the content and select **Edit Assignment** from the drop-down actions menu. Select the **Assignment** tab and enter the number of licenses to place on hold for use later. For **Add Assignment by**, select the **License Codes By Smart Group** to assigned managed distribution codes. Select the **Assignment Type** as **Auto** or **On-Demand**. Select **Remove On Unenroll** to remove from the device when unenrolled from AirWatch and optionally select to prevent backups of applications and the ability to use VPN for iOS 7 and greater.

   2. Click **Save** once complete.

5. **Publishing managed distribution content**: Navigate to **Apps & Books | Applications | List View | Purchased** or **Apps & Books | Books | List View | Purchased** and select **Publish** from the actions menu.

 Your users will need to accept the invitation to join and register with Apple VPP in order to receive the published content.

6. **Renewing sTokens before expiration**: You will need to renew your sTokens as they expire every 12 months. To renew, ensure that you are in the correct organization group and navigate to **Apps & Books | Settings | Catalog | VPP Managed Distribution**. Select **Renew** and upload the new sToken and then click on **Save**.

7. **Deleting sTokens**: To delete tokens, ensure that you are in the correct organization group and navigate to **Apps & Books | Settings | Catalog | VPP Managed Distribution**. Select **Clear** to remove the sToken.

 You can reuse managed distribution codes by revoking the current ones. You can revoke distribution codes by organization group, user, manually, VPP application or book, sToken, unassign, or by smart group.

Advanced application deployment

Advanced application management includes the ability to use AirWatch's SDK and app wrapping features to customize iOS and Android applications as well as AirWatch Applications. To customize and apply these advanced options, navigate to **Apps & Books | Settings | Settings and Policies | Profiles**, click on **Add Profile**, and select the option to configure an SDK profile, application profile, or app wrapping profile. Once configured, you can apply the profile to an application.

The following default options are available for configuration:

- **Security: Authentication Type, Single Sign On (SSO), Integrated Authentication, Offline Access, Compromised Detection, AirWatch App Tunnel, Content Filtering, Geofencing, Data Loss Prevention** and **Network Access Control**

- **Settings: Branding, Logging, Analytics** and **Custom Settings**

Advanced application management doesn't fall within the scope of this book. To learn more about advanced application management, log in to the myairwatch portal and navigate **Resources | Documentation | Application Management** to view the available resources.

Application management

Once you have configured and deployed applications and/or books to your users and devices, there are multiple ways and options to manage them:

1. To view and manage all internal, public, and purchased applications or books, navigate to **Apps & Books | Applications | List View** or **Apps & Books | Books | List View** and perform the following steps:

   1. Click on each of the tabs to view and manage applications in each category.

   2. Options available to manage applications and/or books are the ability to manage devices, notify devices, add versions, manage feedback, retire, deactivate, user ratings, view analytics, view logs, view events, view other versions, run reputation analysis, and delete (not all these options will be available for each category).

2. All your orders and redemption codes can be viewed and managed within **Apps & Books | Orders | List View** or **Products** or **Redemption Codes**.

3. Application logs and SDK analytics can be viewed by navigating to **Apps & Books | Applications | Analytics | Select Apps Logs** or **SDK Analytics**.

4. Application grouping allows you to whitelist, blacklist, require applications, or enable custom MDM applications (custom MDM needs to be enabled in **Groups & Settings | All Settings | Devices & Users | General | Enrollment | Select Customization | Enable Use Custom MDM Application**) for your deployment) and perform the following steps:

   1. To add an application group, navigate to **Apps & Books | Applications | Settings | App Groups** and select **Add Group**.

5. You can enforce polices against your applications using the compliance engine, as shown in *Chapter 4, Mobile Security*.

   1. To add compliances, navigate to **Devices | Compliance Policies | List View** and click on **Add**.

6. To manage all **App Catalog** settings, navigate to **Apps & Books | Settings | Apps | Catalog**.

   1. Within **Catalog**, you have the ability to configure the **General Catalog** options, configure a **Standalone Catalog** to the users if desired.

   2. Configure the **App Restrictions, Applications Categories and Workflow**, an **External App Repository**, add **Featured Applications**, manage your **VPP Managed Distribution** settings and enable **App Reputation**.

The second part of this chapter will cover MBM using the AirWatch Browser.

Mobile Browser Management overview

As we've discussed multiple times throughout this book, mobility is providing us with new and more productive ways to do business. This is also true with MBM within the workforce. Traditionally, you may not have been able to provide access to internal websites/intranet to users from outside the corporate network because of security reasons. As mobile usage grows, we are expected to be able to provide solutions and opportunities to users to allow them to become more productive in their job.

One of the more obvious challenges faced by organizations has always been the ability to control access to the Internet. Browser management within the organizations has always typically been managed at a proxy level, by an enterprise appliance that sits between the users and Internet-blocking or allowing access to the sites. Moving into the mobile world only expands upon this challenge, and it's critical as an organization that you can provide as much security and control around browser management on these devices. With AirWatch, the ability to better control, manage, and secure access to the Internet is part of their **Mobile Browser Management (MBM)** vertical.

AirWatch provides full control over your browser deployments and what can and can't be accessed on the Internet. For your corporate-owned devices, you can disable access to other browsers only allowing users to access resources through AirWatch Browser. You can control which sites the users can access along with multiple DLP options. For your BYOD users, you can provide access to the users to internal corporate resources through AirWatch Browser and DLP controls to meet your security needs. What traditionally may have been blocked for access externally can now be accessed using AirWatch by providing the extra security that wasn't available before.

You can deploy AirWatch Browser in two modes: kiosk or restricted. With the **Kiosk** mode, you have the ability to configure AirWatch Browser to only allow access to a specific website, preventing any other websites being accessed. This configuration is ideal for instances where you need to deploy access to a website in a public area to allow for check-in. The second available mode is the **Restricted** mode, which allows you to manage access to websites using whitelists or blacklists. This mode will make more sense for your BYOD users by providing a whitelist of internal sites they can access from AirWatch Browser on their devices.

With MBM, you can expect the following with AirWatch:

- Kiosk or restricted modes available
- Full control over secure browser
- DLP enforcement
- Force content to open in SCL only
- Allow the ability to accept or deny cookies
- Customize users experience with an easy-to-use interface
- Secure access to internal resources using through a proxy
- Integrated authentication and SSO
- The ability to deploy and remove content without effecting users personal information

Mobile browser configuration and deployment

Before deploying browser management, you will want to set up your app tunnel to proxy your web traffic to allow your external devices to access internal resources. With AirWatch, you have the following options to use a standard proxy, F5 proxy, or MAG, as well as the ability to integrate with Websense for enhanced content filtering. Since this book is about learning AirWatch, we will be using MAG as the app tunnel. If you would like to set up a third-party proxy or tunnel, you will need to add it within the Admin Console. To do this, complete the following steps:

1. Log in to the Admin Console and navigate to **Groups & Settings | All Settings**.

2. Navigate to **System | Enterprise Integration | Proxies and Tunnels** and click on **Add**.

3. Select the function you would like to use, either **Content Filter** with **Websense** as type or **AirWatch App Tunnel** with **Standard Proxy** or **F5 Proxy** as type.

4. Complete the required information and click on **Save**.

Since we will be using MAG, you will need to ensure that you have MAG for proxy and content set up and configured to allow your external mobile users securely access your internal resources through AirWatch Browser. MAG for proxy and content was covered in *Chapter 8, Mobile Content Management*. To review the configuration on MAG for browser management, complete the following steps:

1. Log in to the Admin Console and navigate to **Groups & Settings | All Settings**.

2. Navigate to **System | Enterprise Integration | Mobile Access Gateway** and ensure that MAG is enabled and review your configuration.

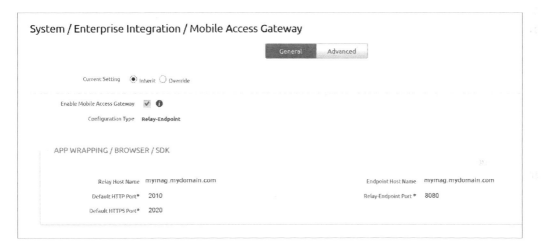

Once we have verified that MAG is enabled and configured correctly, we will need to enable AirWatch App Tunnel and select MAG. To do this, complete the following steps:

1. Navigate to **Apps & Books | Settings | Apps | Settings and Policies | Security Policies**.

2. Select **Enable** for **AirWatch App Tunnel** and then select **Mobile Access Gateway** as the App Tunnel mode.

3. Verify the details and enter the URLs of the sites that will proxy through the tunnel (all other URLs will go directly to the Internet) or leave blank to force all through the proxy. Click on **Save**.

If you configured AirWatch to use Websense, you would enable this within the content filtering option below the AirWatch App Tunnel configuration.

Now we can start to configure the Admin Console for browser management. To configure the settings for browser management, complete the following steps:

1. Navigate to **Groups & Settings | All Settings | Apps | Browser**.

2. The first page will present the following **Browser** options:

    ° **Settings and Policies**: To use the default application profile settings and policies, select **Default**. Otherwise, select **Custom** to select the iOS and Android profiles and apply legacy settings and policies (**Disable Copy, Disable Printing, Force Download to Open in SCL, Enable Mobile Access Gateway and iOS SDK Profile**)

 If you are using AirWatch Version 6.5 or less, you will need to select this as you will not be using the Shared SDK profile.

    ° **General**: This will consist of the following options:
    ° **Accept Cookies**: Enable this to accept cookies from accessed sites.
    ° **Clear Cookies Upon Exit**: This removes all cookies when the user exits the browser.
    ° **Clear Cookies and History if idle**: This clears cookies if the browser is idle for a specified time period.
    ° **Encrypt Cookies**: This encrypts cookies on the device (for Android only).
    ° **Remember History**: This allows the device to remember the history of visited sites for past day, week, month, or all.
    ° **Caching**: This allows data to be cached for increased web performance (for Android only).

- ◦ **Mode**: The first option is to enable or disable Kiosk mode.

If Kiosk mode is enabled, you are presented with the following options:

- ◦ **Return Home After Inactivity**: If this is selected, it allows you to enter the time in minutes you will return back to the home screen with inactivity.

- ◦ **Clear Cookies and History with Home**: This clears the previous user's session when the user clicks the home button.

- ◦ **Home Page URL:** This is the web page that will be made available to the users on the home page.

- ◦ **Selection Mode**: Select **Allow** or **Deny** to add whitelisted and blacklisted URLs to the available section below. Domains need to be separated with a space, comma, or new line and wildcard characters are supported.

- ◦ **Allow IP Browsing**: This allows you to whitelist IPv4 addresses. Wildcards are supported and IP whitelisting takes precedence over domain blacklisting.

If Kiosk mode is disabled, you will be presented with the following options:

- ◦ **Home Page URL**: This is the web page that will be made available to the users on the home page.

- ◦ **Selection Mode**: Select **Allow** or **Deny** to add whitelisted and blacklisted URLs to the available section below. Domains need to be separated with a space, comma, or new line and wildcard characters are supported.

- **Allow IP Browsing**: This allows you to whitelist IPv4 addresses. Wildcards are supported and IP whitelisting takes precedence over domain blacklisting.

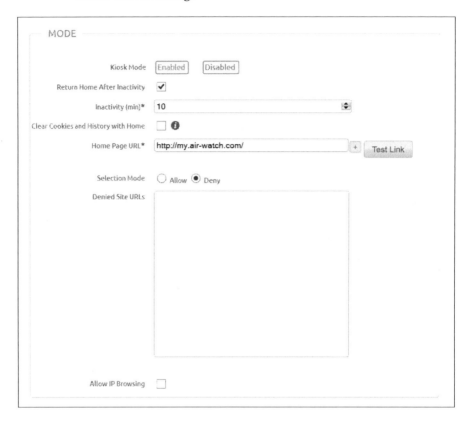

- **Terms of Use**: Select the terms of use if one is required. You will need to configure the terms of use before you can select it.

3. Click on **Save** and then click on **Bookmarks** at the top of the screen:

   1. Here you can add bookmarks to AirWatch Browser.

   2. Enter the name of the Bookmark and the URL and then click on the plus sign.

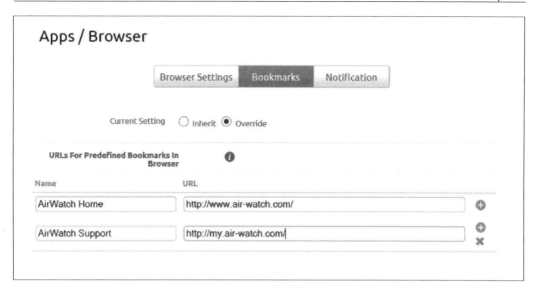

4. Click on **Save** and then click on **Notification** at the top of the screen. This is where you can configure notification settings, currently iOS only.

5. Click on **Save**.

Now that the Browser configurations are complete, we can deploy AirWatch Browser to the devices. AirWatch Browser is available for the following devices:

- iOS 6 or greater

- Android OS 2.3 or greater

- Windows RT/8.1 and Windows Phone 8/8.1

For a more efficient deployment of AirWatch Browser, it's recommended to deploy the Browser automatically, or make it available through the AirWatch App Catalog as described in the previous section.

As with the previous chapters, we will continue to demonstrate the deployment using the currently enrolled iOS and Android devices in our test organization groups. As reminded multiple times, validate that the settings you made for the Browser have been applied to the correct organization groups.

If you haven't deployed AirWatch Browser using AirWatch, it can also be downloaded from the App or Play Store:

- For the enrolled iOS, complete the following steps:
  - ○ Open the App Store and search for and install AirWatch Browser.
  - ○ Once installed, open the browser. It will automatically configure based on your enrollment. Authenticate if required.

- For the enrolled Android OS, complete the following steps:
  - ○ Open Play Store and search for and install the AirWatch Browser.
  - ○ Once installed, open the browser. It will automatically configure based on your enrollment and authenticate if required.

iOS with Kiosk mode disabled

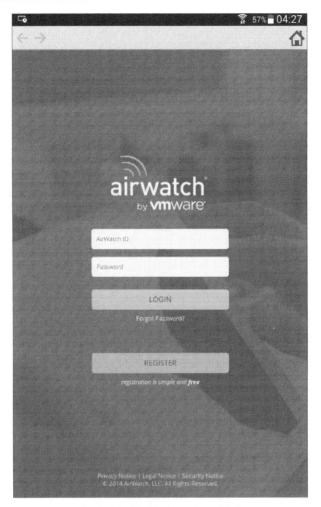

Android with Kiosk mode enabled

For corporate-owned devices, you will want to restrict the users from using the native browser on the devices to force them to use the AirWatch Browser. To do this, you will need to create a restriction profile. When you create a new profile, select the **Restrictions** payload and deselect **Allow use of Safari for iOS devices** and **Allow Native Android Browser for Android devices**.

Summary

In this chapter, we covered how to deploy applications and content to users with application management and the deployment of the secure browser for access to internal resources to users. Application management and deployment in the enterprise has become a critical component of enterprise mobility, and the demand from the workforce to use business apps on devices is increasing. Users are also requesting the ability to access intranet and portals from their mobile devices that may not be available externally, but this is all possible with AirWatch Browser.

This chapter provided an overview of MAM and how to set up and configure the MAG per app VPN for iOS 7 and greater devices. We then looked at the different application types available with MAM and how to deploy the apps to users' devices. We finished off the MAM section with application management within AirWatch.

The second part of the chapter covered MBM. We first looked at an overview of what MBM is before going into detail on how to configure MBM within AirWatch. Finally, we finished off the section with how to deploy MBM to the users in your environment with AirWatch Browser. We will now move onto the last chapter of the book, where we will look at how to set up shared devices for multiple users to be able to log in and use the mobile device and finish off with the opportunities available in AirWatch with laptop management.

10
Multiuser and Laptop Management

In this final chapter, we will look at multiuser and laptop management with AirWatch by VMware. Multiuser management will allow you as an organization to set up and configure a device for multiple users to share, allowing you to customize each user's experience and access depending on their role. This setup prevents the need to purchase devices for every user and allows for devices to be shared between users. Laptop management allows you to enroll Windows and Mac devices into AirWatch. This allows you, as an administrator, to enforce custom settings and security to these devices. This adds to the overall portfolio of EMM.

In this chapter, we will review multiuser management and look at the opportunities available within the organization. We will then set up and configure a multiuser device that can be deployed to your users. The second half of the chapter will cover laptop management with AirWatch and where it can fit within the organization. We will then end the chapter with the configuration and deployment of Laptop Management and the options available for this.

The following topics will be covered in this chapter:

- Multiuser Device Management overview
- Multiuser device configuration and deployment
- Laptop management overview
- Laptop configuration and deployment

Let's get started with the first part of this chapter that will cover Multiuser Device Management using AirWatch.

Multiuser Device Management overview

In the early versions of AirWatch, it was only possible to enroll devices with a single user account. This made it challenging with users needing to share devices as it forced administrators to use service accounts or it required an individual to enroll their username and password for everyone else to use. Using a single service account or requiring a user to sign in can create a potential security risk as well as additional administration overhead with shared service accounts. Today, AirWatch has the ability to set up devices to allow multiple users to log in with their directory credentials.

There are multiple options available with multiuser device management. You can configure the enrollment for all users to be fixed, which means that they will all get the same configuration when they log in, or you can configure custom configurations for each of the users for their log in. By setting up multiuser devices in your environment, you are creating a more secure deployment. At the same time, you are providing a more efficient environment by allowing the users to authenticate with the same credentials they use within the corporate network if the directory integration is configured.

A good use case of this is the need for a team of users who work different shifts needing access to different resources. By configuring a shared device with multiuser capabilities, you can allow the users to utilize the same device, providing cost savings to the organization. Another example is within education — a class that has been provided with iPads for the students. Setting up these iPad devices to be used as shared devices will allow the students to log in to the iPad devices and receive their specific resources as needed for class.

With multiuser management, you can perform the following with AirWatch:

- Configure a device to be used by multiple users
- Allow users to sign in using their corporate credentials
- Provide a simple checkout and check-in of devices
- Ensure that devices are always secure
- Use the same configuration for all users
- Configure a personalized experience for each user
- Provide access to corporate resources as demonstrated throughout the book

Multiuser device configuration and deployment

In this section, we will configure AirWatch to allow a device to be enrolled for multiuser capabilities. To use multiuser capabilities, your devices must meet the minimum specifications:

- Android 2.3 and higher with AirWatch MDM Agent 4.2 and higher
- iOS with AirWatch MDM Agent 4.2 and higher

The first thing you will want to do is create a separate organization group for the shared devices that are going to be set up. Creating an organization group was covered in the *Organization and Smart Groups* section of *Chapter 5, Mobile Device Management*. Go ahead and configure a new organization group based on these instructions for your multiuser devices.

For your deployment, you have a couple of options available, which are as follows:

- **Fixed Configuration**: A configuration that provides the same configuration for each user that logs in to the device
- **Dynamic Configuration**: Provides a customized configuration to each user that logs in to the device based on permissions specified in AirWatch

The organization group configuration for multiuser

Next, we will configure the organization group created for multiuser use.
To configure the organization group, complete the following steps:

1. In the Admin Console, ensure that you are in the correct organization group you created for shared devices.

2. Navigate to **Groups & Settings** | **All Settings** | **Devices & Users** | **General** | **Shared Device** and select **Override** and configure the following options:
    ◦ **Group Assignment Mode**: This will consist of the following options:
        ◦ **Prompt User For Organization Group**: This allows the user to enter the organization group provided by the admin.
        ◦ **Fixed Organization Group**: This uses the same organization group configured by the admin.

- ◦ **User Group Organization Group**: This uses the organization group configured for the user by the user group to provide configured settings and content.

- ◦ **Always Prompt for Terms of Use**: This will always have the user accept the terms of use.

- ◦ **Auto Logout Enabled**: This configures when the user will be logged out automatically.

- ◦ **Enable Single App Mode**: Select this to configure the single app mode. This locks the device and only provides access to a specific configured application. This is only available for supervised iOS devices.

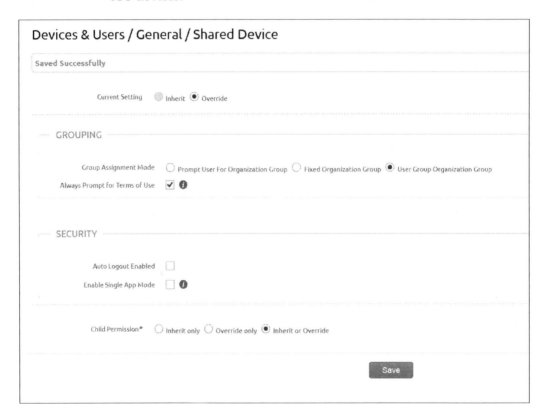

3. Click on **Save** once complete.

The device configuration for multiuser

To set up your devices for multiuser usage, you need to set up and configure a user account that can be used to enable the device for staging for multiple users to log in:

 Set up a separate account for device staging as the user configured for device staging cannot enroll devices for themselves.

1. In the Admin Console, navigate to **Accounts | Users | List View** and search for the user to configure for device staging.

2. Click on **Edit** (the pencil icon) and select **Enable Device Staging** and then **Multi User Devices**.

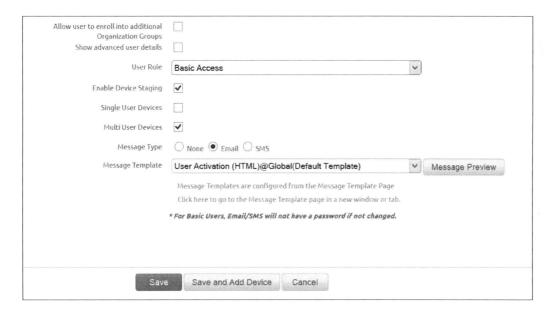

Once the user has been configured, download AirWatch MDM agent onto the device to be used by multiple users and launch it once the installation is complete. We will walk through an iOS deployment in this example:

1. Open the downloaded AirWatch MDM agent on the device.

2. Enroll with the server and group ID options:

    1. Enter your AirWatch server URL.

    2. Enter the group ID configured for multiuser usage.

3. Click on **Continue** and on **Continue** again. Enter the username and password configured to stage multiusers and then click on **Continue** and then again on **Continue**.

4. You will be prompted to install the multiuser profile. Click on **Install** and then on **Install Now** (enter device password if prompted). Click on **Install**, then on **Done**, and on **Continue** on the **Success** window.

The following screenshot shows the multiuser profiles that will be installed onto the device:

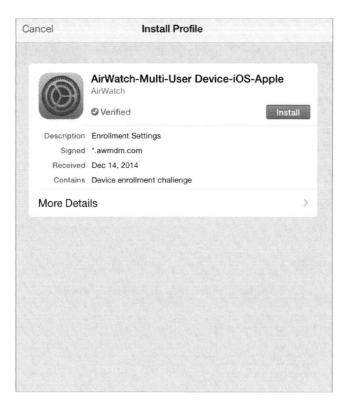

5. You will then be prompted with the multiuser login screen:

 How you configured the settings for the shared device will depend on the login screen. If you configured prompt user for organization group, you will be presented with the **Group ID** field. Otherwise, you will only be required to enter your username and password.

Logging in and out of a multiuser device

To log in to a multiuser device, open up AirWatch MDM agent if the login screen doesn't appear and enter the required login information. Accept the terms of use if required. To log off, open AirWatch MDM agent, select **Log Out**, and then select **Yes**.

Next, we will look at laptop management within AirWatch.

Laptop management overview

As we look at the overall portfolio of EMM, we need to ensure that we include laptops as part of these discussions. A lot of organizations have already created BYOD programs that also include laptops. Many more are looking at the opportunities that allow users to select their own laptops for work usage. Users bringing their own laptops for work creates new challenges with the ability to secure them and efficiently manage them. In today's organizations, teams are dedicated to managing and enforcing device configurations and security on corporate-owned devices. With BYOD, this creates different challenges as organizations can't expect to take ownership and control of these devices as they traditionally have.

Additional challenges include the rapid growth of Mac devices in the consumer world that has slowly grown into the enterprise for specific functions. Another challenge includes consumers wanting the latest Windows OS. Enterprises are typically way behind on their OS versions for various reasons, providing different experiences to users. As the growth of technology continues at a rapid pace, it is critical that enterprises provide options for their users to stay current with the latest technologies available and at the same time provide them with options to use what allows them to be most productive.

Laptop management with AirWatch takes a different approach to the traditional imaging process used within enterprises today with Windows laptops. AirWatch laptop management provides a similar concept to that of its MDM by administrators configuring profiles with payloads that are deployed to the laptops. These profiles allow for a dynamic deployment with access to multiple different corporate resources securely.

Although laptop management is available for Windows 7 and 8.1/RT, it also provides management for Mac devices. Mac devices have slowly found their way into the enterprise environments over the years, but the manageability and visibility of these devices have been extremely limited. With AirWatch, you now have the ability to take full management over these Mac devices in providing the users the needed access along with security to the resources they need.

With laptop management, you can expect the following with AirWatch:

- Management of Mac OS and Windows laptops
- Leverage profile configurations just like MDM
- Automatic software deployment and updates
- App Catalog deployment
- Full asset tracking within AirWatch Admin Console
- Remote assistance and troubleshooting capabilities
- Enterprise or device wipe laptop
- Enforce security and compliance policies
- Deploy AirWatch apps
- Full content collaboration
- Self-service user portal

Laptop configuration and deployment

In this section, we will cover the enrollment of Windows 8.1/RT and Mac OS X laptops.

Mac OS X

Mac OS X devices have traditionally been managed on a need-by-need basis. With AirWatch, we can centrally manage and configure deployments for Mac OS X devices in the enterprise to provide access to the needed corporate resources with the required security.

The following Mac devices are supported with AirWatch:

- MacBook Pro with OS X 10.7 Lion and higher versions
- MacBook Air with OS X 10.7 Lion and higher versions
- Mac Mini with OS X 10.7 Lion and higher versions
- iMac with OS X 10.7 Lion and higher versions
- Mac Pro with OS X 10.7 Lion and higher versions

The first step is to create a new organization group as described in the *Organization and Smart Groups* section of *Chapter 5, Mobile Device Management*. This will allow you to begin enrolling your Mac OS X devices.

Profiles

Before you enroll, you will want to set up and configure the Profiles for your Mac OS X devices. You can, at any time, add/remove/configure settings for your Mac OS X devices. You have the option of deploying user or device payload with Mac OS X. The payloads available for a user profile are **General, Passcode, Network, VPN, Email, Exchange Web Services, LDAP, CalDAV, CardDAV, Web Clips, Credentials, SCEP, Dock, Restrictions, Parental Controls, Security and Privacy, Login Items, Finder, Accessibility, Printing, Messages, Global HTTP Proxy, Mobility, Managed Domains, Content Filter, AirPlay Mirroring, Custom Settings**.

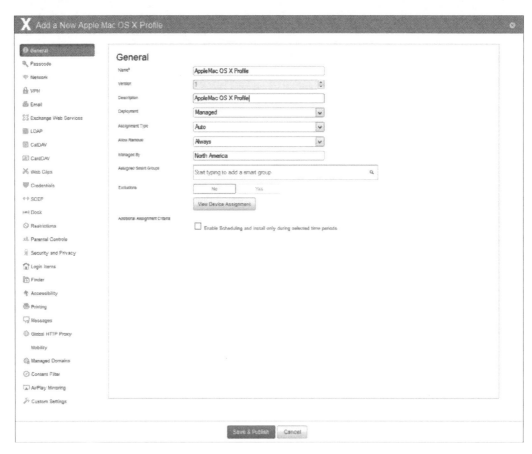

Payloads available for a device profile are **General, Passcode, Network, VPN, Credentials, SCEP, Dock, Restrictions, Software Update, Parental Controls, Directory, Security and Privacy, Disc Encryption, Login Items, Login Window, Energy Saver, Time Machine, Finder, Accessibility, Printing, Global HTTP Proxy, Mobility, Managed Domains, VMware Fusion, Content Filter, AirPlay Mirroring, Custom Settings**

There are three steps needed to enroll your Apple Mac OS X devices. The first is to obtain the MDM profile:

Obtaining the MDM profile

To obtain the MDM profile perform the following steps:

1. Navigate to **Devices | Settings | Devices & Users | Apple | Apple Configurator**.

    1. Select **Override** if not already selected.

    2. Select **Enable Automated Enrollment**.

    3. **Staging Mode**: In this select **Single User Device**.

    4. **Default Staging User**: In this select **Default Staging User**.

    5. **Platform**: In this select **Apple Mac OS X**.

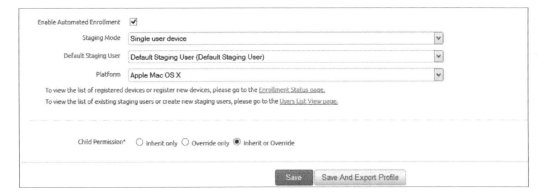

2. Click on **Save And Export Profile** to save the .mobileconfig file.

Configuring standard or advanced staging

Standard staging provides the users with a login screen to complete the staging process while advanced staging allows you as an administrator to enroll for the user:

 Before deploying standard staging, it is recommended that you create a **Directory** profile (for users to log in), **Security and Privacy** profile, **Login Items** profile, and **Restrictions** profile.

To configure standard staging, complete the following steps:

1. Create a user account that can be used for staging by navigating to **Accounts | Users | List View** and then clicking on **New** (you can use a directory-enabled account or basic user account).

2. Click on **Edit** (the pencil icon) on the user account to be used for staging.

3. Select **Enable Device Staging** and then **Single User Devices**. Ensure that the **Standard** option is selected. Click on **Save**.

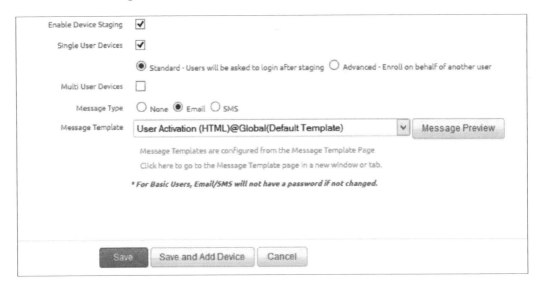

 For a more efficient deployment, you can configure the enrollment using Apple **Device Enrollment Program (DEP)** with standard staging. Using DEP, you can apply standard images to devices, skip setup assistant panes during installation, enforce enrollment for all users, and customize and streamline the enrollment process to meet the organization's needs. Your Apple representative should be able to provide additional information.

To configure advanced staging, complete the following steps:

1. Create a user account that can be used for staging by navigating to **Accounts | Users | List View** and clicking on **New** (you can use a directory-enabled account or basic user account).

2. Click on **Edit** (the pencil icon) on the user account to be used for staging.

3. Select **Enable Device Staging** and then **Single User Devices**. Ensure that the **Advanced** option is selected. Click on **Save**.

Download the agent and enroll

You have the following options to download AirWatch agent:

1. In the Admin Console, navigate to **Groups & Settings | All Settings | Devices & Users | Apple | Apple Mac OS X | Agent Application** and click on **Download Agent**.

2. Open a web browser and navigate to `https://awagent.com/` to download the agent.

Once downloaded, launch AirWatch Agent and complete the following steps:

1. **Standard Staging**: Enter the URL and group ID and enroll the device using the staging account created for staging. Have the user log in with their credentials to complete the staging process.

2. **Advanced Staging**: Enter the URL and group ID and enroll the device using the staging account created for staging. Enter the username of the end user device owner and complete enrollment by installing profiles.

 You can apply compliance policies to laptops just like you would for your mobile devices.

Windows 8.1/RT

Windows is still the primary OS used in the enterprise today and I don't see this changing in the near future based on the number of business applications written specifically for Windows OS. Although enterprises have traditionally managed these devices through imaging, AirWatch has created an opportunity to use the device out of the box and apply configurations and settings based on profiles.

The following Windows platforms are supported:

- Windows 8.1 Core (Pro or Enterprise)
- Windows 8.1 RT Core (Pro or Enterprise)

 There is also the ability to enroll Windows Vista and Windows 7 devices into AirWatch. For additional information, log in to the myairwatch portal and navigate to **Resources** | **Documentation** | **Platforms**. Download *Win32 Platform Guide*.

The first step is to create a new organization group, as described in the *Organization and Smart Groups* section of *Chapter 5, Mobile Device Management*, that you will be enrolling your Windows 8.1 devices.

Profiles

Before you enroll with your Windows 8.1 device, you will want to set up and configure the profiles. You can, at any time, add, remove, or configure settings for your Windows 8.1 devices. The profiles available are **General**, **Passcode**, **Wi-Fi**, **VPN**, **Credentials**, **Restrictions**, **Firewall**, **Encryption**, **Automatic Updates**, **Web Clips**, **Exchange ActiveSync**, **SCEP**, **Custom Settings**. Here is a screenshot for your reference:

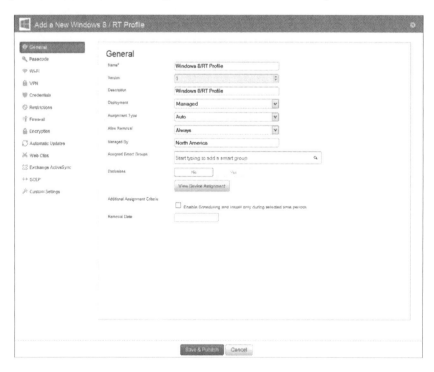

AirWatch protection agent

For additional protection on your Windows device, you will want to require AirWatch protection agent (not available for RT devices). Using AirWatch protection agent, you can create profiles for BitLocker, Windows Firewall, and Windows Update. To use the AirWatch protection agent, complete the following steps:

1. Navigate to **Groups & Settings | All Settings | Devices & Users | Windows | Windows 8 / RT | Agents Application**. Put a check mark in **Publish AirWatch Protection Agent** and click on **Save**.

 To configure AirWatch protection agent settings, navigate to **Groups & Settings | All Settings | Devices & Users | Windows | Windows 8 / RT | Agent Settings**.

To enroll your Windows 8.1/RT devices into AirWatch, you have the option of enrolling using the native Workplace app, Windows Auto-Discovery Service, or Enrolling on Behalf of Others.

 You are required to have local admin permissions on the device to enroll. Do not enroll the device using store agent.

The native Workplace app

To enroll using the native Workplace app, complete the following steps. This Microsoft update is required for this enrollment: `http://support.microsoft.com/kb/2955164`.

1. On the Windows device, navigate to **Settings** | **Change PC Settings** | **Network** | **Workplace**.

2. Enter your **User Principal Name** (**UPN**) or the username provided by the administrator in the `user1@mydomain.com` format.

3. Turn **Automatically detect server address** to **Off**.

4. Enter the server address in the `DeviceServicesURL/DeviceServices/Discovery.aws` format, for example, `ds345.awmdm.com/DeviceServices/Discovery.aws`.

5. Click on **Turn On** and then enter your group ID. Click on **Next**.

6. Enter your username and password and then click on **Next**.

7. If prompted, select **Device Ownership** and then click on **Next**.

8. If prompted, accept **End User Agreement** and select the **I understand** option and then **Turn On**.

9. If AirWatch protection agent is required, click on **Download Protection Agent** from the **Device List** view and install it.

The Windows autodiscovery service

To enroll using Windows auto-discovery, complete the following steps:

1. On the Windows device, navigate to **Settings** | **Change PC Settings** | **Network** | **Workplace**.

2. Enter your UPN or the username provided by the administrator in the `user1@mydomain.com` format.

3. Leave **Automatically detect server** address to **On** and leave the **Enter Server address** field blank.

 The last bullet requires this Microsoft update to be installed: http://support.microsoft.com/kb/2955164. If it's not installed, the bullet can be skipped.

4. Click on **Turn On** and then enter your group ID. Then, click on **Next**.

5. Enter your username and password and click on **Next**.

6. If prompted, select **Device Ownership** and then click on **Next**.

7. If prompted, accept **End User Agreement** and select the **I understand** option and then **Turn On**.

8. If AirWatch protection agent is required, click on **Download Protection Agent** from the **Device List** view and install it.

Enrolling on behalf of others

This method allows you to enroll on behalf of the users, so all they have to do is log in. To enroll on behalf of others, complete the following steps:

1. Configure the Windows device as you would for any other Windows device.

2. Create a standard local user account with a temporary password.

3. Install the latest OMA-DM from Windows updates.

4. Configure the device to enable management and enroll-on-behalf:

    1. Open the command prompt and run the following command replacing `'username'` with the account created previously:

        ```
        wmic user account where name='username' get sid
        ```

    2. Launch registry editor and create the HKEY_LOCAL_Machine\ SOFTWARE\Policies\Microsoft\Windows\CurrentVersion\MDM key.

3. Add the following entries to the key just created:

   ○ MachineMDMEnrollment: The type is DWORD and data is 1

   ○ MachineMDMEnrollmentUserUPN: The type is String and data is userUPN

   ○ MachineMDMEnrollmentUserID: The type is String and data is UserSID

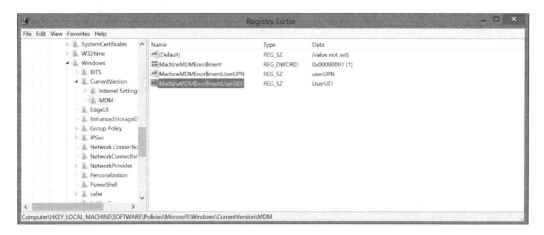

5. Enable management by navigating to **Settings | Change PC Settings | Network | Workplace** and enter the administrators UPN. Select **Turn On** and enter the administrator's credentials. Accept the dialog and if Windows protection agent is enabled, download and install it. Log off as the local administrator and log in as the user.

Summary

In this chapter, we covered how to deploy multiuser devices to the users and how to set up and configure Windows 8.1/RT and Mac OS X laptops for management with AirWatch. Multiuser management can allow your organization to get more out of fewer devices by allowing users to share a single device. Laptop management provides an opportunity to manage devices differently from the traditional method of imaging and allows for more options with a BYOD program.

This first section of the chapter covered multiuser management and provided an overview to the reader. We then demonstrated how to configure multiuser management within AirWatch before finishing with how to deploy multiuser management within your environment.

The second part of the chapter provided you with an overview of laptop management within AirWatch. The chapter then provided instructions on how to configure laptop management within the AirWatch environment before finishing off the chapter with deploying laptop management into the enterprise.

This chapter concludes the primary content of this book and learning AirWatch. We will finish off with an appendix that will touch upon the future of mobility and where it is potentially moving towards.

The Future of Mobility

As you have completed your journey through this book, I have demonstrated the importance of mobility within the enterprise. Mobility has grown significantly over the past 7 years since the release of the original iPhone. Traditionally, enterprises were able to better control and manage smart devices that they were providing to end users as they typically owned them, especially the familiar Blackberry with their enterprise deployment and management. Within the last 7 years, there has been a significant shift from enterprises that dictated the use of mobile device to the end user to now dictating the use due to the consumer market of smart phones. Now that everyone is able to afford and purchase a smart device, the push to do more with smart devices in the enterprise is creating new challenges for organizations.

As technical professionals within the enterprise, we are being tasked and challenged to provide more access to internal corporate resources from mobile devices. This is not an easy task when you look at the possibility of data loss and the continued growth of breaches occurring in the world today. Security is a significant factor in the world today, and we all want to ensure that our organization is not listed in the news for a breach, especially when it's under our ownership. Other challenges include the vast majority of different mobile platforms and the inconsistency between all of them (iOS, Windows, multiple flavors of Android, Blackberry, and so on). Being able to provide corporate information to a user's personal device without affecting their personal information brings up questions of invasion of privacy and possible legal issues, which is something we have to be very careful about.

Over the last few years, we also saw a shift in the ways IT has traditionally deployed its services. IT has always been in an operational role, architecting and deploying services. Once deployed, the focus of what the service is to the end users always tends to become a lower priority as we find ourselves constantly dealing with patching, updating, repairing, and upgrading the service. This is because the services have traditionally lived within the organization's data center and always need operation on the backend. As we move forward, the growth of cloud services is becoming a large footprint for many organizations. At first, it is certainly difficult to understand and accept this change, especially if you are part of the change occurring to your services. However, the reality is that it only makes sense in the long run. As you start shifting your services to SaaS/Cloud models, you are now able to eliminate the operational role of those services that have always consumed the team's time. This allows you to start focusing on the services being provided and allows you to provide better solutions to the users within your environment. Now you can focus on what the customer's needs are and how you can deploy the service being provided to create efficiency and exceptional service.

As you can see from this book, AirWatch by VMware has realized the importance of mobility in the enterprise. AirWatch started with MDM, which was a great start with the management of mobile devices, but it soon realized the bigger picture and has shifted its mindset to EMM. EMM has grown way beyond MDM and now MDM is only a portion of EMM. With AirWatch and its EMM suite, you are able to better strategize and provide solutions to meet the demand of the consumer in the enterprise. The solution provides for a very flexible deployment, meeting the needs of all mobile case uses within your organization.

One of the advantages of AirWatch is the ability to deploy solutions based on the device ownership. Organizations have realized the opportunity of the ability to eliminate corporate-owned devices that have traditionally been provided to users for work usage. With more and more users purchasing their own preferred devices, it makes no sense for users having to carry around multiple devices. Because of this, organizations are starting to provide a stipend back to its employees for the use of voice and data on their personal devices that have been granted access to corporate resources. With the increase of personally owned devices in the organization, there is also an increase in the number of corporate-owned devices that are being used for initiatives within the enterprise. Since the release of iPad, organizations have been purchasing iPads for multiple reasons. With these devices being owned by the organization, the expectation is to be able to fully manage them, just as laptops and PCs have traditionally been managed. With AirWatch, you are able to provide and manage access to corporate information using a personally owned profile to users' personal devices without affecting their personal information and at the same time providing and managing access to corporate-owned assets by maintaining full control of the device.

With AirWatch, you also have the option of deploying on-premise or in the cloud. On-premise will obviously create a large amount of additional work and management, which is why it is recommended that you opt for the cloud solution. Unless there is a legitimate reason for not being able to deploy in the cloud, your AirWatch environment should be deployed in the SaaS environment. The ease of deployment and the reduction in the management of the infrastructure will be significant as you focus on and deploy solutions to your users. Just as I mentioned previously, moving to the cloud is being adopted more and more and is certainly a shift in the way IT is providing its services today. This is something everyone should be considering as they grow.

As you continue to focus on the end solution and provide more access and solutions to your users, you will also be providing a significant increase in productivity to your users. Yes, the employee's time has to be taken into account. However, I find myself being able to be more productive and responsive in general, since I have access to the corporate resources on my personal device. Being able to access my e-mail and corporate documents allows me to easily filter and view information from the click of a button on my mobile device. This is the same for users who are expected to travel a lot. Being able to easily access and respond to information makes a significant difference in productivity, especially when it's available on your mobile device.

Today, I'm continuously surprised as I learn and hear what organizations are able to do with mobile initiatives. Working in the health care industry, I see an increased growth in mobile usage and case uses continue to grow. Recently, I have been involved with mobile solutions that include e-signatures, patient entertainment, patient surveys, stock inventory, video usage, and so on, and we are seeing more and more demand to access all patient information from mobile devices to improve internal workflows and provide a better patient experience. Mobile devices are also being piloted for telemedicine and the discussion around more usage is upon us. When you look into the future of health care, we can possibly expect at some point to be able to use mobile devices for virtual doctor visits, wellness programs, and possibly change the way health insurance works. Mobile devices are going to allow us to better monitor our health and share that information with health organizations to help provide a healthier prolonged life.

In other industries, there are multiple different deployments of mobile usage already today. In the transportation industry, we see airlines use mobile devices for their in-cabin service and flight books being eliminated and replaced with mobile devices. In the retail industry, we are already paying for merchandise with debit/credit cards through mobile devices such as the POS. A recent shift is also the ability to use Apple Pay with your iOS device to pay for merchandise in supported retail locations, eliminating the need to carry your debit/credit cards. Within the hospitality industry, we are starting to see mobile devices sitting on customers' tables for entertainment, ordering, and the ability to pay your check at the end of the service. All these initiatives are playing a big part in the shift and transformation of mobility for our future.

The industry that is going to force a change in the future of mobility the most is education. In education, we see a significant growth with the adoption of mobile devices in the classroom. Mobile devices are creating opportunities to eliminate textbooks (including library books), providing the ability to communicate more efficiently between the students and teachers, better online learning experiences, better tools to the students for more efficient learning, deploying and assigning projects and homework more effectively, and so on. With these devices being put in the user's hands at such a young age is only going to set expectations for our younger generation to use them in the workplace. Our younger generation will be extremely familiar with and expect that mobile devices will be part of their everyday work life as they are with their learnings.

This also leads me into the discussion on how our younger generation is growing up. They are part of a society that includes the usage of mobile devices and they are becoming extremely dependent on them. We see more and more children with their own mobile devices, and the way they use them is going to change and shape the way we manage and deploy these solutions within the enterprise. Communication methods are also changing with the use of mobile devices. Texting, video chat, and social collaboration are the preferred methods of communication with the younger generation, which will start to become an expectation as they become employed by organizations.

Today, we've come along with mobility in the enterprise but there is still quite a lot to accomplish in my opinion. For BYOD, the MDM approach has been extremely invasive and the concern for invasion of privacy is always questioned. With AirWatch, the workspace approach is bridging the gap between defining work-related information and personal information on a single device but it still has room for maturity. I expect to see a larger adoption of the workspace deployment and for it to become a norm for personal devices with BYOD. For corporate-owned devices, the preferred method of device has traditionally been iOS. These devices have caused significant challenges to be efficiently managed in the enterprise, as they are designed for the consumer. The management has continued to improve over the years but there still are challenges for an enterprise to fully control these devices. As the market becomes more competitive and the choice of tablets has increased with Android and Windows, I expect to see alternate devices being selected, which will provide more efficient management in the enterprise.

As we continue to build and deploy solutions with EMM, you will realize the opportunities are endless within your organization. As you work closely with your business units, you will be presented with the ability to improve workflows, provide cost savings, create a more efficient environment, and allow for more efficiency with your users and customers. With AirWatch, the technology has been provided to allow you to develop and be as creative as your team's innovation will allow for. The opportunities are becoming endless as we truly move into a more mobile workforce and world.

As we continue to grow with EMM within AirWatch, we can continue to see much more growth with content, the deployment of video to the users, the availability of chat within the product and more integrations with cloud services to access corporate information. Growing beyond this, we should expect to see new and innovate ways to communicate with mobile devices with enterprise social collaboration and the ability to do more with video communication. It is also critical that we are up to date with the latest security enforcements, as the latest mobile devices are starting to leverage finger printing, biometrics, and voice control to name just a few. Being able to integrate these features as part of your security for your enterprise deployments will only allow for a better user experience.

It is critical as experts in the field that we drive innovation with mobility within the enterprise. Ensuring that you provide the latest opportunities within the mobile space to your end users will provide a more efficient workforce and one that will want to continue to stay around. Staying ahead of the curve and making the technology available to your workforce will provide value to both your team and the organization. Always think outside the box and present new opportunities as they arise; this will only allow you to grow and become as successful as you would like to be.

Index

Y

Thank you for buying
Learning AirWatch

About Packt Publishing

Packt, pronounced 'packed', published its first book, *Mastering phpMyAdmin for Effective MySQL Management*, in April 2004, and subsequently continued to specialize in publishing highly focused books on specific technologies and solutions.

Our books and publications share the experiences of your fellow IT professionals in adapting and customizing today's systems, applications, and frameworks. Our solution-based books give you the knowledge and power to customize the software and technologies you're using to get the job done. Packt books are more specific and less general than the IT books you have seen in the past. Our unique business model allows us to bring you more focused information, giving you more of what you need to know, and less of what you don't.

Packt is a modern yet unique publishing company that focuses on producing quality, cutting-edge books for communities of developers, administrators, and newbies alike. For more information, please visit our website at www.packtpub.com.

About Packt Enterprise

In 2010, Packt launched two new brands, Packt Enterprise and Packt Open Source, in order to continue its focus on specialization. This book is part of the Packt Enterprise brand, home to books published on enterprise software – software created by major vendors, including (but not limited to) IBM, Microsoft, and Oracle, often for use in other corporations. Its titles will offer information relevant to a range of users of this software, including administrators, developers, architects, and end users.

Writing for Packt

We welcome all inquiries from people who are interested in authoring. Book proposals should be sent to author@packtpub.com. If your book idea is still at an early stage and you would like to discuss it first before writing a formal book proposal, then please contact us; one of our commissioning editors will get in touch with you.

We're not just looking for published authors; if you have strong technical skills but no writing experience, our experienced editors can help you develop a writing career, or simply get some additional reward for your expertise.

Citrix® XenMobile™ Mobile Device Management

ISBN: 978-1-78217-214-7   Paperback: 112 pages

Gain an insight into the industry's best and most secure Enterprise Mobility Management solution

1. Deploy and manage the complete XenMobile solution.

2. Learn how to customize and troubleshoot your XenMobile apps.

3. Step-by-step instructions with relevant screenshots for better understanding.

Mobile Security: How to Secure, Privatize, and Recover Your Devices

ISBN: 978-1-84969-360-8   Paperback: 242 pages

Keep your data secure on the go

1. Learn how mobile devices are monitored and the impact of cloud computing.

2. Understand the attacks hackers use and how to prevent them.

3. Keep yourself and your loved ones safe online.

Please check **www.PacktPub.com** for information on our titles

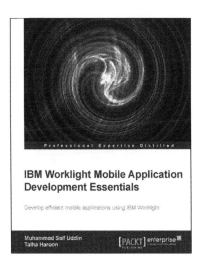

IBM Worklight Mobile Application Development Essentials

ISBN: 978-1-78217-760-9   Paperback: 144 pages

Develop effecient mobile applications using IBM Worklight

1. Develop Mobile Apps that can be deployed on multiple mobile platforms quickly and easily.

2. Build Enterprise mobile apps to ease data transactions and manipulation.

3. Create advanced modules for mobile Enterprise application.

Learning Windows Azure Mobile Services for Windows 8 and Windows Phone 8

ISBN: 978-1-78217-192-8   Paperback: 124 pages

A short, fast and focused guide to enhance your Windows 8 applications by leveraging the power of Windows Azure Mobile Services

1. Dive deep into Azure Mobile Services with a practical XAML-based case study game.

2. Enhance your applications with Push Notifications and Notifications Hub.

3. Follow step-by-step instructions for result-oriented examples.

Please check **www.PacktPub.com** for information on our titles

Printed in Great Britain
by Amazon